T0314891

DOREEN HOLT

PENNIES
IN
THE GRASS

A reluctant immigrant in Canada

DOREEN HOLT

PENNIES
IN THE GRASS

A reluctant immigrant in Canada

MEREO
Cirencester

Mereo Books

1A The Wool Market Dyer Street Cirencester Gloucestershire GL7 2PR
An imprint of Memoirs Publishing www.mereobooks.com

Pennies in the Grass: 978-1-86151-232-1

First published in Great Britain in 2014
by Mereo Books, an imprint of Memoirs Publishing

The address for Memoirs Publishing Group Limited can be found at
www.memoirspublishing.com

The Memoirs Publishing Group Ltd Reg. No. 7834348

The Memoirs Publishing Group supports both The Forest Stewardship Council® (FSC®) and
the PEFC® leading international forest-certification organisations. Our books carrying both the
FSC label and the PEFC® and are printed on FSC®-certified paper. FSC® is the only
forest-certification scheme supported by the leading environmental organisations including
Greenpeace. Our paper procurement policy can be found at
www.memoirspublishing.com/environment

Typeset in 10.5/15pt Bembo
by Wiltshire Associates Publisher Services Ltd. Printed and bound in Great Britain by
Printondemand-Worldwide, Peterborough PE2 6XD

INTRODUCTION

When I was a little girl, many years ago, every story book began with the words ONCE UPON A TIME. Then followed the adventure or the fairy story, which usually ended with... THEY LIVED HAPPILY EVER AFTER. Although my life has not exactly been a fairy story, it has provided me with many challenges and adventures, both happy and sad.

My story begins when I was just a young child growing up in England in the Great Depression of the 1930s, living through World War II, many years of food shortages, air-raid sirens and the awful sound of bombs whistling downwards to their targets, and finally to peace. It also portrays the joys of Christmas, the games we played and the frightening experience of that first day at school, which should have been a happy experience, but wasn't. It covers the teenage years, the discovery of boys causing both joy and tears before finally finding the right one to marry. Then the sadness and stresses of being a very reluctant immigrant to Canada in the 1960s, the struggle to survive in a new environment, the path to eventual financial and family stability, and of course the various magical and unexpected experiences in my long life - the 'pennies in the grass' of the title.

It also delves into the social history of Great Britain in the mid-twentieth century, the difficulties of being an immigrant and the medical systems of Canada and England, and takes an unsparing look at the evolution of marriage over a period of 50 years and the massive changes in so many areas of life, which I hope the reader will find interesting, familiar, inspiring and valuable in this book of memories.

CHAPTER ONE

BEGINNINGS

My birthplace was Liverpool, a large city on the north-west coast of England. It is a port city with a waterfront we called the Pier Head, where the buses and tramcars terminated their journeys before returning to the particular district they served in the suburbs.

There are several impressive buildings lining the waterfront. The Liver Building with its mythical bird on the top of the high tower is familiar to most residents next to the Cunard Building and Mersey Docks and Harbour Offices, known as the Three Graces. Another easy-to-spot building is the Roman Catholic Cathedral, sometimes referred to affectionately as 'Paddy's Wigwam' because of its resemblance to one. No one seems to take offence at this unseemly name and the reference is usually accompanied with a humorous smile, for it is a very unusual piece of architecture.

Another interesting building on the waterfront is the tall red-and-white-striped home of the White Star Shipping Line, which commissioned the *Titanic*, the ship which was built in Belfast and declared 'unsinkable'. This huge and magnificent liner, on her maiden voyage from Southampton to New York hit a huge iceberg and tragically sank, taking the lives of many, many people. That was over one hundred years ago, but it has not been forgotten and probably never will be. Liverpool Port used to be a bustling one. Across the River Mersey in Birkenhead there was a large shipbuilding company called Cammell Lairds, which went into decline after World War II.

Nowadays the port has recovered somewhat and the waterfront restored to a great extent, attracting visitors year round, and hopefully is now back to being a thriving part of the City. There are ferries which cross the short span of the Mersey to Wallasey and New Brighton which many people use, both for pleasure and for transportation purposes.

This important city has a very mixed population. It is home to the very rich, the very poor and everything in between. It is of course, now well-known because of the Beatles, who monopolised the airways and the headlines, and millions of teenagers' hearts, from 1962 onwards. They performed in the Cavern right in the City – it is still there and now has a place in Liverpool's history books. Their thick accents were familiar to me and I can still spot a 'Scouser' when I hear one!

This city is jokingly referred to as the 'capital of Ireland' because of the large influx of Irish folks who crossed the sea to swell the ranks of the unemployed. They are largely of the Roman Catholic faith and had many children to support, since birth control is forbidden in their religion, something the later generation seems to have ignored to some extent – and who can blame them. Like many immigrants, they left Ireland for better things but I imagine that few would achieve them in Liverpool.

Its citizens are called Liverpudlians and are affectionately referred to as 'Scousers', which I think originated from the fact that the poor population fed their hungry broods with a diet of cheap cuts of beef, cut into small cubes and simmered for several hours in

Oxo, or if you could afford it, Bovril, a much richer version, cooked in one pot on the stove-top. Any kind of vegetables, and lots of potatoes, lentils, barley and split peas were all added to the mix to make a rich stew, which for some reason or other was called Scouse. It is nourishing and delicious and it was always enjoyed in our house, from when I was a child right up to the present time.

The only thing I disliked about it was the barley my mother insisted on including in the ingredients. I hated the feel of it in my mouth and would pick it out and place it around the edge of my plate. It would look like a cheap string of pearls by the time I'd finished my dinner. I was often scolded for doing this, but I never would eat it.

There is a variation of this dish called hotpot, which uses the same ingredients but is layered into a large dish, finishing up with several layers of thinly-sliced potatoes, cooked slowly for several hours in the oven. The potatoes on top turn brown and crispy and this is often my choice of dinner. Once everything is prepared, there is nothing more to do other than wait for it cook. During the war when beef and all meat was severely rationed, these dishes would still be made minus the meat, when they earned the name of "Blind Scouse", still substantial and nourishing but less expensive to make.

The city dwellers are well known for their rich sense of humour. Many have quipped that you have to possess one to survive in Liverpool! It actually has spawned many comedians who have risen to fame, including Ken Dodd and Jimmy Tarbuck, to name just two, but there are many others who have made their names in show business. Theirs is a special kind of topical humour which often only the locals understand or relate to, but something I can still chuckle about. They see the funny side of life in their own poverty-stricken and often harsh lives and make jokes about themselves. They are usually generous, goodhearted people who welcome you into their homes and share whatever they have with you. The first thing they do is put the kettle on the stove, because a cup of tea is the solution to every problem under the sun, according to them! They are the real salt of the earth and would give you the shirt off their back if you needed it.

They speak a dialect uniquely their own and difficult, even impossible, for strangers to understand. The thick nasal tone in their voices is said to be caused by the large amount of salt and pollution in the sea air. The poorest people used to live clustered in rows of tiny brick terraced houses, fairly close to the docks and waterfront. They often shared a toilet and washing facilities with several other families, and strung their washing from the bedroom windows to dry, across the grimy street below. Along with the label of Scouse, they are sometimes called "Whacker" – another term of endearment, believe it or not. I've no idea what it means in Liverpudlian terms, but it sounds a bit ominous to me! The dictionary states that it may be alteration of the word 'Thwack' which means a sharp blow. I told you it was ominous!

I used to feel uncomfortable and embarrassed to admit I was born in Liverpool, even though we, as a family, were regarded as middle-class and lived in a quiet area of the city, very law abiding and respectable. I no longer feel ashamed of my birthplace because no one has control over that, only their parents before them.

The tragedy of losing both parents forced my mother in her early teens to leave her beautiful pristine Isle of Man, where she was born and raised, to seek work on the mainland, where she eventually met and married my father, who was a Liverpudlian. Such earth-shaking events change lives and destinies and certainly changed my mother's life completely. She was a reluctant immigrant to England and loved the Isle of Man until she died, her roots still in the place of her birth.

I was born into the Strevens family on Sunday, December 9,

1928, the third child and third daughter. Sadly, their firstborn child died during the birth, an unnecessary death caused by the midwife attending my mother, who had left her alone, remarking she still had a long way to go before the birth. During that absence the baby girl arrived and strangled on the umbilical cord. I can only imagine how painful it must have been for my parents. Mum never liked to talk about it.

They waited two years before having my sister Brenda. Four years later I arrived and then two sons, Roy and Raymond, completed the family. The last arrival was a big surprise, certainly not planned at all, in fact, my parents had got rid of the baby carriage and all other items connected to raising babies, and bought bicycles to enjoy the local countryside on Sundays when Dad was free to do so. That and a half-day on Wednesday were his time off work. They had barely started this new lovely routine before they found there was another baby on the way to upset their plans. Raymond, the last of the children, is eight years younger than I. The best laid plans certainly went awry for them but I'm sure he was a welcome addition to the family.

I recall Raymond's arrival and the weeks which followed for several memorable reasons. Mum's younger sister Marjorie, who had always had health problems, died of pneumonia two days after his birth. She was only thirty-two years old and left a daughter Jean, who was about eleven years old at the time and living with her father. Mum, of course, was confined to bed for two weeks, which was normal in those days. Father arranged for a Home Help to come in and look after the rest of us children. Mrs King was a buxom 'no nonsense' type of woman and Brenda and I took an immediate dislike to her. We didn't like her cooking from the first meal she put on the table. The gravy was revolting to look at, like something the cat had thrown up, white and lumpy, not at all like the rich brown sauce Mum made. We looked at the pallid liquid and Brenda immediately piped up "Don't give me any gravy, I don't care for it", then she went on "Give Doreen plenty, she really loves gravy". It was the very opposite of the truth. I couldn't eat my dinner because it was swamped in the awful gravy and received a telling off from the harassed Mrs King, whom we hated more as the days went by. She certainly couldn't cook and I was usually on the receiving end of her wrath, really my sister's fault. She constantly got me into trouble with Mrs King. She played some awful pranks on her with Brenda as the ringleader and me as the reluctant follower, too scared to do anything about it. She put salt in her coffee and again I got the blame for it!

Poor woman, she was very relieved when her time was up and we no longer had to tolerate her awful meals. We were also thankful she hadn't told Father how badly we had behaved. I just kept my mouth shut and hoped it would all go away. If Father had found out we had misbehaved, he would have been terribly angry with us both, even though I was the innocent party. Luckily he was too preoccupied with having to go to work and still take care of Mum, the new arrival and the rest of us in the evening when Mrs King departed.

Of course, thankfully, everything eventually returned to normal at 13 Kelso Road. Another new baby-carriage was soon standing in the hallway, a dark green streamlined model, much higher than the low burgundy one which had been around for years. I could barely reach the handle, but I was dying to wheel the new baby. Mum promised I could do so when he was a few months older.

We were a close family growing up in a Liverpool suburb in the 1930s and Sunday was my favourite day. It had a different feel to it from any other day of the week, a silence and a stillness broken only by the church bells ringing and the twittering of birds. The roads were empty of traffic - not that there was much during the week, the shops were all closed with the exception of the newsagents', which would be open for a couple of hours in the morning for the sale of newspapers. Dressed in our best clothes worn only on Sundays, my sister and I would walk to Sunday School, compulsory for the eldest children in the household. I don't recall my parents attending church, except for christening the new baby or functions requiring their presence.

When Sunday School was over we would hurry home and run up the back entry. As soon as we got inside, we could smell the lovely aroma of Sunday dinner. It was usually roast beef, cooked in dripping, with Yorkshire pudding, roast potatoes, brown and crispy also cooked in dripping, mashed carrots and turnips, and a jug of rich brown gravy made from the meat drippings, dark and gooey at the bottom, from the roasting pan, kept in a basin on the cold larder slab. It was absolutely delicious! Mum liked to eat it spread on a piece of toast late on Sunday evening, though she didn't share it with us. I imagine it wasn't a very healthy thing to eat, but no one cared about that in those days.

Dessert was usually a thick, creamy rice pudding, made from evaporated milk, baked slowly in a blue enamel dish kept specially for it. The skin on top formed a brown crust, coveted by each of us, including my father, and he was frequently the lucky one to scrape the dish, since quite often he would be last to finish and eat his portion straight from the container, especially if he was late arriving home from work during the week when we sometimes had rice pudding again.

The best part of Sunday was the long-awaited walk during the late afternoon in Newsham Park, where we always found pennies in the grass. Not just once in a while but every time we went! To an innocent four-year-old it was a magical place to visit. It stayed in my mind as I grew up and still I can conjure up that feeling of excitement and joy of finding those pennies. They are among the treasures which I liken to all things which have blessed my long life.

I have been so fortunate to have a family and friends who have contributed to the rich fabric of my being. Earlier this year, when I began writing this revised edition of my book, I read in the newspaper that the United Kingdom and Canada are sending the penny coin into obsolescence by the end of 2013, since it is now regarded as worthless. I know it is true of Canada, but here in England it still seems to be available. I was sad to read that news, even though I realise the tiny coin now has very little value compared to what it had during the 1930s. To me, pennies from the past will always bring back precious memories of those happy, carefree childhood days and the mystery of finding all those pennies in the grass each time we visited the park.

We never doubted for a single moment that we were finding those pennies. But years later we learned that Dad had dropped the money ahead of us and if we missed any he would help us find each of them, exclaiming "I thought I saw something shining just about there!" We were so naïve and trusting and never questioned our good fortune walking in the park on Sunday afternoons. Neither was I disillusioned when I found out the real reason for our wonderful luck; it just made those pennies seem even more precious to me.

On the way home we would visit the Jubilee Ice Cream Parlour in Kensington to spend our pennies. A cornet of vanilla ice-cream was topped with delicious red raspberry sauce. I always thought the topping was the very best part and licked it slowly to make it last.

I have a heart-warming memory of Dad making his own ice-cream on his half-day off on Wednesday, from the large shoe store where he was manager for many years. Shirt sleeves rolled up tightly on his white, skinny arms, showing his bulging muscles, he would patiently turn the handle of the metal container inside the brown wooden ice bucket, round and round, churning the ingredients until they finally thickened. It would take a long time for that to happen. Eventually when it was ready, all the neighbourhood kids would run up the narrow, cobbled back entry into our back-yard with their assortment of cups for a helping of his delicious ice-cream treat. He was the Pied Piper with his adoring flock of kids every Wednesday afternoon.

He had the energy of ten men in spite of his small stature, and couldn't bear to be idle. I don't recall ever seeing him just sitting down and doing nothing. Every day he cycled fifteen miles to work and back, in all weathers. In the winter, when it was exceptionally wet and very cold, and sometimes snowing, he would wrap newspaper and brown paper around his legs, tying it securely with string to protect him from the elements on his long ride from Fairfield to Walton Road, approximately five miles. Beneath all this he would be dressed in a suit, shirt and tie, as was befitting for the Manager of the Co-op Shoe Store. I never once heard him complain. He was as tough as nails!

I don't recall ever seeing my Dad actually listening to music. The only song I ever remember hearing him sing was a funny little ditty which consisted of about four repetitive lines, which always made us giggle and sing along. I don't know whether he made the song up himself or whether it really existed on the air waves. I think not. It was called "When we get married we'll have sausages for tea"! There was a second verse which I cannot recall. Maybe it's just as well! Apart from that very undistinguished jingle, I realise I haven't a clue about his taste in music, or whether he had any favourites at all.

Another source of music in our young lives would be a trip to the cinema, and again from a small child's perspective, it was another unforgettable experience. Not because of the movie, I never cared what was on when I was very young, but Mum would take us once in a while when my father was working late with stocktaking chores and I would look forward to it, but only to watch the man sitting at the organ, dressed in a smart black suit and white shirt, coming up through the floor in front of the stage, appearing like magic out of nowhere! That was the fascination for me.

As if that wasn't magical enough, the beautiful draped velvet curtains covering the blank screen would change colour every few minutes. I never took my eyes off them, waiting for the next colour to start rippling up from bottom to top, like a rainbow. It was breathtaking to me as a young child, and certainly the best part of going to the cinema. The lights would eventually dim and the organist would disappear, going back down through the floor, waving his hand to the audience as he went. The curtains would open and make way for the roar of the Metro Goldwyn Mayer lion (MGM for short), which usually heralded the start of the big picture. It was all part of the wonderful world of make-believe.

We've come a long way since those days. The world is a much noisier place. Cellphone and I-phone conversations disrupt any possibility of having a quiet ride home from work, if you are using public transport. They talk so loudly! As if the whole bus needs to hear what is going on! Fat chance of snatching forty winks after a day's work. Music comes at us from everywhere, in stores, elevators, boom-boxes in cars and of course on the end of a telephone, patiently waiting for a real person to speak to, instead of a voice interrupting the awful music repeating itself over and over to reassure you that you are a valuable customer, so please continue to hold on for the next available person. Occasionally I have held on for almost an hour before that happens. It makes me absolutely livid and I complain bitterly to the person who is receiving my wrath. Even trying to get a bank balance is like having the third degree, and sometimes you are speaking to someone in India instead of your actual branch. It is quite mind boggling at times! I think my father would have hated it all and I cannot imagine him ever sitting with a phone held to his ear for even ten minutes for any reason. He would have gone ballistic and I'm certain would have caused a revolution in this modern world.

He taught me a great deal about life and values. I looked up to him and respected his advice and did what he expected of me; I accepted that he knew best. I have to admit there were many times when I wanted to do something quite different to his wishes, but I was born in that generation where the male dominated the household. It wasn't resented – it was just accepted as being normal. Quite different to what I now feel at my present age, some of which would have been totally life changing, but that is hindsight and useless to think about.

My dad was from a large family of ten children. His father was a sea captain, a drunk who kicked his wife about when he was home. She had to collect jam-jars and buy his beer with the money. I never met either of them and my father never talked much about his past. My mother told me that his mum died of stomach cancer before she was fifty years old and my dad left home at the age of ten and went to work in a hotel in the city, where he polished shoes and washed dishes to keep himself. He slept in a cupboard, just big enough for him and his few belongings to exist, until he reached the age of sixteen.

The First World War was raging and he enlisted in the Army, lying about his age to be accepted. He was a Dispatch Rider and served in France. I can't imagine what life was like for him, a boy pretending to be a man, fighting for his country at that young age.

I have an old snapshot of him sitting on his motor-cycle dressed in army uniform, looking quite cocky as teenage boys often do at that age. He was definitely a self-made man, pulling himself up by the bootstraps to educate himself and make a success of it.

One of his most treasured possessions was a set of encyclopaedias, bound in brown leather, which were kept locked up in a glass cupboard. Occasionally he would let me look at them. I would sit on the carpet and hold them in my arms because they were very heavy. I loved reading them, especially the medical section, which showed a skeleton which named all the bones in the body. By the time I reached the age of seven I could recite almost all of them.

He was a very strict parent but kind and compassionate, especially with children. He really did love children and spent his free time entertaining them. Mum used to say if he had his way, he would have had enough children to form a football team! However they settled for five.

CHAPTER TWO

MOTHER

My mother was a Manx woman, born on the small ancient Celtic island which lies in the Irish Sea between the North of England and Ireland and is known as the Isle of Man. Those born on the island were usually black-haired and brown-eyed, with skin which tanned very easily in the sun, and small in stature, much like my mother. It is a small island, only thirty-three miles long by sixteen miles wide, but it's a paradise of emerald green hills, white beaches, turquoise sea, lighthouses, rocks, coves and quaint villages. Its residents have a very relaxed lifestyle and have a philosophy most seem to follow - never do anything today if you can put it off until tomorrow!

They have managed to keep this philosophy intact and one gets the impression that most of the island is still many years behind the neighbouring countries. Only the capital, Douglas, which caters mainly to tourists, ever appears to be busy and of course this changes in the winter months.

Approaching by ferry you arrive at Douglas Head Harbour to see the long promenade with its green boulevards and colourful flowerbeds on the sea side and miles of Victorian hotels on the other. My mother was the middle child of three daughters, born in the small fishing village of Peel, famous for its delicious smoked kippers, eaten mainly for breakfast, everywhere on the island. The harbour is dominated by the dark and rather forbidding ruins of Peel Castle situated on the cliffs, high above the village. Their father was William Halsall, the Station Master of the small railway station in Peel. He died when he was thirty-five of pneumonia, leaving his wife Annie-Eliza, to raise three young daughters, Doris, the eldest, Vera, my mother and Marjorie, the youngest, a frail child who suffered from asthma.

Grandma Halsall must have been quite the entrepreneur. She converted the front parlour of their very modest house into a general store and Post Office, baking bread in the early hours of the morning to be delivered to customers each day. This was my mother's job and she told me stories of her walks along the lonely cliff tops before going to school to deliver the loaves, and how afraid she was sometimes on that isolated journey. Even in those days in the early 1900s, there were sexual predators in this idyllic place.

She told me of one incident when walking on the path she took on her bread round, of how she came across a man lying in the grass exposing himself. She dropped the basket of bread and ran home screaming, as fast as her young legs would carry her, and it was a long run to safety. After that, Doris accompanied her to make the deliveries.

She laughed when she first told us this story, many years later, because she thought when she came across him that he was the Three Legs of Man – which is the island's symbol and proudly stands on top of Government buildings and elsewhere, unique and easy to identify.

Celtic folk are very superstitious and believe in fairies, elves and goblins and most certainly, in good and evil spirits, tying a talisman on their front doors on certain days of the year to ward off and remove the evil kind which would cause bad luck and sickness.

Tragedy struck the family again when Mum was in her early teens. They woke up one morning and found their mother still in bed, which was very unusual. They thought at first she was still asleep, but when they couldn't rouse her, they ran next door for help. She had died some time during the night. She was forty-one years old. The doctor assumed she had died of a blood clot or a heart attack, but this was never verified, since an autopsy was never carried out.

Her tragic and sudden death left Mum and her sisters alone to fend for themselves and Doris, being the eldest, decided they would have to move to the mainland of England to find work. Apparently, there was little in the way of money to help them start this new life. Marjorie was too delicate to work, not even able to go into service, as they called it, in any of the big houses requiring help, and she stayed at home. They travelled by sea to the bustling port city of Liverpool, and eventually found lodgings in a small suburb across the River Mersey, in a place called Rock Ferry. Their new home was infested with cockroaches, but it was all they could afford at the time. They were not familiar with vermin, coming from their pristine environment, and Mum told me of leaving the light on all night, since the pests would only leave their hiding places when it was dark and scuttle away when the gas-lamp was lit.

Mum and Doris then began looking for work and were eventually taken on at Lever Brothers' Soap Factory in nearby Port Sunlight, which they hated, but since they had no skills of any sort to offer, had to tolerate it to survive. It was their only option. I can only imagine the awful contrast this new life in a grimy city must have been to their idyllic, tranquil green island – and all that conjures up. Their innocent lives changed so suddenly and drastically with the deaths of both parents.

When I was growing up, I perceived my mother to be a gentle, quiet person, rather meek and mild in manner, very much dominated by my father, whom she met and married in Liverpool through her sister Doris, who was courting a fellow called Joe Seymour. He eventually became our uncle. As children we didn't care for either of them and thankfully they didn't visit us more than twice a year.

Auntie Doris was a very fussy person and on the only visit I made to her house, when I was about eight years old, I remember I had to stay out in the garden until it was time to go home. She was fluffing up the cushions the moment my mother stood up to leave! She couldn't even wait until we departed to do it.

Mum didn't seem to have any friends of her own, except a lady who lived across the road from us in Kelso Road. Her named was Mrs Titherington, but she was usually called Mrs Tithie. She didn't have any children of her own and sometimes she would invite me over and give me a piece of apple pie. I ran messages for her occasionally and Mum was really fond of her. She was very tall and held herself in a very stately manner. Her blonde hair was always beautifully curled, with never a hair out of place in the manicured waves. She wore lovely dresses with matching coats and a small matching hat, even when she was just going to the local shops for groceries.

The only other person who visited our house when Father was at work was an ex-policeman who had lost his wife after many years of marriage. He was very tall, well over six feet, very thin and bony, with sparse gray hair. He would arrive with a small bag in his hand which contained his embroidery. At that time he was working on a cushion. My mother was doing the same; she did a lot of embroidery and produced lovely table runners and tablecloths. It was a popular pastime.

They were chatting away about the various stitches used and all of a sudden out of nowhere Mr Walker exclaimed "I can't abide doing Lazy Daisy Stitch". I found it so hilarious and rushed to hide beneath the dark green chenille table cloth which almost hung down to the floor, trying to stop my laughter. I've never forgotten that episode and the explosion which came from Mr Walker's rather sedate countenance, and any time I see anything embroidered I remember the large ex-policeman, not with a truncheon or helmet but with a needle and thread and his bag of assorted silks, ready to wrestle with the awful Lazy Daisy Stitch. A rare kind of criminal!

The only other visitor I can recall was Uncle Archie, my father's brother–in- law, who was married to Dad's sister Annie, though she never came with him. He was small and slim with straight gray hair brushed back off his forehead above his nice pink complexion, and whenever he came to our house, usually Saturday evening after tea, he brought little wooden gifts he had made himself. They were really beautiful. The one I liked and remembered the best, was a trapeze artist, a small male figure in a frame, much like a swing, which had a knob at one side and when it was turned the little man did somersaults, going over and over whenever you turned the knob. It was a very clever piece of work.

He spent his retirement days making such things. Sometimes he would sit and talk to me, giving advice from one old man to his niece, and something he told me remains in my mind to the present day. He said "Always drink a cup of hot water first thing in the morning, it will keep you healthy, as well as give you a nice complexion". I was nearly fourteen years old when he gave me that advice and I began drinking hot water each morning and continue to do so, never miss it to this day. It's strange how something can stick in your mind as a child. He was the only relative who visited our house, despite my father's very large family. He didn't seem to care about them or miss them and never encouraged Mum to make friends with neighbours. He seemed to be contented with having just his own family around him.

As I grew older I found Mum had a great sense of humour and would make us laugh with some of her stories. It amazed me when I found out she actually enjoyed watching and listening to boxing and wrestling. Such a contrast to her nature. She was a gentle soul who wouldn't kill a spider – they were always moved gently out of the door to freedom! Her four children were her whole world.

I realise now that she had suffered a great deal and was very much a survivor. I love and admire her greatly for that. Mum remained superstitious all her life, just as her sister Doris did, they shared many of the same beliefs. She just differed in small ways. She would never have white flowers of any sort in the house, not even a bunch of wild daisies brought home, clutched in a grubby little hand, as a gift for her. She insisted they were unlucky and would bring sickness. I could never understand some of the weird superstitions though, and decided early in my teenage years that I was not going to be influenced by them. However, memories leave their mark and whenever I see white flowers, especially in someone's home, I immediately think of my mother. I also recall that hospital ward staff did not like to see red and white flowers together in a vase. Apparently it was bad luck! Mum wasn't the only one with that particular superstitious belief.

She was very afraid of thunder and at the first flash of lighting heralding a storm, all pictures and mirrors would be hastily covered with sheets. She would rush to open the front and back doors to let any thunderbolt pass through the house, then shepherd us all into the larder, where we stayed until the storm passed over. I had no idea what a 'thunderbolt' looked like and come to think of it, I still don't!

Mum's sister Doris would not have anything green in her house, not even a child dressed in green clothing. She thought the colour brought illness! Paradoxically, it was my mother's favourite, and she called it God's colour. They both shared another superstition, one which scared them a great deal whenever it happened. They would anxiously wait for the results they felt would most certainly follow if a picture fell down off the wall, for they would shortly be certain to hear of the death of someone they knew. A cracked or broken mirror would upset them too, bringing seven years of bad luck to the unfortunate one responsible for the breakage.

Mother was also afraid of the dark, even in her own home, and would send one of us upstairs to the bedroom where she kept the nappies (diapers) for my youngest brother, Raymond. Too scared to go herself. Of course, she passed her nervous fears to us all, and we grew up afraid of the dark too. I can recall when it was my turn to fetch anything from the bedroom, going upstairs slowly and then coming down like a bat out of hell, jumping the stairs two at a time, or sometimes sliding down the banister rail in my haste to get back to the kitchen, not for the warmth, but to get away from my own fear of the dark.

I remember one occasion when my father was in the hospital having a nose operation and was staying there overnight. She took all four of us to sleep in her bed, locking us in the bedroom for the night. All of a sudden we woke when something made a loud noise, jolting us from sleep. Mother whispered to us to be very quiet and we all listened, hardly daring to breathe, terrified that there was someone downstairs in the house. She didn't investigate. We eventually must have fallen back to sleep, still waiting for something awful to happen. The next morning it was discovered that a pair of Dad's trousers had dropped off the door hook to the floor, and the sound we heard was probably the buttons and his braces hitting the linoleum!

Women's lives were often difficult around the home. Housework was a chore which was accomplished without appliances or any help at all. They worked so hard back in those days. Mum had a routine, a job for every day of the week, as well as taking care of all the cooking, shopping and raising a family. It was very much a full-time occupation. Looking back I realised she never had any spare money to spend on anything she would like to have for herself and in fact, one of the saddest memories I have is knowing that each and every day she had to write down what she had spent on the daily groceries and other small necessities on a piece of paper and give it to my father. I remember seeing her do it, but I was in my teens when I became aware of that demeaning task and also the rows which sometimes followed, which were usually about money. As a young child I thought everything in our house was rosy and happy and as an adult I realised that certainly wasn't the case.

For a very long time, Mum, then in her late fifties, wasn't feeling at all well. Eventually she visited the doctor several times with the same symptoms. This lady doctor she had at that time, kept on telling her she was going through 'the change of life', now referred to as the menopause, in spite of the fact that she had glaring symptoms of diabetes. She had a terrible thirst and took a large bottle of lemonade to bed each night, which was usually empty in the morning. She finally collapsed at the shops one morning and luckily there was a doctor's practice in the same area which called an ambulance to take Mum to hospital. There she was diagnosed with Type II diabetes.

It was never completely controlled, in spite of her strict adherence to diet and injecting insulin twice daily. She had always been very slim until she had the diabetes, but then she gained a great deal of weight. At one period she had alopecia and lost every bit of the beautiful long black hair which I used to brush and play with for hours. She always enjoyed that and would urge me not to stop. It must have been a terrible blow when she lost it all and had to wear a wig. She hated it and to be truthful, it looked false.

In the late nineteen sixties there was very little choice in wigs. Luckily, she had always worn a hat and continued to do so outside but when she was home she would cover her head with a scarf. Poor Mum, it must have been devastating for her when her beautiful locks never came back. Nowadays it is much more common to see bald heads on women, many of them cancer victims receiving certain types of chemotherapy. Thankfully, loss of hair is not now the major event in the scheme of things, when cancer strikes and beautiful wigs are now available.

Diabetes definitely shortened her life. It also seems to be in our family because I have two brothers with it. I always hope I take after my father, because he lived to a great age, in spite of having a very sweet tooth which he passed on to me!

CHAPTER THREE

VISITS TO THE ISLE OF MAN

I recall with a great deal of fondness our childhood holidays on the Isle of Man, accessible then only by sea. The chosen two weeks were usually during the school breaks in the summertime. There was just my sister, younger brother and myself at that time. We would travel to Liverpool Docks after my father finished work on a Saturday evening at six o'clock and eventually we would board the Manx Steamship, which sailed at midnight.

The journey was long and very cold, four hours or even longer when the seas were extra rough, and huge waves would wash over the lower decks. We would spend it on the long, slatted, brown, shiny wooden benches, huddled in blankets, cuddled by our parents to keep warm, on the top deck which had only a roof to keep out the elements. In spite of the bitter cold, my parents chose the fresh air as a deterrent to the sea-sickness which overtook many of the passengers in those swollen, heaving seas. On the deck below the smell of vomit filled the air as the journey progressed and there were many green faces at the end of the trip, many times, ours included.

But as the ship sailed into Douglas Head Harbour in the early morning light, all discomfort was quickly forgotten. We would flock to the rails of the ship, eager to catch that first glimpse of the clear blue water and the long, sweeping Promenade with its Victorian hotels stretching as far as the eye could see. We had arrived in the heart of the island.

This was not our final destination though. We would board the horse-drawn tram, nicknamed, for some reason, the Toast Rack, and this would take us along the promenade and then onward to the small suburb of Onchan Head, where we stayed at a large house on Royal Avenue. Our hostess, Mrs Camp, took in boarders. She was a plump, jolly lady who wore a pinafore and always seemed to be laughing. She would greet us with smiles and hugs and then take us upstairs to the bedrooms which were to be ours for the next two weeks. I remember the bright pink fuchsia and the purple foxgloves which grew in profusion in gardens and wild in the country lanes. The air smelled fresh and clean. It always seemed to be sunny there. I never remember it raining, though I'm sure it did. The countryside was emerald green and a feast to the eyes.

Each morning, after breakfast, we would set out with our parents to spend the day at the beach. My brother, sister and I dressed in our bathing suits, made of fine wool to preserve our modesty. They clung tightly to our bodies. Mine was green and it lasted for years until I grew out of it. I remember though before it was finally thrown out, it sported several tiny holes where the moths had got at it. Happily not in strategic places!

We always carried our buckets and spades with us and we would spend hours making sandcastles, running back and forth to the blue water to fill our buckets to make a moat, a task which never seemed to be accomplished, since the water would vanish into the warm almost white sand. When we tired of this, we would splash and play in the beautiful warm water, and often our parents would join in. Our long days were very simple but we loved every minute of them.

On the walk to the beach we would stop at the small corner store, where the sidewalk was made of red tiles, to choose a lollipop from the jar standing on the counter, to suck on the walk down the many rickety steps from the cliff top to the beach coves below. I always chose blackcurrant flavour. I remember the sharpness on my tongue as I sucked it until it was just a tiny sliver of coloured glass clinging to the stick. They were the very best lollipops in the whole world!

We must have had the run of the kitchen because I remember my father, shirt sleeves rolled up tightly on his thin but muscular arms, cutting endless slices of white crusty fresh bread to satisfy our hunger when we returned from the beach. As fast as he cut them, we three kids would make sandwiches - butties as we called them - usually lathered with strawberry jam, sometimes just with thick, red tomato sauce straight from the tall, glass bottle. They always tasted good and satisfied us for a while, until dinner was ready.

Sometimes in the evening, when it was dark, we would have a very special treat. We would walk to nearby Groudle Glen, a fairyland of lofty trees, lit by tiny lights, paths and walkways lined with rustic rails and the constant sound of water rushing over stones. This was the place where the elves and fairies lived, according to my Celtic mother, and although I never saw any, I knew she was right. It was a magical place.

They were golden days and all too soon it would be time to wash our buckets and spades for the last time. The shells, the souvenirs we had gathered on our visit and the sticks of peppermint candy rock we had bought to take back to our friends were all packed. The goodbyes and hugs were exchanged and we were on our way. We travelled back in daylight and the journey home always seemed so much shorter, the sea not as rough, allowing us to roam about the ship to pass the time.

Our yearly visits to the island ended with the start of World War II in 1939, since it was too dangerous to make the journey because of the German U-Boats which frequented the Irish Sea waiting to torpedo any passing ships. They succeeded many, many times in doing so.

Many years later in 1989, I revisited the Isle of Man, together with my husband and daughter, wanting them to capture some of the magic of my childhood visits which had never been forgotten. We spent time in the small quaint fishing village of Peel where my mother was born and raised, and actually found her home, a small gray stone house sandwiched between identical others in a long row on Glenfaber Road where time had virtually stood still. The small harbour, with its cluster of fishing boats, smelled strongly of fish, seaweed and salt, and the air was filled with the screeching cry of the gulls as they swooped down to capture the fishy tidbits available to them. The fishermen sat around smoking their small clay pipes, waiting for the tide to turn, before heading out to fish for herring and mackerel. The Isle of Man was still famous for its delicious kippers, which we ate for breakfast.

The tiny cottages, whitewashed or painted with pastel colours, were strung out like beads, leaning against each other on the narrow streets. We explored the ruins of Peel Castle which dominates the village, up on the surrounding cliffs and walked along the cliff heads where my mother delivered bread before going to school each morning. On the day we found Mum's house, I stopped and on impulse, walked up the short path, and knocked at the door, my heart beating very fast as I waited to see whether it would be opened. It was, by an old lady with short gray hair and a kindly, pleasant face. I explained why I was there. To my utter surprise she remembered my mother and her family and invited me inside the house. I had goose bumps just spending those precious moments in the cottage where Mum had been born almost 90 years earlier.

She had made a few changes, but it was essentially the same. The small front room, which had been a shop and post office in my mother's childhood, had reverted to a sitting room and she had installed modern plumbing. Other than that, it was the same little house where my mother and her two sisters had spent most of their carefree days before tragedy changed their lives forever.

I thanked her for letting me see her home and left feeling as though I had peeped into the past and could visit it in my mind whenever I wished to and think about Mum and her sisters growing up and the struggle their mother must have had after their father died.

I have visited the island several times since that discovery of where my mother was born. One of those visits was somewhat unexpected and quite different to any other I had made. I was staying with my brother in Old Colwyn, North Wales and had arranged to see my old next-door neighbour Bridgette, who was then living in the Isle of Man with a friend. She had lost her husband Bernard several years earlier, very suddenly, and I had not seen her for quite a while, though we still remained friends. It is a long journey from North Wales to the island and my day began with the alarm clock gently beeping at the ungodly hour of 5.15 am in my bedroom. It was a cold, wet windy morning and I had to remind myself that this was a holiday!

I washed and dressed quickly, left the house, taking care that I didn't wake my brother or his wife, and caught the early train to Chester and then another train to Lime Street, Liverpool, without a hitch. I followed the 'Exit' sign out of the station, humping my heavy case up two flights of stone steps, went through a door and found myself on the street, but not the one I had been expecting to see. It was lashing down with rain and I wrestled with the umbrella as well as my luggage. I was almost doing a 'Mary Poppins' impression. It was so wild and windy it lifted me off my feet, billowing my raincoat out. My hairdo also took a beating.

I was looking for a taxi among the mass of cars whizzing past me in the early morning rush on the very busy streets. The sidewalks were full of people hurrying purposefully to their destinations, while I was dithering about, not knowing where the closest taxi stand could be found. Suddenly, I spied a familiar black cab on the other side of the street, going in the opposite direction, and I hailed it, instinctively imitating actions I had watched many times in past movies, usually in New York. Miraculously the driver saw me waving my free arm frantically, did a U-turn in the middle of the busy street and stopped in front of me. In seconds I was safely inside with my baggage and on my way to the Pier Head, some ten minutes' drive away. What a relief that was!

The driver was a typical Liverpool 'Scouser'. He called me 'Love', asked me twenty questions and wished me a good holiday. He got his large tip! Eventually I boarded the Superfastcat Manx Ferry and we sailed up the River Mersey, once more leaving the buildings which line the waterfront I had seen many times before. The Liver Building with its twin cupolas on the towers topped with the marble liver birds, which look like huge seagulls but which are, in fact, mythical creatures, is one of the landmark buildings of Liverpool's waterfront and familiar to residents and visitors alike.

The sea crossing was really pleasant and surprisingly smooth. The rain lessened and then finally disappeared and before long we had sunshine. The Seacat looks like a luxurious plane inside, with soft navy blue leather seats set in rows with fold-down tables on the backs. There were a number of staff dressed just like flight attendants, serving breakfast and other light meals right at your table. No having to line up for coffee or food! What a complete surprise it was to me. I was wishing I hadn't slapped a solitary slice of ham between two pieces of dry bread at 5.30 that morning and ate them just as soon as I boarded ship before I became aware of the amenities to be had. I told myself I would look forward to the return journey and sample the food.

As the journey progressed and the outline of the Isle of Man loomed into sight, my excitement grew. I knew Bridgette, my long-time friend, would be at Douglas Head harbour with her friend Charles to meet me. We sailed into the harbour some two and a half hours after we left Liverpool. My childhood memories filled my mind. It looked exactly the same as it had done on the many holidays I'd spent in the Isle of Man so long ago. The vast sweep of Victorian Hotels overlooking the wide boulevards, the green verges and the turquoise blue sea were still the same. The horse-drawn tram, nick-named the 'Toast Rack', was still clip-clopping its way, taking visitors up and down the long promenade to view the sights. From the rail of the ship it all looked unchanged and my heart sang with pleasure and anticipation.

Soon I was disembarking and waiting for my case to appear on the carousel in the large waiting area. I looked around for my friend and spotted Bridgette standing beside a tall, slim, gray-haired man in a navy blue raincoat, whom I guessed was Charles. I had spoken with him the previous week, but of course we had never met before. He had also written me a letter assuring me of a welcome in his home as a friend of Bridgette's and followed this up with a phone call, relieving my slight apprehension and it was much appreciated.

Bridgette looked much the same, slim and tiny with a healthy complexion, blue eyes and light brown hair now taking the place of the long black mane she had had as a young bride some forty-odd years ago. She wore it now in a thick ear-length bob which suited her. She was still a very pretty woman at sixty-five years old. To my surprise she was wearing jeans and a white fleece jacket. I had always seen her dressed in skirts and dresses, never pants, but this was the new Bridgette I was soon to learn. She wore them almost throughout my visit of twelve days.

Of course, I had packed skirts and dresses not to feel out of place, instead of the pants I would normally choose to wear! We laughed about this a few days later and since we are the same build she loaned me pants and jackets and I abandoned the contents of my carefully-packed case. Their welcome was warm. Charles had a nice open face, with a healthy pink complexion, and a firm handshake. He spoke without an accent of any kind and I learned later he'd been well educated at public school in England. He was very interesting and articulate and easy to talk to and we had many long conversations during my visit.

Soon we were driving away from Douglas, through the green countryside, towards the village of Port St Mary, which I had not visited before. My first glimpse was of a small harbour. The tide was out, leaving a few dozen small boats marooned in the soggy sand. There was a strong smell of seaweed and the fish and seagulls wheeled constantly overhead attracted by the odour. The sun was shining for my arrival. Surely a good omen for my visit, I thought. Their house was one road over from the harbour and sea front which stretched away for about a mile, lined with small shops. It was sandwiched between other homes and it was tall and narrow, built of thick, dark gray stone quarried on the island. It had three floors, white lace curtains on the small windows and a freshly-painted bright blue front door which sported a large brass knocker shaped as a lion's head. Inside was a fairly long dark hall, with a sitting room off to the left, stairs to the right with maroon carpeting and straight ahead a large rectangular kitchen and eating area, also painted the same bright blue of the front door. There was a patio door on the left leading into a small walled garden with a tiny green lawn and borders with newly planted lobelia, alyssum and geraniums, as well as some fading daffodils – all the work of Bridgette, I suspected.

There was another door off to the right of the kitchen which led into what I can only describe as a junk yard. Old tyres, several car parts I didn't even recognise, a garage which was stacked tight with more of the same and a shining black motor-cycle standing in the middle. It would definitely qualify as an 'unsightly premise' under Council By-laws. It was a mass of clutter! All this belonged to Charles of course and pretty soon it wasn't hard to see that he was an absolute pack-rat who seemed totally reluctant to throw anything away!

There were stacks of books and papers on tables, shelves and any other available surfaces. Bridgette, who is the exact opposite in nature, had tried to make a dent in all this, but it probably was a losing battle. It made me feel good about my own clutter, which looked very minute by comparison.

Bridgette is a calm, serene person who never raises her voice, never hurries or appears to get flustered and often wears a Mona Lisa smile. It is hard to imagine her getting upset about anything. Many times she would ask whether I would like a cup of tea. I would reply in the affirmative, then she would start telling me a story of some happening and I would make the tea and pour it out! I swear she didn't notice I was doing it!

We had some wonderful long talks and she understood the tears for my husband who had died not too long before, since she had lost her husband Bernard, very suddenly three years earlier. We both were living new lives now and doing our best to adjust and survive in the present situation.

My first impressions of the house were that it felt very cold and damp and had a musty smell to it, as though there was mould somewhere, especially upstairs. It looked run down and in need of much tender loving care, but then it was a hundred years old. "I shouldn't be too critical", I told myself.

Soon I was to learn that Charles and Bridgette lived a rather Bohemian lifestyle. We ate lunch out every day around 2 pm, taking turns to pay. We usually had it in a country pub. Charles had an enormous capacity for red wine and drank three glasses with his lunch, seemingly unaware that he could lose his driver's licence for doing so. My seat in the back of his sixteen-year-old Scirocco was devoid of seat belts. I tried not to let that worry me.

Dinner, which I cooked a few times, could be anywhere between seven and nine pm and never seemed a planned affair, decisions only being made after peering into the tiny fridge to see what edible items could be in there, when hunger pangs finally made an appearance. There was, however, an abundance of red wine to calm the pangs!

I managed to survive all these changes to my very orderly life. I even enjoyed it after a few days and decided that the best thing to do was to adopt the old cliché of 'When in Rome...' What I didn't think I would survive were the first nights in the ice-cold bed, in a freezing bedroom, even with two of their three cats sleeping on top of my legs. It was cold with a capital C, bone-chilling cold. I lay in bed that first night in my long flannel nightdress and woollen bed socks and felt as though I could easily die of hypothermia from just lying there! Luckily, I only needed three trips to the bathroom during the night. The rest of the time I lay numb with cold, thinking of what kind of an emergency I could possibly come up with to get me away from there. My apartment had never seemed so attractive to me as it did that night!

The next morning my whole body was stiff as a board with the cold and I staggered out of bed into the frigid air, feeling very much under the weather, and made my way into the bathroom, hoping to thaw myself out in the bathtub. The bathroom was equally cold. Central heating was not part of their lives and when I ran the water it was just lukewarm. I gave up on the bath and washed myself in the basin, reviving myself only slightly before wrapping myself tightly in the fleecy dressing gown loaned to me by Bridgette and then crept downstairs to start my day. Bridgette was already dressed and pottering around the kitchen. Charles had left for work at 8 am and would return at noon, or thereabouts, and then go back again at 4 pm until around six o'clock. He worked at a small grocery market, looking after the books and being useful in general. He was sixty-three years old and just filling in time until he retired in two years.

Bridgette greeted me warmly and asked whether I would like a bath. I replied "That would be lovely" but I mentioned I had found the water quite cool. "Oh" she explained, "the switch to heat the water is in your bedroom, we only put it on when we need hot water. I didn't want to disturb you in case you were still asleep!" Well, at least I had control over something - a hot bath would surely be on my agenda each morning.

The second night came and I knew that I was coming down with something. My throat and chest were raw and scratchy and it proceeded to get worse, but I didn't want to make a fuss and I was enjoying the wonderful outings we had taken in the car those first few days. The hedgerows and hillsides were emerald green, thick with bright yellow gorse. There were primroses, bluebells, harebells and a variety of other wild flowers and blossom everywhere; it truly was a feast for the eyes. The weather was sunny and reasonably warm, in fact, it was much warmer outside than it ever was in the house!

The coves and beaches around this island are a delight. There are lighthouses perched on rocky cliffs, still in use around the island. The villages are quaint and picturesque with picnic spots which look out to the blue sea and are easy to find. Each day there was a plethora of things to see and enjoy. Another trip was to Peel, the little fishing village, home of the celebrated Manx Kipper. We explored the Laxey Waterwheel, which is the largest in the world, built in 1854 to pump water from the mines of the Great Laxey Mining Company. It is easy to spot from long distances away since it is painted bright red, black and gold and it is huge.

One day Bridgette and I rode the steam train from Port Erin to Douglas and enjoyed the journey through the countryside as it slowly chugged its way along, churning out plumes of smoke into the clean air. But it is still a great favourite with the tourists.

We walked through the shopping mall and eventually caught a bus back home. The roads had little traffic since it wasn't the height of the tourist season and the big event of the year on the island, which are the TT Motor-Cycle Trials held late May into June, over a very punishing course, had been cancelled because of the foot and mouth disease outbreak, so the island was even quieter than usual. It has a population of 73,000 people and I always hoped that 72,997 of them were home asleep when I was in the back of Charles' car, especially after his large intake of wine!

Although I was coping with the days, the nights were still a problem. On my third night I coughed constantly for three hours with my head under the clothes most of the time, trying not to wake my hosts, and by morning it was obvious to me that if I didn't do something, I could end up in a strange hospital with, at the very least, pneumonia. I hadn't planned to leave this beautiful island feet first in a pine box! Again, I felt as stiff as a board as I got out of bed and thankfully ran a deep, hot bath to restore my circulation. Dressed and feeling warmer I headed downstairs to Bridgette and the three cats, Thomas, Shuey and Bluey.

I explained apologetically that I was feeling the cold – the understatement of the year – and needed to go to a pharmacy or chemist for some cough mixture. She was very sympathetic and gave me two sheepskin blankets for me to sleep between that night and promised to light the stove in the lounge which would filter warmth up to the bedroom. She had no idea I had felt so cold, because obviously they didn't notice it, but I was grateful for her response.

We made the visit to the local pharmacy and armed with a jar of Vick's Rub, cough mixture and a hot water bottle, I hoped for a better night and less of an endurance test.

During my stay, I persuaded Charles to let me set up his computer on the large old desk in the lounge, instead of it sitting in the corner of the kitchen, where he had to re-connect the monitor each time he used it, for lack of space on the shelf he was using. He kept the monitor under a chair in the kitchen! All part of the incredible clutter. He agreed, and was delighted with the new set-up. I showed him some basic tasks such as how to transfer documents on to the floppy disks being used at that time, and how to defrag and a few other useful things he hadn't been able to figure out. He called me a genius! I had to smile, since I would never call my computer skills anything but basic. I also showed him how to send E-mails from the computer in the local Library, since he didn't have Internet service, and he was really tickled pink with that.

We got on like a house on fire and although we were three very distinct and different personalities, we enjoyed each other's company. The big love of Charles' life was definitely his motor-cycle, a big black, shiny BMW, which he rode over the switch-back roads on the famous TT course, whenever he got the chance, sometimes with Bridgette as his pillion passenger. He also collected old cars and swore he would build something really special out of them, when he retired in a couple of years' time! Bridgette just smiled her Mona Lisa smile. They seemed to have a really wonderful friendship.

Towards the end of my visit, I ventured to ask Charles whether I could have a ride on his motor-cycle. He looked surprised but very pleased, and on my last Sunday there, I got dressed up in Bridgette's black leather motor-cycle kit, donned the very heavy crash helmet, climbed on to the back of the bike and had a wonderful time. We rode thirty-five miles to Douglas and back, through some of the racing circuit, going at speeds of eighty-five miles an hour on the winding roads. It was totally exhilarating and I didn't want it to end. I had last been on a motor-cycle when I was seventeen years old, and now at seventy-five I hadn't forgotten what to do – or more importantly – what NOT to do. It was all about instinctively knowing how and when to lean in the right direction. For a while, I was just a teenager again, alive and completely without fear. It was something I will never forget.

My hosts were such lovely people and day by day I enjoyed their relaxed attitude to life. It was almost stress-free because 'mañana' was their favourite word. I never heard a raised voice or a sharp word during that twelve days and when it was finally time to leave, I realised it had helped me a great deal.

I know, if it is possible, I will return to the Isle of Man and again visit some of the nooks and crannies of the island. Next time I hope to walk some of the winding paths over the green hills which on that occasion, were closed because of the Foot and Mouth outbreak. I have picked up a book of walks and checked the hotels in Port Erin who lease apartments for long and short periods, in the hope that my family can share some of the fascination I feel for this magical place. I will perhaps visit Charles and Bridgette and maybe cadge another ride on the BMW motor-cycle and feel young again for a little while.

CHAPTER FOUR

MEMORIES OF CHILDHOOD PLEASURES - CHRISTMAS

Christmas was a wonderful event when I was a small girl growing up in England during the 1930s. We were just an ordinary family, neither very rich nor very poor, just like thousands of others. I was too young to know about riches or poverty at that particular time.

As the Christmas season grew near the shop windows would be dressed with sparkling tinsel, Christmas trees and decorations, giving them a festive air. We didn't have shopping malls in those days. The local shops were in long rows, each painted a different colour, joined to each other, stretching away on either side of the road. They had large plate glass windows, decorated year round, following the seasons of the year and it was a favourite pastime in the evening, when the stores were closed, just to look in the store windows at the display of merchandise. Hence the expression 'window shopping'.

There was very little traffic on the streets then, just the tramcars taking people on their journey to work or to shop in the downtown area of the city. There were a few trucks on the roads, but often deliveries were made by horse and cart. Big dappled gray work horses with huge feet, clip-clopping along the cobblestone streets, pulling very heavy loads. They were Clydesdale horses, especially bred for heavy work, used in the city as well as work on the farms.

The Lamplighter would appear each night as dusk descended, with the long pole he used to light the gas lamps. He rode a bicycle from lamp to lamp. In the winter when the days and nights were sometimes very foggy, the lamps cast a weird, eerie glow and made it difficult to see if you were unfortunate enough to be out.

In those days, when coal fires were one of the main sources of heat, together with paraffin lamps, thick pea-soup fog was very frequent and very harmful to the health. I do remember when it was extra cold we had a fire plus the smelly paraffin lamps, which would be placed at the foot of the stairs. The smell pervaded the whole house, but did take the chill off the air. Mum would make us wear a scarf around our nose and mouth when we went out, which was supposed to avoid breathing the foul air. I don't think it helped very much.

In the heart of Liverpool City there were many big department stores, all fairly close to each other on London Road and Church Street, usually eight or more stories high. Each floor would contain certain items and if you took the lift (elevator) there would be a man or sometimes a woman, dressed in a smart dark uniform, usually black or brown, to call out the various merchandise as the lift moved from floor to floor. For instance, "China" meant the whole of that floor would be devoted to cups, saucers, teapots, glasses and dishes and porcelain or pottery. You always knew when to get off as long as you were sure of what you were going to buy and it made shopping a lot easier.

As Christmas came close these large stores would transform a whole floor into a grotto. This was a lovely place for kids to visit and we always looked forward to it with great anticipation, excitement and a little trepidation. Each store would choose a theme from the many story-book characters we all knew and loved – Red Riding Hood, Jack and the Beanstalk, Cinderella, Sleeping Beauty, Snow White and the Seven Dwarfs and many others. So much to see with wide eyes, as we slowly walked through long, twisting, turning passageways, much like long tunnels, lit with masses of tiny coloured lights, listening to Christmas music as we slowly made our way to Father Christmas, otherwise known as Santa Claus or St. Nicholas.

I have to admit, when it was my turn to visit with him, that my stomach would be doing little flip-flops and I didn't really want to sit on this large stranger's lap and talk to him, but that was what this visit to the grotto was really all about. I thought if you didn't go to the grotto, you wouldn't receive any presents on Christmas Day.

Father Christmas would be sitting on his large throne-like chair, dressed in his bright red clothes, trimmed with white fur. He always wore a wide black belt around his fat stomach and had black boots on his feet. His bushy white beard hid most of his face. When it finally was my turn he would ask what I wanted for Christmas and his elves, usually wearing green, who were the helpers, would write it down. Then he would ask that all important question – "Have you been good all year?" I would just nod my head, too shy and much too scared to speak, just waiting for the moment when I could slide off his knee and return to the safety of Mother's arms; she was always close by urging me to answer properly. His elves would then reach into a huge sack and give you a parcel wrapped in tissue paper – usually red for the girls and green for the boys. Inside would be a small gift to take home. Our magical, but scary visit to the Grotto was over for another year and we could now really look forward to Christmas Eve when Father Christmas would be paying a visit to our house.

Two weeks before the big day we would help our parents decorate the living room with stretchy, crepe paper streamers about two inches wide which we made ourselves in every colour imaginable. They would be criss-crossed, corner-to-corner, up close to the ceiling and fastened with drawing pins to the wooden picture rail. We would also make paper chains with paste and coloured paper and these would be draped over mirrors and pictures with a bunch of holly in the middle. Sometimes we would have clusters of red and green balloons in the corners of the room. The finishing touch would be a bunch of mistletoe hung over the doorway. It was the custom to try and catch someone under the little white berries and make them give you a kiss.

We had an artificial Christmas tree with real candles, small spiral ones about four inches long, usually white, in small green metal holders which clipped to the branches of the tree. Each evening Dad would light the candles carefully, and it would take him quite a while to do this. The soft flickering lights made the coloured shiny balls we'd hung on the tree twinkle and the whole room looked different - cosy and somehow mysterious, casting shadowy shapes on the walls.

On Christmas Eve right after supper, we would have a bath in the big zinc tub in front of the warm kitchen stove which always had a fire glowing in it. Mum would boil water in big black iron pots on the hob especially for this and of course it took a lot of water, and she spent a lot of her time seeing to it. Then, dressed in clean flannelette pyjamas, we would each be given a clean white pillow-slip to take upstairs to bed, ready for the visit from Father Christmas. We would put it on the end of the bed where our feet could nudge it to check whether he'd been, whenever we woke, usually quite frequently!

Before we went to bed we helped Mum make up a small treat for Father Christmas when he came. A small glass of port or sherry and a piece of homemade bun loaf, which is a fruit cake full of nuts and candied peel, with marzipan on top, would be put on a tray with a napkin. It was very rich and always cut into tiny pieces. It was always gone when we got up the next morning!

I shared a bed with my sister and on Christmas Eve we would have a terrible time falling asleep. We were so afraid that we would still be awake when that all-important visit to our house was made. I remember us pulling the bedclothes right up over our heads, nearly suffocating, trying not to breathe, and many times thinking we could hear reindeer bells coming closer. It was an exciting time but rather frightening as well. We were told if we weren't asleep, Father Christmas wouldn't leave us any presents.

Eventually sleep would claim us, but early morning, as soon as it was getting light, sometimes even before that time, we would check the pillow case, nudging it with our feet, then feeling something there, we would shout, full of excitement "he's been!" and we'd grab our pillowcase and dash to our parents' bedroom and push in between them in their large very soft bed, to open up our presents. Usually there were only one or two gifts, but no matter what we received we loved whatever was there. We didn't expect much in those days. Our gifts always included a small mesh bag full of chocolate money wrapped in shiny gold foil, a tangerine, a red apple and a handful of nuts which we would shell later and eat.

I remember one Christmas, just after my eighth birthday, finding a beautiful doll with a porcelain face with deep blue eyes fringed with thick black lashes, which opened and shut when you moved her to a sitting position. She had long golden hair curled into thick shiny ringlets. Her body and legs were made of cloth and she had long white lace pantaloons under her pink dress and tiny white shoes on her feet. I loved her on sight and called her Valerie because I had a best friend at school with that name. I later knitted tiny coats and bonnets with pale pink baby wool, which had silver thread running through it. I had her until I was fifteen years old and gave her, and my other toys away to some orphaned children during the war years, at the suggestion of my father. It was hard to part with them but it seemed a good reason to do so at the time.

I learned many years later that Mum and Dad had spent four nights at a visiting fairground where my Dad had persevered on the rifle range until he had enough points to have two dolls to take away as prizes, one for me, the other for my sister Brenda. Now, that's what I call a beautiful gift.

Another memorable Christmas gift one year was a wrist watch – the very first one I'd ever owned. I had asked for it, but wasn't really hopeful it would be there. Sure enough in the bottom of the pillowcase, was a slim black leather case lined with matching velvet. Inside was a watch with a round face and black leather straps each side. I was thrilled that year and walked around for days with my left arm stuck out showing off my prized possession, asking everyone "do you want to know the time?" and telling them anyway!

Looking back to that period in my life when I was a child, I feel very blessed with everything I had, which really, by today's standard, wasn't a great deal. Each gift was appreciated and treasured. Sometimes receiving just one precious gift is better than having a whole bunch of things which you get tired of soon.

There was one gift I longed for which never materialised. I always yearned to be like the film star Shirley Temple. She was the cute, precocious child, beautiful to look at, with a mop of blonde ringlets, laughing eyes and dimples in her round cheeks, who tap-danced her way into millions of hearts through the movies, for many years. I bore absolutely no resemblance to the lovely Shirley Temple with my dark brown, very straight hair and plain little face, redeemed slightly by large hazel eyes, but I longed for a pair of red tap-shoes fastened with ribbon bows, utterly convinced that if I had them I would be able to dance like her. I would tap my feet, twirling around in front of the long wardrobe mirror in my parent's bedroom, arms outstretched pretending I was Shirley Temple, trying to smile, beguiling and charming just like her.

In spite of asking many times for a pair of tap shoes, they never appeared. My shoes were always the sensible kind, made to last and keep the feet dry on the long walks to and from school, chosen by my father because of being manager of a shoe store. Twice yearly he would bring home a small selection of shoes for our growing feet, usually lace-ups or buckle-strapped black ones and of course the knee-high rubber boots we called 'wellies' (short for wellingtons) for the wet weather. They were good for stamping through puddles on the way to school but quite heavy and ugly. One year Brenda and I looked like a pair of Nuns, in new matching raincoats, navy-blue ones with a hood, down to our ankles, worn for several years and disliked intensely. When she eventually grew out of hers I inherited it and wore it for several more winters, until finally it was thrown out and replaced with another long suitable raincoat.

I loved everything about Christmas; the lights, the tree, the stores, the visit to the Grotto, even if it scared me a lot. The children who came to the door in December to sing carols, the lovely smells of favorite food in the kitchen, the eagerness and anticipation as Christmas Day came closer and closer and you felt you would burst with excitement when you went to bed on Christmas Eve.

Finally I gave up asking for tap shoes. Instead my sister and I were enrolled in an Acrobatic Dancing Group and became Co-op

Sunbeams, not what I really wanted to do but we did eventually enjoy it and performed quite a few times in front of adoring parents, Mum included, usually gazing up at us from the front row. She had to sew costumes for us both, every bit done by hand – no sewing machine in our house.

When I think about it now, it must have been a heck of a lot of work. For one show number we had ice-blue short satin flared-skirted dresses and for an Egyptian number she sewed cream-coloured muslin pantaloons with emerald green satin sleeveless bodices, trimmed with gold braiding around the armholes and neckline. We practised hard and became really good at forming a pyramid, with me, the smallest and lightest dancer, on the very top. We had to hold that position like statues for what seemed ages, before dismantling the pyramid in graceful fashion and bowing to the audience in unison.

I loved being on stage and was never shy or nervous about performing. It must have been the 'ham' in me as I was a shy child as a rule, who hid under the long dark green chenille tablecloth edged with tassels, which hung down over the table nearly touching the floor, whenever anyone came to the house.

My thoughts of becoming 'Shirley Temple' gradually faded with time, but not my love of dancing. At the age of sixty-five I joined another dancing group of senior citizens under the dubious title of 'The Golden Girls' and finally fulfilled my childhood dream of learning to tap-dance. My favorite number was dancing to Frankie Vaughan singing 'What's Behind the Green Door?' I absolutely loved every minute of it and the black patent-leather tap-shoes, tied with ribbon bows, mine at last, were my prized possession for a long time. Friday mornings were the high spot of my week. I only stopped dancing when my husband's long illness made it impossible for me to get to class. The shoes stayed in the cupboard for years before I actually parted with them.

My next venture, many years later, was to join a line dancing class, and for a while I enjoyed it, although I found it rather difficult to remember all the different steps. The teacher taught us one or two new dances each week, a lot to digest at my age and reluctantly I eventually stopped going.

My very last adventure on the dance floor was confined to just one appearance. It came about through my old friend Bridgette, who phoned to tell me she had found a beginners' class about to start a new session in a week's time. It was a belly dancing class! She was very enthusiastic and had been to classes for the same thing, where she lived, for a number of years. I really wanted to decline but she was very persuasive and I didn't want to hurt her feelings so agreed to try it.

Bridgette said she would go with me the first night and gave me instructions on what I should wear. I went shopping for a full length, down to the floor, cotton skirt and bought a nice flouncy one in a dark pink shade to go with my black velvet top, and a pair of very light flat slipper-shoes. Apparently some students danced in bare feet, but I didn't fancy that thought and settled for the slipper-type footwear. Now I was all set to belly dance!

The class was to start at 7 pm and I met Bridgette outside the hall just ahead of time. She handed me a small brown-paper parcel, the contents of which were to be tied around my hips on top of the skirt. It was a broad band of black velvet, liberally scattered with small gold hoops, which apparently would jingle with the correct movement of my torso. She gave me the name of it, but I soon forgot it. Topping it off was a pair of castanets for my fingers to produce even more sounds as I danced. I felt very daunted as we climbed the two flights of stairs to the 'ballroom' for the one and a half hour session. It felt a bit like my first driving lesson in 1963, too many things to remember and not enough hands to accomplish them.

There were about a dozen women assembled, all of them much younger me. At 78 years old that wasn't a big surprise! What soon became a surprise – a big one and very obvious – was that this was not a beginners' class. Everyone, without exception, knew exactly what they were doing, while I hadn't a clue! The teacher who had greeted me knew I was a beginner. I explained that I had never belly danced before. "Don't worry, you'll soon catch on, just enjoy yourself" she assured me, and that was it. I scuttled to the very back of the lines of dancers, feeling way out of my depth. There was no help coming my way and I just tried to imitate the four ladies immediately ahead of me. I waved my arms to the music in graceful fashion while trying to remember to click the castanets and drum my feet very fast, in an effort to make jingling sounds from the hips. It was totally exhausting, but I carried on as best I could for the remainder of the session. The longest one and a half hours I can ever remember!

I found out at the end of it all – just as I had suspected – that the class was not for beginners at all, it was actually an advanced class! Bridgette, or someone, had made a mistake. We had turned up on the wrong night! It was my only attempt at belly dancing. I had no desire or inclination to try it again, in spite of the teacher and Bridgette reassuring me that I had done well, under the circumstances. The long flouncy skirt still hangs in the closet, never worn since that night. The slippers were worn around the house until they fell apart, destined for housework – not for belly dancing! I think my dancing days are over.

As a child I was never tired or bored with life and usually was very happy and contented. Our lives and the pastimes and games we played were basically very simple. Of course life wasn't totally carefree, I had my fears and was afraid of the dark and a visit to the toilet wasn't anything to look forward to but that couldn't be avoided. The red brick terraced house we lived in had a back yard with high brick walls in which our outside toilet facilities were located. This was a place I absolutely hated and feared, not only for the short walk from house to the toilet, dark in the winter months, but because of the huge spiders which made their home there, lurking in the corners of the whitewashed outhouse, watching me I thought. I was also frightened of falling down the large black hole beneath me as I sat on the wide wooden seat, bleached white with frequent scrubbing. The toilet paper was thick and often homemade squares hung on the wall by string threaded through a hole. During the war we had to use newspaper for the same purpose. This was never a place to linger!

Beyond was the cobblestoned back entry, which ran the length of the street. The only garden we had was the size of a postage stamp, and had a foot-high brick wall around it, alongside the front step which went straight on to the pavement where we played hopscotch. It was quite a long road of identical houses which looked pretty much alike. Lace curtains and aspidistra plants must have been high fashion at that time, since almost every window of every house on the street looked virtually the same, the long thick green leaves of the plant sticking straight up between the draped white lace curtains.

The front step was our playground, our world of make-believe, where I and my friends would play House, Doctors and Nurses or Hospitals, mimicking our own parents and life in general. Our dolls were our babies who got sick and needed the doctor, or they were naughty and had to be scolded. They had to be dressed and undressed, and diapers (which we called nappies in England) had to be changed. Sometimes we would have tea-parties, using candy from a store called Daltons, located not far from home. They sold sweets shaped like miniature vegetables, potatoes, green peas and tiny brown lamb chops. They all tasted the same, but we didn't care about that. We even had pretend cigarettes, thin white sweet sticks with a red end, glowing like the real thing. Just like the grown-ups around us we would mimic them, inhaling and exhaling the pretend smoke. Sometimes we'd do the same with liquorice pipes filled with tiny coloured balls for tobacco. It was proof that parents and adults in general do influence their children.

There was always so much to do; a favourite was playing marbles in the gutter and coveting the red ones the most. We called them "Pollies" and at night we'd wash them, sorting them into colours and counting them, before putting them into the small, home-made cotton bag, with the drawstring, and stowing them away carefully for the next time.

Top and whip was another favourite pastime. We would decorate the plain wooden top with small pieces of coloured paper, preferably the kind that glittered, and the top would look like a kaleidoscope of colour and changing patterns as it spun on the pavement. I never got tired of watching or playing with this simple toy.

In the summer months when fruit was available, we would collect the pits from apricots and plums, patiently rubbing one side flat on the concrete step, then making a hole with a darning needle and scraping out the soft white contents inside, until we had a tiny canoe. It took a long time to accomplish. When we had our armada complete, we would spend hours sailing them in a dish of water.

Skipping ropes and yo-yos all had their turn throughout the year and as all kids do, we all became very proficient. None of our games required much in the way of materials. Most were just simple and inexpensive toys, sometimes given at birthdays and Christmas; otherwise we used what we had, plus our imaginations, which took us anywhere we wanted to go.

On fine summer days when we were out of school, Mum

would pack us off to the local park with a bag of fish paste sandwiches and a bottle of water or lemonade for lunch. We'd take a ball and a cricket bat and play rounders, the English version of American Baseball. That event would keep us occupied for most of the afternoon.

When I was about ten years old I received a pair of roller skates for my birthday which I absolutely loved. I would skate to the shops for a couple of items Mum needed and save her the effort. One particular afternoon when I came home from school, she was about to make a pudding for supper that night. She had just discovered she needed eggs and told me to run up to Pegrams Grocery to pick a half-dozen up. I asked whether I could go on my skates because it would be quicker and she said 'No' at first then gave into my pleading request to go on them. I said "Don't worry, I will be very careful Mum, I never fall on my skates any more".

I left for the ten minute journey, picked up the eggs and put them in the small shopping basket she had provided and skated back home very carefully, down Wyndham Avenue, then on to Hilary Avenue, which was a bit longer, and finally arrived safely with the eggs on the doorstep of our house. I stretched my hand to press the bell, losing my balance as I did so and dropped the basket on to the tiled floor! Most of the eggs were smashed and I did expect Mum to be very angry with me, but I was so upset that she just told me that would be the last time I went for anything breakable on my skates. For once I didn't argue!

I had another adventure on the way to the shops. This time it involved my baby brother Raymond and the fancy baby carriage, the handle of which was rather high for me to reach. In spite of that, I kept asking my mother to let me take him for a walk. Finally she gave in, warning me to be very careful when crossing the road and getting the carriage off and on the sidewalk at the top of

Wyndham Avenue, just prior to reaching the shops, where I was picking up a loaf of bread for my Mum. It was perfectly safe in those days to leave the baby outside of the store while you shopped. Getting the baby carriage up and down the curbs was difficult and the worst happened - my baby brother slid backwards on to the pavement, screaming his head off. I was absolutely petrified and held him until he stopped crying and put him back into the pram. There wasn't anyone around and I rocked the carriage gently all the way home until he fell asleep. I never told my mother what happened and hoped she would never find out.

There is an old adage with says 'Be sure your sins will find you out'. Weeks later when Mum was wheeling Raymond up to the shops, a lady stopped her as she got to the top of Wyndham Avenue – scene of my accident – and asked my mother whether the baby was all right. To cut a long story short, she had been looking out of the window and saw the whole thing happen. My secret was no longer safe. My mother of course was very angry with me and I never asked again to wheel the baby carriage. Thankfully my brother hadn't appeared to be any worse for his experience, but I had learned a valuable lesson.

As an adult, with children of my own, I have visited families and friends with children. In most cases, the living rooms were cluttered with a vast assortment of toys - some of them huge replicas of the real thing, like vacuum cleaners, cars big enough to sit in, telephones - so many things, yet the children kept asking their mothers, "What shall I play with?" I was happily surprised though to find one little guy, two-year-old Luke, sitting on the kitchen floor, spinning the lid of a saucepan over and over again, with a look of complete absorption and happiness on his lovely face. I witnessed this on my three visits to this particular home, and it brought back a vivid memory of my own son, Christopher, who, at the same age, played for hours on my kitchen floor with pots and pans just as Luke had done forty years later. I thought many times there was a message here for parents that all children want and need to be creative and really don't require the excess of toys given to them by their doting parents and grandparents. They simply want to be given the time to be just kids, to use their imaginations and to feel safe, wanted and loved by their parents. This is the need of every child whether they are rich, poor or somewhere in between, though I know that isn't always the case.

As I write this chapter I know that life as become even more complicated with the arrival of electronics into our midst and I am amazed at the sight of practically the whole generation of young and adults, all with cellphones sticking out of their ears or technology of one kind or another. I am quite happy not to be part of all. I do have a computer, mainly used as a typewriter, and while I do keep in touch with friends by email I have no desire for other new devices which seem to appear on a steady basis. Some of them have scrumptious names like Blackberry, something I only relate to in a pie or a pot of jam! I do appreciate that the new technology is probably wonderful but it arrived too late for me to want to be part of it. At least that is how I feel at the present time. Who knows, I might change my mind!

CHAPTER FIVE

MEMORIES OF THE KITCHEN

The kitchen has always been one of my favorite places and Thirteen Kelso Road was the first one I really remember. It was a large square room with a black iron range at one end, which had an open fireplace and ovens each side in which Mother cooked. It took up the whole wall and dominated the kitchen, which was the hub of the house, the room we used the most. There was always a pot of something simmering on the hob and all our hot water came from the same source. The ashes were removed first thing in the morning every day and once a week my Mum would blacklead the whole range, making it shine like ebony. The floor was red tiles, cold to the touch even on warm days, and food was kept in a larder off the kitchen.

A small room with shelves and a cold slab made of concrete, on which Mum would keep meat and other perishable items, on plates and dishes, was always covered with mesh to keep away the flies. She hated flies in the house and there was always a long sticky fly catcher hanging in the kitchen from the ceiling, near the light.

It did its job very well, but I hated seeing the flies struggling as they tried to get free of the sticky, killing glue. I would look away and was always happy when the old fly strip was taken down and a fresh one put in its place. For a little while, it would be empty of the horrible insects.

We had a large radio which in those days required a huge battery, the weight of several heavy books, which had to be taken to Appletons' Chandlers Shop to be recharged every few weeks. It was the only means of communication in that time.

I always knew what day it was in our house by the smells in the kitchen as I entered the back door from school. I hated Monday with its smell of wet washing, which took all day and a great deal of energy. Mum would be wearing rubber wellington boots and apron and would be hot and tired after scrubbing the clothes before putting them to boil in the huge zinc tub, which was heated by gas, and afterwards they would all have to be rinsed over and over by hand until all the soapsuds had completely disappeared. Finally they would be put through the mangle or the wringer. It was my job to help her wrestle with the heavy flannelette sheets, folding them before putting them through the rollers, to make the process easier, trying to hold the wet sheets away from me as Mum turned the handle, which took all the strength she could muster.

In those days pillow cases, tablecloths, linens, collars from Father's shirts and even handkerchiefs, were put into a bucket of starch. This was usually the last thing to be done. Washing day was an awful lot of hard work, and it took many hours to complete the job. When it was finally finished, the washing would be placed on a pulley which came down from the kitchen ceiling and then hoisted up again as high as possible. There it would stay until the clothes dried, sometimes overnight since the heat from the stove would rise up and dry them quickly. The heavy things and the sheets took much longer.

Of course that wasn't quite the end of washing day. The water had to be ladled out of the washtub, the floor mopped and the mats put down and it would be time to start the dinner for when my dad came home from work. A few years later we had a new washtub which had a tap on the front and the water could be emptied into a bucket and put down the sink or the outside grid in the yard. That was a big improvement but still a big chore. In this day and age of large washing machines and dryers, we should all count our blessings that we don't have to endure the hard labour previous generations, like my mother, had to endure each and every week.

My favourite day for lovely aromas in our house was the day Mum baked bread. The smell of yeast and fresh loaves would fill the kitchen and she would give me a crust from the end of a new loaf as a special treat for helping her with the washing. My second choice would be the smell of clean sheets, dried on the line outside, blowing in the breeze. It wasn't until we moved to a house with a garden in 1939 that the washing was dried that way with a line which stretched the length of the back garden. What a difference that made! I would help bring it in when it was dry and always bury my head in the clothes to inhale the fragrance of the clean scented air.

One other item I recall being in the kitchen for a short time one winter when I was about four years old was a swing, the kind you see in a children's play area. Ours was just inside the back door. One evening before my father came home from work late my sister was pushing me back and forward on the swing and I slipped off backwards, hitting the back of my head hard on the red tiled floor. In minutes I had a lump the size of an egg and my mother rushed me to the nearby chemist, happily still open, where Mr Prebble, who was as efficient as any doctor, held cold compresses on my sore head before talking to my mother about what to do if the lump didn't go down and/or any other symptoms appeared. My mother was terrified of my father knowing about the accident – for that's what it was – warning both of us not to mention it to him. We never did of course and I did not suffer any ill-effects, other than a sore head for a few days.

I realised as I grew older that Mum was afraid of my father and his quick temper which flared up occasionally, especially if he found one of the drawers messy. He would empty the contents on to the floor and she would rush to tidy them all back in their proper place.

The swing was dismantled shortly after, but the two pleasant things still remain on the top of my list of special memories of Mum's kitchen, when I was a child: the lovely aroma of newly-baked bread and the smell of clothes dried in the fresh air in the garden, when we eventually had one.

CHAPTER SIX

THE CHIMNEY SWEEP

Nothing caused more chaos or mess in our house than a visit from the chimney sweep, and yet it was an absolute necessity to have him twice a year, in the days of coal fires. Mum hated that day because it meant an awful lot of extra housework, cleaning up the mess after him. Soot, like dust, only worse, made its insidious way into every nook and cranny, in spite of precautions taken ahead of his visit. Mum would have prepared the room, moving the furniture back against the walls as far away as possible from the fireplace, covering everything with sheets, old curtains and even old newspapers, as far as the front door. Rugs would be rolled up and put well out of harm's reach. Still, as I said, if you were burning coal in your fireplace, it had to be done. I can recall what it was like when the build-up of soot in the chimney did catch fire, dropping down on to the hearth in red-hot smouldering lumps. It was very frightening because the chimney would roar and the sparks would fly out of the chimney-top, along with hot glowing lumps of soot falling down. The rugs would hastily be pulled out of the way, and Mum would grab the package of salt and throw handfuls of it on the fire to kill the flames.

Within the next few days the chimney sweep would appear at our house. Most chimney sweeps were small, thin men who always had traces of their trade in their appearance. Even if our house was his first call, as it often was, we could see traces of soot on his hands and in the creases of his thin face. He wore black, grimy clothes smelling of sulphurous soot, arriving on his bicycle, with his collection of long, stiff brushes, hanging over his shoulder. Usually he would be accompanied by a younger version of himself, often just a young lad, who had the job of climbing up on the roof to make sure the brush was coming through the chimney top, the assurance that the job was being done properly. Our chimney sweep bore no resemblance to Dick Van Dyke, who played the same role in Mary Poppins, flying above the rooftops on his bicycle without a trace of soot on his face!

The job would take about forty-five minutes and when it was finished there would be a small mountain of black soot sitting in the grate, spilling over on to the floor. The air would be foggy with soot which had been forced down the chimney, leaving a coating of black dust everywhere. The sweep would shovel the soot into a sack, collect his money and leave Mum to clean up the horrible mess, which would take hours.

Later, when we moved to a house with a garden, Mum would ask the sweep to leave the soot behind and my father would put it in the soil, around the onions he grew, which had marvellous benefits. He won prizes for his onions when he entered them in gardening competitions, showing he was probably correct.

As the years passed, steps were taken to provide cleaner air to eliminate the pea-soup fog we used to endure, especially in the wintertime, causing lots of health problems to the population, especially the elderly. It was a product called coke, and looked like large lumps of gray cinder toffee. Still a derivative of coal, but much cleaner burning, although not as bright as coal, it did eventually glow red and gave off the much needed warmth. Central heating had never been heard of, especially by the working class, in those far-off days. I still remember those pea-soup fogs even as a teenager. Sometimes it was so dense you couldn't see a hand in front of you and we had to tie a scarf around our mouths to avoid breathing it.

It was particularly frightening to be out in the dark when it was foggy, it was so creepy and eerie with just the street lights, which weren't particularly bright. even on a clear night. The yellow fog formed halos around the lights at the top of the iron lampposts and you hardly see them until you were really close up. The fog muffled the street sounds and I seldom went out alone when it was really bad. Like my Mum, I was afraid of the dark and venturing out in the black foggy night was definitely a no-no.

Once the Clean Air Act came in force in Britain, coal and the chimney sweep became obsolete, a thing of the distant past, along with those pea-soup fogs, but I remember him as a regular visitor to our house for many years.

CHAPTER SEVEN

STARTING SCHOOL

I had reached my fifth birthday in December and it was my first day at Infants School. It was also the first day for several other children and for a boy named Georgie Borne. There were no kindergartens or play schools in those far off days, nothing to prepare you for what lay ahead. When you reached your fifth birthday you simply started school the next term, and for me that was early January. On that morning I left the safe familiar world of home, to be thrust into a new strange environment a very daunting world for a sheltered shy five-year-old girl.

That first day I joined the small group of new students waiting in the front hallway, holding on to my mother's hand tightly, until she gently but firmly told me it was time to go. That was a long time ago, but I still remember the introduction into that new world away from my mother. I remember that I wore a long-sleeved light brown sweater with a collar which had a tie at the neck striped with a rainbow of colours. I wore long black woollen stockings for the first time, held up by wide, home-made elastic garters which made my legs itch and left red marks around the tops of my legs.

My very straight dark brown hair had been cut to a mid-length bob, complete with a fringe which never did lie flat on my brow, as it was supposed to.

I remember the music the teacher played on the piano as we marched in to take our places in the big hall for our first assembly. It was called 'In an English Country Garden' and it soon became very familiar, because she played it every day after that for us to march into Assembly. Her name was Miss Threlfall and she had a kind, smiling face and a head of fair curly hair. She was to be my Class One teacher and I liked her from the start. When all the students had gathered in the big hall the Headmistress, Miss Nairn, appeared. She was quite a contrast to the piano teacher. Short and fat, she wore a long-sleeved, brown woollen dress which almost reached her ankles. It clung to her body and made her look lumpy. It had a vee-neck, which showed some of her large bosom. Her straight, black hair was snatched back into a tiny bun at the back of her head. She looked very stern and formidable. Nothing about her suggested warmth or laughter. Her small, dark eyes roved around the large room, seeing everything. lingering for a few moments on the group of new pupils.

After the Lord's Prayer was chanted, Miss Nairn launched into her Rules and Regulations. We were never to run in the hallways; that was to be kept for the playground. Food was not allowed in class, but at ten thirty each morning we would be given a small bottle of milk to drink. This was free to the children who came from poor homes, otherwise your mother had already arranged to pay each week for the milk. Whenever there was a murmur in the hall she shouted for silence, and she made it very clear that any disobedience would be rewarded with a visit to her office and several strokes of the cane. I was already scared to death of her and vowed to myself never to do anything wrong and be on the receiving end of her wrath.

Suddenly, there was a loud snicker from behind me, breaking the silence between her sentences, and Miss Nairn's eyes swivelled in the direction of the culprit. I knew it was the new boy, Georgie Borne. She gave him the opportunity to raise his hand and confess, but he didn't move or show any sign that he was the guilty one.

Miss Nairn knew. She walked slowly towards him, never taking her eyes off the culprit until she reached him. Then, without a word, she marched him into the centre of the room by his ear, and stopped by one of the floor to ceiling, massive black and white marble pillars which dotted the hall. Raising his hand, she rapped his knuckles over and over, against the hard, marble surface. It must have hurt terribly. Her face was red and puffy with anger.

There was complete silence in the hall. You could have heard a pin drop. He didn't flinch or cry. With this act of punishment she had established her power over every pupil - every pupil but Georgie Borne.

As he made his way back to his place behind me, the hall was completely silent. His face was very pale beneath the unruly mop of black curly hair but he was determined not to cry - and he didn't. In fact, he had a slight smile of defiance on his face, as though he was already familiar with that kind of treatment. The whole episode had lasted just a few minutes, but I was trembling with fright, really worried she would do it to someone else, that this was a normal part of school and this was how it was going to be.

I felt terribly sorry for Georgie that first day, but soon I realised he was always in hot water, usually for being late in the morning, when he came in looking as though he'd just got out of bed having slept in his clothes, which always looked rumpled. His knee-socks were usually in a heap around his ankles, his big mop of lovely black curls in desperate need of combing. He always wore a look of defiance on his face which only got him into worse trouble. He spent a great deal of time sitting outside Miss Nairn's office, waiting to be caned.

For a while he made my life a misery. Georgie sat immediately behind me in class and every day for the first weeks of school, he would lean forward, pull my hair and pinch my bottom, when teacher was writing lessons on the blackboard. I never complained because I couldn't bear the thought of him being caned or worse, on my behalf. The memory of his knuckles hitting the marble column stayed with me, burned into my mind, so I suffered in silence, telling no one.

Eventually, he stopped tormenting me. He even became my admirer, following me around the playground wanting to play with me and the little group of classmates I had made friends with. I was always worried he would get me into trouble, but I did stay friends with him from a distance. As an adult I have wondered what became of Georgie Borne. Whether he grew up destined to be in trouble - a criminal even - at odds with society and the world.

I've also wondered whether his antics in school were really a desperate cry for attention or even help. In those days no one cared about possible causes of bad behaviour, perhaps because of a home situation. He was simply labelled an unruly trouble-maker from that very first day in school. A label which stuck with him for as long as I knew him, a period of five years before we moved away from the area to greener pastures further away from the city.

As for me, I developed a bad stutter very soon after I started school, which my father helped cure with his coaching and patience. It took a while and no one knew why it had happened in the first place. Thinking it through with the wisdom acquired as an adult, I wonder whether the trauma of witnessing physical violence for the very first time in my life, on that first day in school, was responsible for my nervous stutter. I'll never know the answer to that. Certainly the violence the Headmistress had displayed on that day had a huge impact on me, and many others, I suspect. I hope Georgie Borne had a happy life and I thank God that the Miss Nairns of the world hopefully no longer exist to terrorise kids in what should be the happiest time of their lives, their first schooldays.

It has now gone completely the other way and teachers are not allowed to punish their pupils, even if they deserve it, and many of them are afraid of the violent attitudes displayed at times. There should be a happy medium for bad behaviour, but it seems hard to establish. My personal feelings are that there should be punishment of some sort, if only to control those pupils who disrupt both the teachers and the rest of the normal students.

In spite of the trauma of my first school experience I loved Miss Threlfall and the time spent in her class and other teachers in the years which followed during the time we lived on Kelso Road. I was a happy student, eager to learn whatever subject was being taught. Unfortunately, I was home sick with yellow jaundice when it was time to sit the examinations to go forward to a grammar school and missed them and there was no second chance for a secondary education.

I stayed in school until I reached the age of fourteen years before leaving to find my way in the working world. The Headmistress, Miss Campbell, sent me home with a letter for my father, full of praise and urging him to send me to a drama school, since she felt I had talent to become an actress. I had played Puck in *Midsummer Night's Dream* and the King's daughter in a play called *Fat King Melon*, which also required me to sing. I was applauded for my efforts by the audience, mainly doting parents, and all the school staff. I was always in my element on the stage, even though they were just school productions.

My father read the letter and immediately tore it up, telling me in no uncertain terms that no daughter of his would ever go on the stage. In his opinion (which of course I accepted as correct) only prostitutes and women of ill repute took up that kind of profession. The subject was never spoken about again and I don't think he even replied to Miss Campbell's letter. She also never referred to it again but she did mention it in my Testimonial, received when I finally left school. I still have it among my various treasures kept in the Safety Deposit Box.

CHAPTER EIGHT

HILARY AVENUE

We moved in the spring of 1939 from the Kelso Road terraced house where I had spent my happy childhood to the new suburb of Bowring Park, still Liverpool but on the very outskirts of the busy roads. 83 Hilary Avenue was new and pristine, semi-detached and identical to the rest of the houses stretching away for half a mile on both sides of the road, which led to the small block of shops on Pilch Lane and also to the 6a tramcar which took you right into Liverpool City, some eleven miles away now, instead of just ten minutes or so, in our other house. They were built by Paradise Estates and had gardens back and front with fields at the back of the house with cows grazing, a source of great interest to the city-dwellers.

We loved it from the first moment we saw it. Most of all was the joy we felt having a real bathroom with a large porcelain bath, separate wash basin, and of course the coveted indoor toilet. No more scary visits to the outdoor facility in the backyard, hanging on to the wooden seat for dear life, looking for the spiders who made their home up in the corners of the white-washed walls. It was heaven!

Not long after we made this happy move from City to the pleasant area of Bowring Park, there was an event which was to change our lives drastically for many years. I remember that Sunday morning in September, 1939, when World War II was declared. I was ten years old and I can still picture the scene in our kitchen very vividly. We were huddled round the wireless, listening to the solemn trembling voice of the Prime Minister, Neville Chamberlain, announcing that Britain was now at war with Germany. I remember how still and quiet we were and the look of fear on my mother's face as the grave news was given. No one then could envisage that the war would last six gruelling years, and that we would all become acquainted with the trappings of war, in just a matter of weeks. Ration books and identity cards were issued. Blackout curtains were hurriedly made for every window. It was an offence to show any kind of light once it became dark outside.

Gas masks were given to every man, woman and child. Oh, how I hated that gas-mask which had to be carried everywhere, in its brown cardboard box! We had to practise wearing it and I dreaded having to put it on. The awful smell of new rubber, plus a kind of chemical smell, made me feel sick and the sensation of being suffocated was a much bigger fear than the thought of a gas attack, but then I was too young and naïve to know the results of that threat.

Life was put on hold for a while, all schools were closed and we took lessons in small groups in homes all over the neighbourhood, while brick, one-storey air-raid shelters were quickly being built at every school. The sky was filled with silver barrage balloons, a deterrent to planes flying too low. Once we had the air-raid shelters at our school and heard the long whooping sound warning sirens went, we filed out quickly and took a place on the benches provided, pupils and teachers all together. We would occupy the time waiting for the long steady sound of the All Clear telling us the raid was over, listening to volunteers singing their favourite song.

I used to put my hand up frequently to sing, and I do remember two of the songs I sang. One was called 'Goodbye Sally' and the other was a Gracie Fields song called 'There was I waiting at the Church' which was supposed to be an amusing ditty about a bride waiting for her groom who never showed up because he was already married. It ended with the line 'My wife won't let me'. Supposed to be funny!

We learned quickly to identify the sound of the sirens warning us of an imminent attack from the skies above, which made our stomachs churn with fear and quickly sent everyone scurrying for shelter. It happened many times, day and night. It was always a huge relief to hear the all-clear siren, and life returned to normal again for a little while.

Eventually there were small shelters issued to every home. They were of two different designs – one for outdoors if you had a garden to accommodate it, which was called an Anderson Shelter, and one for indoors to add protection as you huddled beneath the kitchen or dining room table, which was called a Morrison Shelter. Ours was erected at the bottom of the garden, Dad having first dug a deep grave-like hole to accommodate the tube shaped piece of corrugated iron which measured approximately ten feet by six feet. He covered it with grass sods to camouflage it. My father made our shelter amazingly comfortable, though I disliked being in it intensely. He made a small wooden ladder for us to climb down backwards into the shelter and three narrow coffin-like bunks for us children to sleep in. He also made a cement floor and covered it with linoleum and a piece of old carpet. The only light we had was from a paraffin lamp which had a wick and glass hood and he made a roll-down shutter for the small opening to hide the light and keep the draught out, but in the winter it was still very cold most of the time.

When the bombing first started we would roll quickly out of bed when the siren went off and head for the shelter, but later when Liverpool was really blitzed and the bombers came every night for weeks on end, Mum would send us down to the shelter right after supper, though I was never able to sleep. I hated being in the tiny space, listening to the sounds and in time I recognised many of those sounds - the drone of the bombers, the gunfire from the ack-ack defence guns, the whistling noise as bombs fell to earth and later in the war, the shunting train-like sound of the deadly land mines dropping on our city, causing terrible destruction and taking endless lives.

My dad, who was an Air Raid Warden and a member of the Home Guard, never joined us in the shelter but stood outside watching for incendiary bombs, which started fires. We kept a long ladder and buckets of sand in the back garden for the purpose of dousing any fire which started in our area, especially on the roof-tops. We would wait for dawn to break which usually would bring the welcome sound of the all clear siren telling us it was safe to return to the house. The long, steady one-note wailing sound was music to our ears. The birds were usually up and singing as we trooped bleary-eyed, dragging our blankets with us, back into the house. Depending on the time, we would either go to our beds or be given breakfast to start our day.

On our walk to school we would search the gutters for the biggest piece of shrapnel and keep it as a trophy until a bigger piece was found. Somehow, we survived and in spite of everything our spirits were high and the idea that we might not win this war never entered our heads, even in the darkest moments. Winston Churchill took care of that with his speeches on the radio to the population of this tiny island, even the sound of his voice reinforced and lifted our spirits. I think without him the outcome of that war might have been a very different story. He was a true leader. The United Kingdom would be better off today with a man of his character, determination and great strength.

But the sounds of war will never be totally forgotten, nor the fear which they brought. It affected me in strange ways. I am claustrophobic in small spaces. I don't like to sit wedged between two people, and always choose an aisle seat on a plane, or a bus or even in church. Just small matters really, a kind of legacy from spending a great deal of time in that tiny Anderson shelter in our back garden as I was growing up.

Not long after we moved to Hilary Avenue, I made my first friend, Hilda. We were the same age and feeling lost and lonely without our old friends in our new surroundings, we were drawn immediately to each other. She and her large family lived on the opposite side of the road to us, the last house before the vacant piece of ground which was slated for more houses but postponed for many years because of the onset of the war. It was to remain that way for many years and as children we played on that empty ground and fished for tadpoles and frogs in the natural pond which emerged after a winter of heavy rains.

When I first met Hilda's mother, I immediately thought how masculine she looked. She was small, compact and quite heavily built, but the thing which fascinated me the most was her black moustache, one which any teenage boy would have been proud to display. As a ten-year-old and not at all worldly, I'd never seen one on a woman before. It was quite long, black, straight and thick, exactly like her bushy eyebrows and the hair on her head. It obviously didn't bother her because she still had it many years later when I left Hilary Avenue.

She wore glasses, so thick you couldn't see her eyes. I'm not sure what colour they were but I'd guess at brown, like most of the children's eyes. She had a deep, husky male voice. I soon learned that she ruled the large household with a very firm hand, but she always spoke affectionately about her meek and mild-mannered husband, Charlie, who usually offered me a hesitant smile whenever I was there, but never volunteered any kind of conversation. He was very thin, with sparse, brown, straight hair. He also wore glasses and was missing a few teeth; perhaps this was responsible for his reluctance to smile or speak more than a couple of words. He worked in a hospital, something to do with maintenance of the heating system, but I never knew his exact occupation, only that he wore dark blue coveralls and came home on his bicycle, looking dirty. He was such an inoffensive, unobtrusive man, someone you hardly noticed at all, though he produced six children, five daughters and just as a last resort, a son, whom they called Frederick.

All the girls were fairly similar in looks, personality and temperament, except one called Dolly, who was the prettiest of them all. Bertha, named after her mother, was the eldest and was in her mid-twenties. She was fairly tall and thin, but quite plain with a blotchy, sallow complexion and straight brown hair. According to her mother she was 'bad with her nerves' and unable to work. She had got married, very early, to a handsome young soldier called Bob, who was eventually sent to the Far East and went missing, presumed killed, up the Burma Road. He never saw his son David, who was born after he left England for the Far East, and was raised by his grandma. This was probably the cause of the stress and sickness to the eldest daughter.

Eileen was a couple of years younger and was the next one to marry. She had the same pale skin and brown hair, which she wore curly, which made her look much prettier. She also wore glasses.

She married Bill, whom she absolutely adored. She used to go around the house humming a popular song at that time, called 'He's Just My Bill'. He was in the Merchant Navy and was torpedoed five times during the war and survived. They eventually had a son Alan, who was born with small custard-coloured growths on his tongue, which was swollen and stuck out of his mouth. We felt so sorry for them and their awful problems with their first born child, but they never complained. They spent years searching for medical help and eventually found a surgeon in the South of England who agreed to do very risky surgery and remove part of the tongue, which of course included the growths. It was nothing short of a miracle and Alan grew up a healthy, normal boy, all traces of his awful problem gone.

Dolly, just a year or so younger than Eileen, was small and slightly chubby with twinkling blue eyes and a mass of fair, natural curly hair which she wore long, down past her shoulders. She was the beauty of the family and was always laughing - that is, when she was awake. She suffered from a disorder called narcolepsy and would fall asleep instantly, anywhere, without any kind of warning. I remember going to their house and was waiting for Hilda just inside the back door. I stood waiting because Dolly was washing the kitchen floor and I didn't want to be a nuisance and walk across it. She was down on her knees with floor cloth in hand and suddenly she slumped over and was fast asleep and remained that way for what seemed ages, but was probably about five minutes. I stood there at the back door, not knowing what to do, then suddenly she opened her eyes, looked around and carried on washing the floor. Apparently, this happened several times a day and I eventually got used to seeing it though it certainly scared me the first few times I witnessed it.

Dolly never married, perhaps because of her health problems, and she had difficulty keeping a job. In spite of it all, she always seemed to be the happiest member of the family. She was really a beautiful person, always pleasant and smiling. Hilda was the same age as I was and she was my friend for a long time. She had the same rather sallow skin, straight dark brown hair and eyes that most of the family had; and was quiet and shy.

We had many adventures together as teenagers, and while I was always scared of my father, whenever we found ourselves in trouble – as teenagers do - she was terrified of her mother's wrath. She would ask me to go home with her when something had to be confessed to her, because she felt it might diminish the punishment if I was there to plead her case. I have to admit, I think it worked sometimes!

I do recall several occasions we got into mischief, climbing up the railway embankment at the back of the houses on my side of Hilary Avenue, separated by a field with cows in it. We had been warned several times to stay away from the railway line, accessed by a steep climb through trees to the actual line where the trains passed. In spite of the warning, the embankment and the actual lines drew us like a magnet. There was usually a 'Cocky Watchman' (a guard) patrolling the line but that didn't deter us until one day, as we reached the top of the steep incline, he was just feet away and shouted for us to stop. Of course we didn't! We turned tail and slithered down the long embankment on our bottoms, then jumped the last ten feet into the cow field and headed for home as fast as our legs would carry us. As we slowed down, feeling safe from the guard, who had given up the chase, we looked at each other in dismay. We looked filthy, covered with soil and heaven knows what, from our adventure and Hilda said "Mum will kill me, what am I going to tell her?"

We sat in the grass at the back of my house, rubbing the worst of the mess off ourselves, before going home to Hilda's house. We both still looked rather dirty but the worst was over. We managed to get away with it telling her mother we had been playing at the pond, looking for frogs that Hilda had slipped and fallen in the mud. She received a telling-off from her mother because of the state of her clothes, but she believed our story.

I recall another occasion when we had a very lucky escape from a disastrous event which happened one Sunday afternoon in early April. Hilda and I were collecting shells to paint and make necklaces to sell, eager to contribute to the Aid to Russia Fund launched by Clementine Churchill, wife of the Prime Minister. Our previous endeavours had been quite successful and this was our third long trip across the River Mersey on the ferry from our home in Liverpool, to add to our supply of sea-shells. As we left to catch the bus on our first leg of our journey, our mothers' last words were not to get our clothes dirty – and we always obeyed. Well, nearly always!

In spite of the fact we were going to the beach, we were dressed in our best clothes. Sunday was after all Sunday, and it required us to be suitably attired, no matter what plans we had. Hilda was wearing a brand new hand-knitted cardigan on top of her skirt and blouse and I was similarly dressed. We both wore lace-up shoes and ankle socks suitable for thirteen-year-olds. It was sunny but cool with the wind blowing off the sea but we had not come to sit on the beach, we were on a mission.

As we meandered across this familiar beach that day, our bags partially full of the desired shells, we had no idea of the terror to come, no signs telling us of any danger in the area. Hilda was just ahead of me. Suddenly, without any warning, she disappeared in front of my eyes and seconds later surfaced, struggling and screaming, covered in sand, seaweed and totally wet. My first thought was 'quicksand'. I screamed for help at the top of my lungs, but my cries fell on deaf ears, even though there were people within fifty yards of us, leaning on the iron railing bordering the long promenade at New Brighton, looking out across the sands to the sea. But no-one seemed aware of what was happening in front of their eyes. I jumped up and down, waving my arms, screaming again, frantically trying to attract someone's attention. Seconds elapsed, although it seemed like hours. I knew if Hilda went down a third time, she wouldn't come up again. Somewhere that knowledge was in the back of my head – something to do with drowning and going under three times - perhaps it was just one of my mother's superstitious beliefs but, whatever it was, it had stuck with me.

At the same time there was a voice in my mind telling me what to do, though I don't know where it came from - something again stored in my memory. I got down on my stomach and lay flat on the sand and inched closely to Hilda. Only her head and neck showed above whatever was in this hole which had swallowed her. She was screaming with terror, begging for help. I told her to stop struggling and I wriggled close enough to grasp one hand, which she managed to get free. Slowly, very slowly, I edged backwards, using every bit of strength I had and more, which came to me from somewhere in my desperate attempt to pull her to safety, and eventually I had both of her hands in mine. I inched backwards, pulling her with me and soon she was able to help herself become free.

We lay in a heap on the firm sand, crying and hugging – trembling but safe. The whole episode had probably lasted about six or seven unforgettable minutes and no one on that beach, or watching from the promenade railing, seemed to be aware of the drama which had taken place. Onlookers perhaps thought we were just teenagers fooling around – even having a good time – when in fact we had come very close to losing our lives.

Shivering with cold and shock we made our way up the beach to the steps and along to the toilets and changing rooms on Victoria Road, where the very kind lady in charge listened to our story. She gave us towels to wrap around us while she dried our clothes, which took a couple of hours, before we set off on our long journey home, across the River Mersey and the long bus ride to Hilary Avenue. Hilda by now had recovered enough to be terrified of what her mother would say at her appearance - wrinkled clothes, ruined shoes and damp hair. I was having similar misgivings. We both looked pretty sorry sights, especially for a Sunday. However, our explanation of what had happened was totally accepted by our parents. After all, who could ever dream up a story like that and live to tell about it?

Needless to say, we never collected shells again. Our patriotic desire to help the Russians waned for quite a while. Looking back, we were incredibly lucky to survive that day. Had we been walking side-by-side and gone into those sinking sands together, instead of me trailing behind, we would not have survived, but I guess our guardian angels were with us that day and we lived to tell this tale. The Ashton family was still intact.

There was one more daughter in this large and varied family. Brenda, the youngest of the girls, was small, dark-haired and very quiet. I didn't know her very well for she was five years younger than me and the age gap seemed very wide at that time in our lives. Then there was Fred, the idolised male offspring and the baby of the family. He was small and thin and had a bad turn in his eye and like most of them wore glasses. He also had straight brown hair and looked the spit of his father. He too lived at home as King of the Castle, single and idle until both parents passed away when he was in his thirties. He married a while after to someone who probably supported and adored him. I often wondered if that marriage lasted. Having grown up in a harem of women, he was the personification of a chauvinist. Certainly he was no oil painting to look at either but love is blind. His wife didn't marry Fred for his looks – or his charm!

They were the largest family in the neighbourhood. We had several nicknames for them – something we bestowed on almost everyone we knew, in ruthless fashion. A habit formed in our teenage years with utter disregard for anyone's feelings, even though this was strictly between ourselves and never broadcast outside our little circle of friends. Apart from referring to Hilda's mother as 'Big Bertha' which really was her Christian name, it was also the nickname given to one of the big guns used to defend Britain from enemy planes coming in to drop their bombs. The term was used to describe her booming voice, which could be heard some distance from outside the house sometimes. We also called her 'Mrs Gotalot' because whenever she cornered anyone into having a conversation with her, she would boast about her rich relatives scattered around the globe. She apparently had them just about everywhere… ..Canada, the United States and New Zealand and, according to her, they were all very wealthy and held very high, important positions. Strange, because she and her family seemed to have very little, apart from the new house, so the wealth certainly wasn't shared!

She would have been the perfect understudy for the terribly snobbish Mrs Bucket of television fame and Charlie would have been the perfect Richard. Outnumbered by his lovely daughters, Charlie seemed contented to take a back seat and offer a toothless smile in acknowledgement of anyone's presence. Life always seemed rather chaotic in this household. It was quite normal to see, at least one member of the family, at any given time, making a meal from a huge slab of bread. They never seemed to have any set times to eat and I don't recall ever seeing the family sitting around the table eating together. Come to think of it, there probably wasn't room for them to do so. Sleeping too, must have presented problems. The house contained two large and one very small bedroom to sleep five females, one son, one grandson, plus parents. That must have been quite a squeeze, to say nothing of the fights to get into the only bathroom each morning.

To give their mother credit, all of the girls grew up with nice manners and were very polite and in spite of her being a bit of a tyrant, they absolutely idolised their 'Mam', as they called her. I know she was a good mother and so proud of her children. They were to me an interesting and loving family and always made me feel one of them and very welcome in their house. Obviously, they made an impression on me which has lasted in my memory all through the years, though I haven't kept in touch with Hilda – or any of the daughters.

Hilda eventually married a quiet studious fellow called John, a tall, thin very shy lad with dark hair and glasses, who blushed whenever anyone spoke to him. Trying to have a conversation with him was painful, he was so shy. However, he studied hard at night school and became an accountant, much to his credit. They moved away to London and sadly we lost touch, it had been a great friendship for a long time after we both married, perhaps realising we no longer had much in common

Next door to that family was an elderly lady who seemed to spend a great deal of time peeping through the lace curtains, looking at anything which might be going on in the street below. She soon got the name of Nosey Parker. In time we got to know a lot of the neighbours on this long avenue and I made another friend, Margaret, who lived at number twenty-two, which was some distance up the same road and on the other side. She was the youngest of three girls. Their mother was a petite woman with short straight gray hair, twinkling blue eyes and apple-red cheeks. She had been widowed fairly young and left to raise her daughters, Lillian, the eldest, who looked quite like her except she had light brown curly hair, Joan who resembled her father, with her mop of fiery red hair, friendly round face with blue eyes and a bubbly outgoing personality, and Margaret, who was short like me and wore her straight fair hair in a bob, blue/gray eyes and a fair skin which burned very easily if she stayed out in the sun too long. They reminded me of the March family in one of my favourite books, 'Little Women'.

Mum was always fussing over her brood like a mother hen, especially her youngest child, always making sure she had a clean handkerchief tucked in the pocket of her navy-blue knickers before leaving the house for school. I would squirm with embarrassment as I stood in the small hallway waiting for her to finish her inspection, and look the other way. Margaret accepted all this attention as normal. They were a very happy family, who hugged and kissed each time they left the house and I envied the ease they had in doing that freely. A perfectly normal gesture, but one I wasn't used to.

I loved spending time in their house, gathered around the piano in the sitting-room as Lil played and we sang until we had exhausted our repertoire and our voices, or it was time for me to leave. Joan had a beautiful contralto singing voice and I'm sure, under different circumstances, and in the modern era, could have earned her living with the gift of her voice. She was like a big sister to me and taught Margaret and me to knit. We made clothes for our dolls, using pink baby wool, speckled with silky white thread – coats, bonnets and booties, all to match.

Whenever I had a problem to solve I would always take it to Joan. She was always smiling and ready to listen. I still have the prayer book she bought me one Christmas. Margaret and I grew into teenagers together, sharing secrets and thoughts as teenagers do. It was a wonderful, carefree existence.

Their mum decided to take in a boarder for a while, the new curate from the Anglican church we all attended. He was a tall, thin, gaunt pale-faced fellow in his late twenties. His nondescript looks matched his personality. His only redeeming feature was his shock of thick, dark straight hair, which he had to keep brushing out of his eyes. He was painfully shy and must have found life difficult in his new digs with three very outgoing females. His grave face would blush every time he spoke, and he always looked slightly puzzled, as though he wasn't sure of what to do next. I never remember seeing him smile. Margaret in particular, didn't like him descending on their all-female domain. The poor curate was a constant target of discussion, both for his scarecrow-like appearance and his inability, we thought, to ever be a proper minister. Youth is cruel, there was no mercy in us at that age. We would giggle all the way to school, and he was often the cause of our merriment.

Not long after the curate arrived on the scene at the house on Hilary Avenue, Margaret decided one evening to have a nice hot bath and since it was a bitterly cold November night, and she thought their lodger had gone to his usual church meeting, she wrapped herself in a towel and ran downstairs to get dried and dressed in front of the coal fire in the living room. She had just dropped the towel from her naked torso when the door suddenly opened and the lodger appeared, took one horrified look at Margaret and rushed out again, without speaking a single word.

She was terribly upset, because she knew they would meet the next morning at the breakfast table and she couldn't bear the thought of having to face him. She pleaded with her mother to let have her breakfast in the bedroom, but in spite of her protests, her mother insisted that she turn up at the breakfast table as usual.

That next morning they ate in complete silence. No one mentioned the incident at all, and Margaret said she didn't know who was more embarrassed. She avoided the lodger for weeks afterwards.

That story was resurrected many times over the years and it would always send us into fits of laughter. The mere mention of his name was enough to start us off. The curate, much to the surprise of everyone, married six months later and moved with his bride to live elsewhere. It was a big joke in the family that it must have been the sight of Margaret naked that was responsible for him looking for a bride. Passion was the last thing we ever thought he would be capable of!

Margaret and I became stenographers, and she eventually married a co-worker, Eric. They moved away from Hilary Avenue to a house in the Wirral and raised three children. We still kept in touch over the years. Joan met and married a lovely man from Egypt. He was a metallurgist, studying at Manchester University. They eventually had a daughter, Elizabeth-Ann, a beautiful child with honey-coloured skin and a mop of dark curls. She was admired by everyone and often people just passing by would stop and say how gorgeous she was. Later my husband Stan and I would sometimes have her for the day and pretend she belonged to us, we loved her so much.

They went to live in Egypt, then eventually to the United States of America. They tried Detroit, which wasn't to their liking, then moved to Los Angeles just prior to an earthquake which they experienced, fairly close to where they had chosen to live. It must have been a terrifying experience. LA was their final stop, in spite of living in an earthquake zone. Anise died quite a while ago and Joan reached her mid-eighties before she joined the angels. They were such beautiful people, much loved by everyone they knew.

We had many visits with them over the years and treasured the time spent with them.

Lil eventually returned to live in Montreal, where she had resided a number of years before. I never met her again but I know she too has passed on. Elizabeth-Ann and I reconnected after her mother died, and we stay in touch with emails. She is married and has two daughters of her own. It is so wonderful for me to have her as a close friend after all these years and she is very much a part of my life once more. I loved her so much as a toddler and I love her now as a grown-up courageous woman who writes me wonderful letters which I look forward to receiving, courtesy of the internet.

CHAPTER NINE

OUR 'SWEET' WALKS

The journey was a familiar one. I had travelled it many times in my early teens, usually with a friend of either sex, a sort of Sunday ritual which we looked forward to for several reasons. We would walk from my home on Hilary Avenue, carrying our hated gasmasks, now in smart leather or cloth cases, much nicer than the original cardboard boxes, which contained our identity cards, ration books and a little money, and set off for the five-mile hike, crossing the main road, passing the big hotel on the corner. Then, leaving the houses behind, we would walk on paths across fields full of cows grazing the sweet green grass, through the beautiful English countryside, with its hawthorn hedges, white with blossom in the springtime, the air full of birdsong. It was difficult not to be happy and contented in those circumstances in spite of the war and the shortages of sweets and other items we no longer were able to have, and those country walks were treasured.

Our walk ended in the very posh village of Gateacre Brow, with its large imposing brick houses, many of them in Tudor style – the real thing, in most cases. I remember the beautiful diamond-shaped leaded windows which were curtained with lace, and expensive looking drapes and shiny heavy oak doors with huge brass knockers, all set in manicured green lawns bordered with flowers and foliage. Some of the homes had tall, black iron gates to keep the likes of us out, but we would peer through the bars anyway and sigh at the owners' good fortune and wonder what it would be like to live in a house like that, even for one day.

Our destination in the village was a small sweet shop, which also served as a Post Office. There we would take at least ten minutes to spend our very small sweet ration, which amounted to two ounces per week, picking and choosing from the jars on the shelf. What should we have this time – it was so difficult because there were so many favourites! Bright yellow lemon sherberts, which felt sharp and good on the tongue when you had sucked through to the white powder deep inside, pear drops, jelly babies, wine gums, licorice cakes and bootlaces made of the same, which clung to your teeth, and gobstoppers, which were huge and lasted for hours if you sucked them carefully, each layer a different colour to be viewed at intervals, until you sucked all the way down to the tiny black spot in the middle, which tasted of aniseed (licorice) and disintegrated quickly on your tongue. And the tiny sweets shaped as lamb chops, potatoes and peas which used to be 'meals' when we were younger and playing house… so many to choose from, such a hard decision to make in those days of rationing.

The quiet elderly man who owned the shop – I think his name was Mr Gaskill – would lean against the counter, never rushing us to choose, and would wait patiently for our big decision and then weigh our tiny 2 oz portions of sweets, tipping them from his metal scale into small white paper funnel-shaped bags. Sometimes we would refrain from taking the sweets that day but part with our coupons to the shopkeeper, who would mark them in his ledger against our names for future spending. This enabled us to save for those special treats at Easter and Christmas towards a box of chocolates to give to our mum as a present. This was an enormous sacrifice to sweet-hungry teenagers, but we were usually rewarded by the shopkeeper. "Hold-on" he would say, as we reluctantly started to leave, and he would shovel a few sweets into a bag to share between us on the long walk back. A reward for our self-sacrifice I guess.

They were golden Sundays and part of the simple pleasures which filled my life in spite of the war going on around us. I have never been back to Gateacre Brow and only once to the area where I lived, to look at the house on Hilary Avenue I grew up in, which I found looking just as I had left it years before. Someone obviously loves it as much as I did. I don't want to shatter the illusion of our Sunday walks through the countryside, for I'm sure it is now just another urban mass of houses, the cows no longer there, and the tiny shop will probably be a supermarket. Some things are best left alone in our memories, where we can return to visit them and enjoy again.

CHAPTER TEN

CHICKENS IN
THE HOUSE

During the war eggs were as scarce as the proverbial hen's teeth. In place of them, we had what the Government called 'reconstituted' eggs, a sulphurous-looking yellow powder which didn't even remotely taste like the real thing. They were like cardboard! Mother used to bake with it and occasionally, as a last resort, she'd make omelets for dinner, when the meagre meat ration had been eaten and 'blind' stew had already fed us several times that week. No matter what Mum added to the omelets, they still tasted, and felt like tough old shoe-leather. We hated them.

My father began talking about having our own hens, using up the last space in the back garden, just beyond the living room window, to house a coop. We already had the Anderson Shelter, which was tucked in the far left corner of the garden, as far away from the house as possible for safety reasons. We also had a sizeable vegetable patch which took up half of the garden, leaving only a small area of grass which would have to go if his plans for a henhouse were to materialise. My mother seemed fairly receptive

85

to the idea until she learned that the baby chicks would have to spend their first weeks of life in the living room, to keep them warm. That was a very different matter. She objected very strongly to the whole idea.

Both of my parents were very houseproud. The modern three-bedroom house was kept absolutely immaculate. Every bit of woodwork, including doors, stairs, banisters and windowsills, was painted a glossy white and kept that way. Floors and carpets were swept and washed every day of the week, except Sunday. Lots of brass everywhere, which Mum cleaned and polished each Wednesday morning after her daily visit to the shops. Without a doubt, cleanliness was definitely regarded as being next to godliness in our house.

You can perhaps imagine the violent disagreement which erupted and went on for several weeks. In between arguments, there was frosty silence in the house, during which time I carefully avoided mentioning anything remotely connected with chickens or eggs. However, I knew my father would eventually win out with the chickens, since he usually did and it had been unusual for my mother to disobey his orders and protest as violently as she had done.

One Wednesday afternoon, which was Father's half-day off from work, I came home from school about 4.30 pm As soon as I opened the back door I knew something was wrong. My mother was standing at the kitchen sink peeling potatoes, looking as black as thunder. I knew why when I reached the living room. The chicks had arrived! Twelve tiny balls of yellow fluff were running around a cordoned-off portion of the room. Thick layers of newspaper covered the pristine coffee-coloured carpet. The large brown armchair which usually sat in the corner had been removed altogether to make room for this new venture. My father had made a cardboard fence about four feet square and just over a foot high.

Another cardboard box, turned upside down, with a light bulb inserted through the top, served as an incubator for the tiny, adorable week-old chicks. Apparently they were Rhode Island Reds, eleven hens and one cockerel, though how anyone could tell at that stage, was a complete mystery to me.

After a few days, even Mum thawed a bit, in spite of the invasion and take-over of her domain, for it was hard to resist the cute little chicks. We were fascinated watching them grow, and they did that very quickly. They never stopped chirping and spent their whole day eating and pooping. My mother was forever changing the newspaper and clucking her disapproval every time she did it!

The chicks were in our living room for six weeks and during that time my father built a henhouse in the garden and made a run of wire netting, and much to mother's relief, she claimed her living room back and perfect order was once again restored, along with peace. The chicks soon grew into hens and my brother Roy and I took turns to collect the large, brown warm eggs, nestled in straw, which they produced each day. They were such a wonderful treat at that time of food shortage. Deep orange yolks which tasted as eggs should. Absolutely wonderful!

These creatures became like pets to us and we named several of them and called the rooster 'Bossy Boots'. He was quite fierce and I was just a bit afraid of him. I think the hens were too! The months went by, and eventually the appearance of those lovely eggs slowed to a trickle then stopped altogether. They had come to the end of their laying period, which apparently was normal. I don't believe my father had given much thought to what would happen to the hens when their usefulness was over. Although we kids didn't know it at the time, he had made plans to kill off the hens one at a time for us to eat. But when that time came, he found he just couldn't do it, so he asked my brother-in-law to kill the first one when Roy and I were not around, and that apparently is what happened.

A roast chicken appeared on the table for dinner, something we hadn't seen for a very long time. I glanced at Mum, who looked very unhappy, and then at Father, who was very quiet, and suddenly I knew the chicken was one of ours. Roy and I began to cry and refused to eat. We called Father cruel. Eventually even my parents lost their appetites.

The whole plan to eat the chickens was a dismal failure. It was a small miracle Dad didn't lose his temper with us, since normally we didn't dare to answer back or question his decisions. Eventually, we calmed down with his promise never to kill another hen, and to this day, I honestly believe, that my parents were just as upset as we were. Without a doubt, they were not cut out to be farmers, they were much too soft hearted.

Even now, I don't know what did happen to the rest of the family chickens. I came home from school one Wednesday a few weeks later and they had gone. My father said he had given them to a man who wanted them. We didn't ask why. I don't think we really wanted to know. Soon the henhouse was dismantled and the area restored to grass, as though the chicken episode had never happened. We didn't talk about it, nor did we grumble about the awful omelets, made from re-constituted egg powder, which returned to the dinner menu.

CHAPTER ELEVEN

LEMON-AID

The weeks passed by, and Hilda and I talked about renewing our efforts to raise money for the Aid to Russia Funds. We had recovered from the terrifying ordeal of Hilda's close call on New Brighton sands, but we no longer wanted to collect shells. We tossed ideas around but hadn't come up with anything we thought would be worthwhile. Then quite by chance a solution was handed to us on a plate, so to speak. Hilda had a brother-in law serving in the Merchant Navy, and returning home from a trip he presented us with two lemons! What a great gift!

We decided it would be perfect to raffle them and send the amount of money raised to Clementine Churchill, who was still asking for donations at that time, on the radio and in the newspaper. We still thought it was a good cause. The prize would of course be the two lemons, which were a scarce commodity, along with bananas, which we rarely saw any more.

We hurriedly got to work, made tickets up and knocked on every door in our neighbourhood, selling our tickets, which sold like hot cakes. We wrapped the precious lemons in a piece of white tissue paper and waited for the day of the draw just two days away. We wanted to give the lemons away while they were still nice and firm! We were very excited about the whole thing which had gone so smoothly and asked our next door neighbour, Reggie Wheat to do the honours.

The winner was a Mrs Harris, who lived almost across from our house. Her face lit up when we presented her with the lemons. She was delighted with her prize and the envy of the neighbours. Imagine getting excited now over winning two lemons!

We had the large sum of eleven pounds (sterling) from our efforts, quite a bit of money in 1942. We sent it off to the Aid to Russia Fund and received a thank you letter back, signed by Clementine Churchill. I still have the letter tucked away in my safety deposit box and from time to time I wonder whether it is of any value some fifty-odd years later. I still remember how proud we felt with our effort and our contribution to help 'the poor Russians'. How times have changed! Now, all these years later, it all seems quite strange to think about that time in our history, but in the minds of two teenagers in that particular era, it seemed like the right thing to do.

CHAPTER TWELVE

THE END OF THE WAR

I remember the end of World War II – the War To End All Wars. What a macabre joke that turned out to be in light of the many other wars and conflicts which have occurred since 1945 and continue to this very day. I can recall the joy we all felt as word filtered through that nearly six years of death, destruction and hardship was over.

Our own small neighbourhood got together and festivities were quickly arranged for a big celebration on the still vacant piece of land just a bit further down our road, originally intended for more houses which would have looked exactly like ours. The frog pond was still there, though Hilda and I no longer visited it and the grass had grown in unruly tufts, but it served a good purpose at that particular time. The war had drawn the friendly neighbours even closer, and good and bad news was passed quickly.

During the food shortage, word that the small produce shop had received a delivery of potatoes or bananas would spread like wildfire and housewives would fling on their coats and hurry to Waterworth's, the fruit and vegetable shop, to stand in the queue hoping they wouldn't run out of whatever they were standing in line for. Standing in line, or queuing as we call it in England, was a way of life and everyone took it for granted. It became a time for exchanging news or airing one's opinion, or just having a good moan about the weather.

English people always talk about the weather! As a teenager, working as a temporary cashier in Blackler's Department Store in the city, I would stand in line the whole of my lunch hour in the hope of getting five cigarettes for my mother, who had never smoked in her life, until ordered by the doctor to do so, because her nerves were so bad when the bombing started. When it was finally my turn to be served I never knew what brand of cigarettes I would be getting. Many times they were Turkish cigarettes called Pasha and were foul when smoked, like smelly socks burning. Conflict and trouble seems to bring out the best in people, and it certainly applied to our tiny corner of the suburbs of Liverpool. There was no such thing as crime in our area, it would have been unthinkable.

The celebration at the end of all this lasted for days. Strangers hugged strangers. There were smiles on everyone's faces and people danced in the streets just drunk with joy – or sometimes, just plain drunk, not offensive though, just talkative!

For our own neighbourhood party, tables were carried onto the vacant land and placed in a long, long row, which we covered with an assortment of tablecloths with chairs of every size and style brought out of the houses. No such thing as garden furniture in those days – these were everyone's precious belongings sitting on a field and no one cared about damage, we were all too happy to worry about it.

We were blessed that day with hot sunshine, as though the gods were sharing our joy. Kitchen pantries were raided, and precious tins of horded rations came from every household. Everyone contributed to our victory party, which went on long after darkness fell. Babies were put to bed and eventually the older children disappeared too. The teenagers, of which I was one, helped with the large job of clearing up and returning belongings to the rightful owners. It was a great celebration, a memorable time, when 'love thy neighbour' really was just that and totally true. The war was finally over and we had all survived it.

Of course Bertha's husband was still missing, but she was still hoping he would return. Sadly that never happened and later he was presumed dead, like so many others who were victims of the Japanese savagery up the Burma Road.

CHAPTER THIRTEEN

SHATTERED DREAMS

I was 17 years old, waiting patiently to reach my 18th birthday some months away, when I was to begin nurse training at Olive Mount Children's Hospital in Liverpool. My rosy future lay ahead all mapped out, or so I thought, until fate stepped in and changed my plans in drastic fashion, without any warning.

I remember every detail of the day it began. It was a warm spring Saturday in April and I had taken the bus into the bustling crowded city of Liverpool, eleven miles from home, to browse the vast array of clothes in the many large department stores on Church Street. The war was finally over and things were slowly getting back to normal. The large glass display windows were no longer blacked out and criss-crossed with broad tape to prevent them shattering when bombs were flattening much of the city and the surrounding suburbs. The windows now displayed elegant mannequins dressed in the latest fashions, to tempt the deprived post-war population, and I was no exception.

I loved clothes and like most teenagers, was very fashion conscious. The hemlines went up and then down, and colours changed with every season. I wore them all, regardless of whether they really suited me. I recall now with a wry chuckle wearing clothes labelled the 'New Look' and feeling very elegant in a double-breasted sea-green coat, trimmed with black, which almost reached my ankles. I was only 5ft 2 inches tall! This was topped off with a black velvet bonnet, tied under my chin and black ankle-strap high heeled shoes. I probably looked like a member of the Salvation Army, but at the time, I thought I was the bees-knees - the very height of fashion!

That morning around lunchtime, I suddenly began feeling very tired. My legs were aching and I developed a headache. Not the usual migraine which plagued me each month at period time, but a thumping pain which filled my head. I decided I'd better go home. I remember passing Cooper's store, on the corner of Paradise Street, which sold a large assortment of coffee beans and other specialty foods. The pungent aroma of ground coffee and spices wafting out onto the pavement (sidewalk) usually delighted my senses, and I would often be drawn into the shop simply to browse and breathe in the delicious odours, even though I didn't drink coffee. In fact there wasn't even a coffee pot in our house. We just drank tea or milk.

On that day though, the smell made me feel nauseated and I hurried by to reach the bus stop. My bus eventually arrived. I sank down thankfully on the soft leather seat and closed my eyes as the lurching, green double-decker bus made the very long ride to Bowring Park. I was so relieved to reach the end of my journey, because by then I was feeling more and more unwell. I still had ten minutes' walk down Hilary Avenue before our house was in sight. All I could think of was crawling into my bed and closing my eyes to stem the awful pain in my head.

My mother was surprised to see me back so early, but she took one look at my face and realised I was feeling ill. She hustled me upstairs to bed, helping me off with my clothes, then left me to try and sleep, telling me to call her if I needed anything. 'You've probably caught a chill' she said as she tucked me in. 'I'll make you some hot lemon and barley water.'

Lemon barley water, home-made of course, was Mum's cure for all illnesses and I didn't want anything just at that moment. I slept fitfully through the night, feeling worse every time I woke, which was often. I was hurting all over, feverish and nauseated, though I wasn't actually vomiting. I had not finished the drink Mum left on the bedside table, it was too much effort to lift my arms even though my mouth was parched.

Sunday finally arrived, and so did large black lumps all over my legs and other parts of my body. They were exquisitely painful, making even the cotton sheet totally unbearable. I could no longer stand or walk. Most of that day and late into the night, my father sat stroking my pounding head with a cloth soaked in malt vinegar.

I don't think my parents knew what to do at that point. In those days help was not available on Sunday. It was a day of rest, in every sense of the word. Everything was closed, except the news agent's store, which opened for two hours early in the morning, but only for the sale of newspapers. We didn't have a phone or a car. No way of contacting our doctor or even a chemist, regarded as the next best thing if you were ill. Clearly, though I was getting worse by the hour, I would have to wait for help until the next morning.

I was much too sick to care but I sensed my parents were terribly worried. There had been a lot of poliomyelitis (infantile paralysis) in the news and my father didn't believe in vaccinations or inoculations of any kind, so of course I had not received any, not even for small-pox or diphtheria – both capable of seeing you off the planet.

Dad must have phoned the doctor as soon as he reached work and early on Monday morning our long-time family physician, Dr Robb, came to see me. He usually joked with us in his clipped Scots accent, and sometimes stayed for tea, but that day he was totally serious, examining me briefly before declaring I had to go to hospital. He said I was a very sick girl, though he didn't say why. Mother hovered at the side of the bed anxiously listening to the doctor. I was too ill to care what was happening to me. I just wanted the pain to stop.

Soon the ambulance arrived. I was wrapped in thick scarlet blankets, put on a stretcher and carried down the stairs by two male attendants into the waiting ambulance for the six mile journey to Whiston Hospital. There I was taken straight to a ward and put into the end bed, where seriously ill patients are kept, close to the Ward Sister's Office which had glass windows all round, so she could see what was going on at all times. This was to be my home for a long time.

Several doctors, all with solemn faces, visited me during the first hours there, asking questions, examining me and eventually explaining that I had rheumatic fever. The explanation meant nothing to me, since I'd never heard of that particular disease.

For the next three months I had to lie flat on my back, perfectly still, without a pillow. The nurses fed me liquids through a utensil resembling a teapot with a much longer spout. Most of the time I didn't know what I was drinking - they put it in my mouth and I obediently swallowed as much as I could stomach. They washed me and changed my gown and sheets daily, taking care to barely move me in the process. I had a cage over my legs to hold off the bedclothes so they wouldn't touch me. I was utterly dependent on the nursing staff. They were absolutely wonderful and very caring.

My only visitor was my mother, who sat by the bed each night from seven to seven-thirty. We didn't talk. She would sit on a chair looking around the ward at the other patients, her thin face a picture of anxiety. Now and then she would make comments just to fill the silence, but we never discussed my illness and I never asked questions.

Antibiotics were not around in those days. I was treated with a medication called M & B tablets, too large for me to swallow whole, especially lying down. I had to chew them. They dyed my mouth purple and it became ulcerated and incredibly sore. The nurse had told me they were too hard to crush so I didn't have a choice. At weekly intervals I would have blood drawn, something I anticipated with a great deal of dread. The same needle would be used over and over on all patients, and it became blunt after a while, hurting like crazy and leaving multi-coloured bruises and sore places, which only began to disappear when the next round of needles were due.

Using a bedpan was my worst nightmare, especially lying flat. Even urinating was a great challenge, never mind the more serious problems. Though thankfully I wasn't eating solid foods. I longed to be able to use a bathroom in the normal way, but I knew it wasn't at all possible. It was a busy ward with female patients stretching away on both sides down the large room to the bottom. Each bed had a small locker at the side for personal belongings and a tray for eating at the foot of the bed, something I didn't need for a while. I could see very little of the other patients from my prone position, and I was delighted when a girl about my own age arrived in the bed next to mine. Her name was Mary. She had pneumonia and fluid on her lungs, which was to keep her in bed for many weeks, before being transferred to a sanatorium. It was wonderful to have someone my own age to talk with occasionally and we soon became friends.

At the end of three months, the resident female doctor, Mary Pringle, stopped by my bed during her rounds. Her usual prim face had a smile on it and her cool gray eyes sparkled behind her glasses, as she told me I was to be given one pillow. You would have thought I was at least receiving the Crown Jewels! I was so excited and cried with sheer joy. Everyone around me joined in the celebration when the pillow arrived, and was presented to me with a flourish, so appreciated after weeks of being without one. The first small victory in a long battle with the illness which had changed my whole world.

The bed was my cocoon. The outside world, and my place in it, had gradually faded. Tiny insignificant things gave pleasure. The pillow was a perfect example, the first victory in an ongoing fight to return to a normal existence.

The road back consisted of a series of small triumphs, often weeks apart, and took another three months to accomplish. Such things as getting a second pillow; being allowed to sit up in bed to eat from the tray; getting rid of the cage and enjoying the feel of crisp, clean sheets on my legs, without pain; being allowed to sit in the chair while the nurses changed my bed and the first wobbly baby steps around my bed, then to the next bed and the next, to reach my most coveted goal, the black and white tiled bathroom at the end of the ward, where I could sit on a toilet, without an audience, and scorn the offer of the hated bedpan.

These small victories gave immense pleasure, and the celebration would be shared by the patients and the staff. In a way, they became my family and almost my whole world.

Now that I could move about I began to think about food again. I asked Mum to bring in a few of my favourite things. I longed for thick slices of fresh white crusty Vienna bread smothered with butter - and something else I craved at that time; thick pieces of raw, crinkly, white tripe liberally sprinkled with malt vinegar and seasoned with black pepper. My mother would wrap it in several layers of paper before putting it in a brown paper bag. I would quickly take it from her and put it out of sight into my bedside locker to enjoy furtively later that night when the day staff departed and lights were dimmed and patients were supposed to be sleeping. Mary and I would have our little feast while we listened for the sound of the Night Nurse's crepe-soled shoes squeaking on the highly polished brown linoleum floors, checking on patients, from her table and chair in the centre of the ward.

We were caught a few times snacking long after lights out, but the night staff were usually more lax and just gave us a short lecture with a hint of a smile. They were often not much older than us and because of our lengthy stay on the ward we knew many of their first names and they would tell us about the latest boyfriend, sometimes from the nearby American Air Force Base at Burtonwood. One of the nurses did in fact, marry 'her Yank' as she called him, and went to live in the USA. She often walked around the ward singing quietly, an American song which must have related to her beloved 'Yank'.

At the end of six months, I had recovered and my thoughts now turned to life outside the hospital ward, which had become like home to me. I wanted to return to normal life, which I had vowed to myself would include all the things I'd loved to do, before this happened to me. I kept a vision of myself dancing, skating, riding my bicycle and of course, dating. More than ever now I wanted to be a nurse. The possibility of not being allowed to do those things was not part of the future I envisioned.

At the end of six months I was finally discharged from hospital and felt elated that my long stay was coming to an end at last. I was shocked and terribly distressed to learn that instead of going home,

I was being sent to a convalescent hospital miles away at the seaside, in a place called West Kirby. There I was to spend another four weeks recuperating further before going back to Hilary Avenue. I cried myself to sleep that night because I was so utterly deflated and disappointed and certainly had had no idea I was to go on to another hospital.

The following day the ambulance made the long journey and deposited me in the new hospital. I detested it from the first day. I was seventeen years old and my only companions were women who looked ancient to me, though I realise now they were only in their fifties. I hated listening to them exchanging stories of their hysterectomies and other gory details of operations they were now recovering from. There was no alternative other than to ask for permission to go for a short walk just outside the building, if the weather was in my favour.

Another insult to my dignity was having to wear not one but two pairs of navy blue fleece-lined knickers, which hugged my knees over long black woollen stockings, plus a bright red flannel under-vest, apparently specially made for me, to be worn next to my skin at all times. Matron would indeed check that I was wearing all these garments. There was no escape. She would stand in the hall waiting to make a show of me in front of anyone who was there. I was miserable now and homesick, oddly enough, for Whiston Hospital, and pining to be back there.

I stuck it for a week, then finally decided I'd had enough. I walked to the nearest telephone box one windy, rainy day, and phoned my father at work. I hadn't seen him for over six months. Maybe that gave me the courage to rebel. I was weeping and almost hysterical as I told him if he didn't come and get me, I was going to run away. Desperation made caution and fear vanish. I remember screaming down the phone as he tried to calm me, coaxing me to stay longer as the doctors advised, using the same words I had heard all my life "to be a good girl". I wouldn't listen and finally slammed down the phone, tears of anger and self-pity pouring down my face, as I trudged back slowly to the convalescent home.

Miraculously my tantrum worked. Mum arrived the next afternoon and after my long absence, I was home again. In a matter of weeks I ignored the list of dos and don'ts I'd been given when I left the hospital, and returned to all of the activities I loved. My sights now were even more set on being a children's nurse. I was devastated when I visited the Children's Hospital and learned from the Matron I had seen previously when I enrolled that I could never become a nurse because of having rheumatic fever. In tears, I protested that I was totally back to normal. She shook her head and repeated it wasn't possible now to take me. I saw sympathy in her eyes and on her kind face as she stood up, putting her arm around me as she walked me down the wide concrete steps to the street, my dream now in shreds.

As for the tripe I enjoyed so much in England, I could never find it in Canada, and haven't eaten it for forty years. I had almost forgotten its existence. The thought of eating raw cow's stomach now is utterly repulsive to me. I can't imagine why I craved it in the hospital – but I do remember it was delicious at the time!

Within a month I had almost returned to my old lifestyle and ignored the long list of activities I was not supposed to participate in. I went back to the Youth Club and Concert Party I had belonged to and where I had learned to do ballroom dancing, which was very popular in those days. I loved being back to normal, seeing old friends and noticing new ones attending the various activities.

One evening I noticed a new face sitting at the piano playing beautiful music, without any sheet music. He was tall, dark and handsome and I fell in love with him at first sight. I had had many boyfriends, none of them serious, though I always took them home for Father to inspect and approve or disapprove. That was a rule of the house and strictly adhered to. I only admired this gorgeous fellow from a distance, but one night he crossed the floor and asked me to dance. I was in seventh heaven!

His name was Gordon and he was nineteen years old and lived about a twenty-minute walk away from Hilary Avenue. We had every dance after that first one and talked without stopping. It seemed as if we had known each other for years. It was definitely mutual attraction, and when he asked to walk me home after the dance, I eagerly agreed, though I didn't take him in to meet my parents. He asked me to go to the Granada Cinema not far from his home, the following Saturday evening. *Gone With The Wind* was playing, starring Clarke Gable, Vivien Leigh and Leslie Howard. He mentioned there would be a long line-up because of the popularity of the film, and suggested he leave early to wait in the queue to make sure we made it. I agreed without hesitation as I was so thrilled and happy and so smitten with this new boyfriend.

The only snag was I already had a date to see that same movie at the same cinema, on the same night, with a boy named Vic, and somehow I had to find a way to cancel that arrangement. Nothing on God's earth would have prevented me from saying yes to Gordon. There wasn't enough time for me to write a letter to Vic, no phone to ring in those days, and his home was a long way from mine and I didn't even know how to get there. The only thing I could think of was to send a telegram direct to his home address cancelling our date. Looking back it was a thoughtless, cruel thing to do because the very sight of a telegraph boy delivering a telegram in those days usually meant bad news.

I never did see Vic again to apologize for my act. I was so desperate to be with Gordon that I didn't care at that moment what it took to cancel a date. The young can be so cruel at times and it was so out of character for me to hurt anyone, but it was done out of desperation. That's how crazy I felt about this new boy in my life.

Saturday arrived and I walked to the Granada Cinema to find Gordon in the line-up. There was a very long queue, but we did get in to see the movie, which I've never forgotten. We were shown to our seats and waited for the main event. The lights eventually dimmed and only the glow from cigarettes could be seen, dotted in profusion throughout the whole cinema. It seems amazing as I write this episode, that smoking was allowed in cinemas and theatres. What a fire hazard that was, but smoking was the thing to do in those days and encouraged everywhere. Every seat had a small metal ashtray attached to the seat in front, for the depositing of ash and eventually the last of the cigarette. The air would be filled with a blue haze of smoke, which must have been bad for health, but of course we were totally oblivious to the dangers and never gave it a thought.

Gone With The Wind had an intermission halfway through because of its length. Attendants, mostly young pretty teenage girls dressed in very short dresses wearing pillbox hats and trays around their necks, walked up and down the aisles selling tiny tubs of ice-creams. That lasted about twenty minutes before the second half of the movie started where it had left off. Gordon took hold of my hand and held on to it throughout the rest of the film, stroking my fingers with his, and my heart skipped several beats each time he glanced at me, with those smouldering brown eyes. I wanted the night to last forever.

The movie thankfully was long, but of course it did end with the famous exit line from Clark Gable to Vivien Leigh – 'Frankly my dear, I don't give a damn'.

That memorable night was the beginning of a long relationship with Gordon. I loved going to their house, which was very modestly furnished, but it was filled with happiness and an abundance of love. I felt it from the start and was completely at ease and very relaxed.

Gordon was the middle child of three sons. All of them were talented musically, along with their father, and every visiting night was like having a party. His mum was a lovely lady, so warm and welcoming, and she adored her husband and boys. Between them they played just about every instrument and Gordon usually took over the piano, playing by ear, he didn't need sheet music. He just sat down, ran his hands over the keys and played anything you asked for. He could reduce me to tears with *Clair De Lune* or make my feet tap in time to his versions of Boogie-Woogie, which was very popular at that time.

It was all a huge contrast to my home and upbringing. I knew my mother liked Gordon, but Father didn't approve of him because he was so outgoing and friendly. Not disrespectful, he was just at ease with his elders. I didn't care, I was so in love with Gordon and wanted to marry him when he finished his apprenticeship, which would occur when he was twenty-one years old, some 17 months hence. He had promised his parents to complete the course to be a plasterer, a valuable trade at that time.

We got engaged about a year after we met, while on holiday with his parents on the Isle of Man. They had left us to walk the long promenade while we were sitting on the beach and Gordon asked if I would like to look for a ring – an inexpensive one we would acknowledge as an engagement ring but not telling my parents for a while. Of course I was thrilled with that wonderful suggestion. We went off to the shops and found what we were looking for, and as soon as we left the store he put it on my finger. We told his parents that day and they were delighted; however, I didn't tell mine until Gordon could ask and receive permission to marry me from my father. He did so, but I could tell my father wasn't overjoyed with the news, even though Mum was pleased, as she had liked Gordon from the start.

We continued to be happy for several months, but then we began to quarrel. He wanted to have a sexual relationship, since he felt we were as good as married. That's how sure we were about our feelings for each other. I had always wanted to walk down the aisle in a white wedding gown still a virgin, entitled to wear white. It certainly wasn't a lack of desire on my part, I really loved him. Above all, the terrible fear of my father, should the worst happen and I became pregnant, constantly scared me to death. Birth control was unheard of and I knew without any doubt he would never forgive me. I could never imagine putting myself in that position. I would have done something desperate rather than bring disgrace on the family.

We continued to argue about it for several weeks and finally I told Gordon I wanted us to just take a break from each other for about a month, give us time to think about the situation, hoping he would understand how stupid it was to keep on fighting. I just wanted to wait until we could be married and then begin on the right foot. I would never stop loving him or wanting him, he was the only one in the world for me at that time.

He didn't like it but he finally agreed, and we promised to stay in touch during the break; both of us knew it was just a temporary parting. It was a very hard decision to make, and although I didn't know at the time, it was to change my whole life. I was miserable during that first long month and missed him terribly, yet there was a sense of relief that the constant demands and quarrels were over for now.

He visited me a couple of times, but we didn't go out together. He told me over and over he was very unhappy without me. I felt just as lonely. In my heart I knew it was just a matter of time before we got back together, because we really did love each other in spite of the problems. I kept telling myself he didn't have too much longer to finish his plastering course and receive his Apprenticeship Certificate, then we could go ahead and marry.

Then two months passed and I didn't hear from Gordon at all. I worried about the long silence but didn't know what to do. I was worried he might be sick. They didn't have a phone in their house.

One day I couldn't bear the waiting any longer and decided to send him a letter. Before I did so, I bumped into his mother while shopping on my day off. She looked really ill and had lost a lot of weight and her sparkle. Very concerned, I immediately asked how she was and she said she'd been in hospital with stomach ulcers. Before I could ask about Gordon, she blurted out some news that absolutely shocked me to the core, robbing me of speech as I tried to absorb what she was saying. Gordon was getting married in a few weeks' time to someone he had met not long after we had parted. She was now pregnant with his child.

It was unbelievable news and I couldn't understand why he hadn't had the decency to come and tell me himself, instead of me accidentally hearing about it from his mother. I was still wearing his ring – our engagement ring – and I couldn't make sense of it all.

The tears fell down my cheeks and his mum held on to me as though she'd never let go. In the end I had to say goodbye, telling her to look after herself and thanking her for always making me so welcome in her home.

As I watched her walk away from me I felt numb and shocked. My world fell completely apart at that moment and I knew my love affair was really over.

Several months later I received a letter from the eldest son telling me his mum had died. It had not been a stomach ulcer, but cancer. He actually said it was probably the shock over Gordon having to get married, especially so soon after the break-up of our engagement, which had upset his family, especially his parents. They had no idea why that had happened either.

It was all very tragic and not even easy to write about it now all these years later, but it was part of my life and even now I feel sad when I think about what might have been in another era like the present one; the stark contrast of the world now when thousands of people have babies before getting married, and in fact never marry at all, even when they have several more children. When I was growing up, getting pregnant before marriage would bring terrible disgrace and shame on the whole family. It was certainly a deterrent to me, but sadly I lost the love of my life because of my high standards, plus an awesome fear of my father's wrath, which I knew from past experience could be terrifying.

The world is certainly a very different place now in many ways. The changes began in the sixties when 'free love' came into society and having sex with anyone became the norm. I wonder if Gordon ever thought about this new world?

I never did see him again after we finally parted but I know he married a redhead and coincidentally, a few years later, so did I. It is now water under the bridge and youth being resilient, I eventually did go on with my life and stopped crying myself to sleep at night, still wishing and wondering whether I had done the right thing.

CHAPTER FOURTEEN

WORKING GIRL

After recovering from my long illness and the subsequent disappointment of no longer being acceptable to train as a nurse, I knew I would have to find work, using the only skills I had. My father had insisted I attend Commercial College, on Dale Street, in Liverpool, to learn Pitman's Shorthand and to touch-type, with keys covered, and music to help develop rhythm when typing. I hated it, but I knuckled down and tried very hard to learn these skills. I knew it was costing my father a great deal of money, money we didn't really have, and as usual I felt compelled to try and please him. Whatever I was faced with in life it was an automatic response for me.

In spite of my dislike for shorthand and typing I learned and absorbed both subjects easily and received an excellent report from the Principal, to help me find my first job. During the months of learning office work, I had one terrifying ordeal which I'll never forget. One morning Father gave me a brown envelope, containing £100 to cover the school fees due that day, warning me to take good care of it. I boarded the tram and went upstairs as usual, sitting on the shiny wooden slatted seat just enjoying the ride into the

City. I got off at my usual stop close to the College on Dale Street, some ten minutes from the terminal at the Pier Head, where it would wait for a short while before returning to Bowring Park, a journey of approximately eleven miles. I walked up the long flight of stairs to where the Office area was located to hand in my payment and suddenly realised I no longer had it. I had been carrying my small purse, umbrella, woollen gloves and the envelope.

My stomach lurched with fear and I ran to the Principal's office to tell her of my plight. She sent me very quickly on my way to the Pier Head to see whether I could catch the tram before it left on its return journey. I ran every step of the way, panting and puffing to get my breath, the adrenaline and fear coursed through my body and I'm pretty sure I was the first person to run a four-minute mile!

Once I arrived at the terminus I could see there wasn't any sign of a 6A tram and when I told the Inspector standing in the area of my loss, he told me it had already left. He added that the best thing to do was to see if the Lost and Found office on Dale Street, not far from the College, had received the brown envelope I was supposed to guard with my life. If that didn't produce anything, he said my only other hope would be to visit the Tram Depot at Edge Lane, located on the route five miles or so out of the city. He said that perhaps if it had been handed in, the driver would have dropped it off there.

I did as he advised, but there was nothing at the Dale Street Office, just a couple of umbrellas handed in that morning. I boarded the tram which would take to the depot and sat gazing out of the window, just terrified at what would happen when I told my father I'd lost the envelope. I couldn't bear the thought of that scenario, and I felt sick to my stomach at my stupidity. I must have let the envelope slip out of my hand without realising, but Father would not take that for an explanation or an excuse. He would be furious with me for being careless, and I couldn't blame him.

My fear grew worse as I reached Edge Hill Depot and rang the bell to be let off the tram. I had no idea where the office I wanted would be found, since it was a large area of sheds and brick buildings, but I eventually located the Main Office and told my sorry tale to the man in charge. He could see I was in a terrible state and sat me down on a chair, while he went to check the log book to see if a brown envelope had been handed in.

He was gone for ten very long minutes before coming back holding something in his hand which looked as if it just could be my envelope. He smiled at me and asked what was written on the front of the item he was holding, and of course I was able to tell him. He put his hand on my shoulder and said 'You are one lucky little lady, but I think you know that and perhaps have learned your lesson to be more careful in future'.

The tears of relief finally flowed and ran down my cheeks and I thanked him over and over. He kept protesting he wasn't the one to thank but rather the honest passenger who found it and the driver who took it to the Depot.

I never did tell my parents about that awful day, not even my mother or my sister. It would be my secret for the rest of my life – until now.

I finished my college course with good marks and knew the next stop was to find a job. At this point I had no idea what kind of office I wanted to work in. I checked newspaper ads and other sources and wrote letters of application.

While I was still getting organised I received a note from the Principal of the Commercial College telling me that Ealing Film Distributors, located on Commutation Row, right in the city, was looking for a Shorthand/Typist. They had set up an appointment for me a few days later. She cautioned me not to accept the low salary this particular situation was offering, urging me to ask for more money.

The words 'Film Distributor' immediately conjured up visions in my teenage mind, like a magnet, of the glamorous life of film stars, an exciting world I was eager to be involved with. Regardless of the salary offered, I knew I wanted this job.

I dressed carefully that day and rode the tram from Bowring Park to London Road, just steps away from the office. It was in a row of storefront businesses, with a large plate glass window with 'Ealing Film Distributors' written across it in large black letters. I opened the single glass door. Inside there was a counter, gray filing cabinets, a table and two desks in a small area.

Sitting at one of the desks was a woman with short dark hair, in her thirties. Not really what I was expecting to see. I thought there would at least be pictures of film stars on the walls in the office, or at least some indication of a connection to the world of movies. It was disappointing, but it did not deter me one bit.

I was directed to the next floor and shown into a large office with black leather chairs and an imposing oak desk. A large, heavy man with a florid complexion, balding, with just a dark fringe of hair and a compensating bushy moustache beneath his large nose, sat behind the desk. He introduced himself as Mr Lee, the manager. He was in his fifties or thereabouts, I guessed.

He appeared impressed with my college marks and after asking me some questions, he offered me the position. He then explained that there was just one other woman working in the office, plus the staff who worked at the rear of the building, separated from the office area, who were responsible for the actual reels of film to be dispatched and returned from the various cinemas who had booked them. There were two salesmen who would be in and out of the office daily.

Mr Lee told me I would be required to take care of correspondence and learn everything there was to know about the film distributing business, which he warned would be challenging. Just as the Principal had predicted, the salary offered was low, but I accepted it – as I knew I would.

I worked for Ealing Distributors for two years, gaining valuable insight and experience of the complicated business. I took dictation and typed correspondence. I also learned to book films for the numerous cinemas in a large area covering the North-West of England Counties of Lancashire and Cheshire - and the whole of North Wales. Movies were thriving in the nineteen forties and fifties, and even the tiniest Welsh village had a picture house, often just called 'The Cinema'.

It was a strict barring system which involved making very sure that the same film was not booked to two cinemas, within a certain radius, at the same time. Once that time had elapsed, the film could then be booked to a second cinema in the same area. All this information was recorded in writing in large ledgers measuring two feet wide by a foot and a half deep.

I enjoyed the challenge of the work and the occasional reward of attending a Trade Show held during the morning, where I was often among the privileged first to view a new film, before it was actually released to the circuit for public viewing. All the cinema owners and the salesmen who worked for the distributor, and quite often the managers of the various distributors, would be in attendance. I got to know most of them, occasionally having a short conversation before we went inside the cinema to view the new movie to be released.

Two years later, the Manager of Columbia Pictures asked if I would like to join them. It was a much larger distributor, located on Norton Street just a few minutes' walk away from where I

presently worked. The salary offered was much better than I was
receiving at Ealing and since the other secretary had left and Mr
Lee had not replaced her, I had found myself in charge of the office
and the dispatchers who worked in the back room, responsible for
sending and receiving the films for distribution. I was only just out
of my teen years and quite capable of doing the job, but I wasn't to
be paid for it. I decided to make the switch.

My new boss was Nathan Levy, a very attractive looking man,
somewhere in his early forties. He was of medium height, with
beautiful wavy silver hair, velvety dark brown eyes and tanned skin.
Like Mr Lee, he was Jewish. The film business had many Jewish
people in the various distributors. He wore a different suit every
day, each one immaculate and expensive. I could tell by just looking
that they were beautifully tailored, usually complemented with a
crisp white shirt and silk tie, often a plain red one. He was a
bachelor who, by reputation, liked women, good food, wine and
cigars. He drove a Jaguar and occupied a very large office on the
ground floor, with windows looking on to the street to his right
and a glass wall facing the stairs on the other side, which his large
female staff used frequently throughout the day. I soon learned he
had dated several of them, but they were all single, as he was, and I
didn't feel there was anything wrong about it.

There was a buzzer system in his office, to summon his
secretaries, which now included me. His most important secretary
was summoned with just one buzz; I was four. Her name was Trudy,
the Office Manager. She had been with Columbia Pictures for
many years and must have been in her sixties when I arrived. She
dressed very smartly in beautifully tailored suits and blouses, her
dark hair cut short in a modern style, always the height of fashion.

Occasionally, as you passed her office there would be an aroma
of urine in the air, even though her door would be closed. It was

rumored she dried her wet underwear in front of the electric fire in her small office. I don't think it was just gossip, I had noticed it myself. I thought it was such a shame because she dressed so immaculately, not a hair out of place. In every other way she was the perfectly groomed secretary.

The first time Mr Levy buzzed for me, I was nervous and knocked at his door waiting for him to say 'come in', then practically tiptoed across the large space to the chair opposite his desk, to take dictation. Later, when I was more familiar with what was expected of me, I would tap and walk straight in. He was always very pleasant and businesslike and I settled down at Columbia Pictures very quickly. I knew the film business now, all the names and locations of the various cinemas and needed only to learn the film titles released by Columbia. It was an impressive list and included not just feature films but shorts, cartoons and of course Pathé News, which always followed the forthcoming attractions, leading into the major movie being shown at that particular time. The system though was the same and the barring rules applied as they had at Ealing Film Distributors.

There was a much larger staff, consisting of four booking clerks, four secretaries and half a dozen salesmen, as well as an office manager, Mr Blackburn. I remember he was very thin, with glasses and a head of sparse straight black hair, greased and slicked back and showing his rather pitted complexion. I always thought he looked as though he needed a bath and a good feed!

He had worked at Columbia for twenty years and still seemed very nervous around the boss. He smoked incessantly, holding it in the corner of his mouth, squinting through the smoke at the papers on his desk, never removing the cigarette. The ash would eventually drop off and he would sweep it away with his hand and only discard the cigarette when it was a tiny stub and in danger of burning him.

It was quite revolting really, even though I didn't find smoking repulsive then, as I do now. At that time almost every person in the building shared the habit. The same can be said about cinemas, theatres, pubs, restaurants and amazingly in hospitals where both patients and visitors could smoke.

Mr Levy usually left the office at midday to eat, returning between one thirty and two o'clock. This seldom varied. However, one particular day when I thought he was at lunch I was coming down from the second floor to the main area, and instead of using the stairs I impulsively decided to slide down on the banister. I don't know what possessed me to do such a foolish thing at that moment. I have to confess it was something I had done occasionally at home since I was about nine years old, but only when my father wasn't around! Usually I did it to hasten the journey from the dark upstairs bedrooms, of which I was very afraid, back to the safety of the living room where my mother would be waiting for the baby's clean diapers and his night clothes. She always sent one of us to do this because she was so afraid of the dark herself.

This particular day however, Mr Levy had *not* left for lunch and as I slid down the banister in my short dress, his dark brown eyes met my hazel ones. I got the shock of my life and spent my entire lunch time agonizing over what I was going to say to him, feeling sure he would at least give me a severe reprimand and perhaps even fire me. My stomach in knots, I waited minute by minute to hear four buzzes, summoning me to his office. I couldn't concentrate on anything, the shorthand notes I was transcribing looked like Egyptian hieroglyphics and I felt like bursting into tears for my stupidity.

I had to wait until three o'clock for the summons from Mr Levy. I picked up my notebook and pencil and walked on trembling knees to his office, tapping on the door before I walked to the usual chair. He didn't look angry, which was an immediate relief, in fact there was just a tiny glimmer of a smile on his face as he motioned me to sit down, and as though nothing had happened, began to dictate a letter. I could hardly believe my luck!

I had learned my lesson of course, and never did that again in the office, nor did I ever tell anyone at home. I would have been in terrible trouble with my father. I do know I got off very lightly that day.

I was now happy both at work and in my personal life. I celebrated my twenty-first birthday with a party surrounded by family and friends. Life had almost returned to normal after the break-up with Gordon and I dated a few young men, but they just didn't appeal to me. I still took them home to be vetted by my father and my mother said I was hard to please, but then she never did know the real story, not until years later in fact. She knew I had broken my engagement off but not the reason or any of the details why we had split up.

I had worked for Columbia Pictures for several years when I was offered another job. This time it was to work for the other side of the film business, for a company called Hamner Enterprises which owned a string of cinemas in Lancashire and Wales. It was the boss, Phil Hamner, who approached me at a Trade Show we were both attending for the release of 'Gilda', starring the very beautiful and glamorous Rita Hayworth. It was too tempting to pass up. Mr Hamner had the reputation of being good to work for and I thought I should at least go and talk with him.

The office was located in stately premises he owned on Rodney Street, a prestigious address on the outskirts of the city, well known for housing the very best medical specialists and successful lawyers in Liverpool. The houses were built of large gray stone blocks, with black shiny doors and brass knockers with iron railings around the basement steps. Inside it was very spacious, consisting of ground floor offices with rugs on the hardwood floors, armchairs here and there, plus a full kitchen and bathroom. The first floor was entirely for Phil Hamner's huge and lavishly furnished office and bathroom, and above that was his apartment, which he used when he needed to stay in the city overnight. His other home was in North Wales. He was semi-retired and loved to play golf, and some weeks he only made a brief appearance in the Liverpool Office.

He interviewed me with George Henderson, his Office Manager, for the position of Secretary. Apparently I would be the only other employee in the office, something which made me hesitate, but not for long. There were so many other advantages to this new position, including a much bigger salary and flexible working hours (plus I liked the thought of working in this elegant house on this particular street) that I agreed to take it.

I loved it from that first day. Being the only female, they treated me like a piece of Dresden china and I know they enjoyed having me there. I was young and pretty and I never objected to making pots of tea for either of them, but it was usually just George and I in the office most of the time and we became really good friends. He occasionally asked me out for a drive in the country and we would have a meal and a drink together.

I sensed early on that he was quite smitten with me. I was of course free at that time but I felt the age difference of sixteen years was too great for me to be really interested. I did enjoy his company and the kindness he showed me. Of course I loved working there. It was home from home - or even better! The best job of three I'd had since I became a working girl.

I was reluctant to leave this place, although I did so when I married, only because my new husband insisted on it, stating he didn't want his wife working. We actually met through his sister

Hilda who worked at Columbia Pictures. She was forever singing the praises of this wonderful brother, this paragon of virtue, and eventually I was introduced to him when I stayed at their house one weekend. He kept asking me for a date after that initial meeting. At first I went out with him because I couldn't bear to hurt Hilda, who thought the world of him.

I wasn't attracted to him physically, though he was quite nice to look at. Stan had a mop of wavy red hair and although I loved it on females, I was not at all keen on red-haired men, especially a boyfriend. Tall dark and handsome had always been my preference.

Stan kept asking me out and I continued to see him, mainly because of his sister. I did find him to be kind, gentle and very caring. He sort of grew on me gradually as time went by and I was fond of him. We got along without any quarrelling or difference of opinion. I later realised that we never discussed anything of importance, but it took a while before that became a problem of sorts. I don't know whether that was enough for a lifetime marriage, but he eventually proposed and I accepted and we married in September 1951 with full approval from both my parents, especially my father, whom Stan treated with the utmost respect. That was important in their opinion.

Stan had joined the RAF as soon as he was old enough and was crazy about flying. Trained in Canada at the back end of the Second World War, he received his Wings after spending time in Cold Lake, Alberta and Regina in Saskatchewan, before returning home to England. He never talked about his time spent in Canada or told me whether he liked it or not, and as usual, I never asked questions. I was much too happy living in England, with no wish or desire to change it. Emigrating to another country was never a subject either mentioned and certainly never discussed. When I thought back to my relationship with Stan I realised he never talked about his family, other than his sister and his older brother George who had also been in the RAF. He was a rear-end gunner, known as a 'tail-end Charlie', and had been shot down over Holland and buried there. Eventually I learned he had left a wife, Joyce, and a new-born baby boy they called Andrew. Shortly after, she died of meningitis and Andrew was raised by his maternal grandparents and lived in Cheshire.

What a terrible tragedy. Hilda had never spoken about it, and neither had her parents, in my presence. I liked Mrs Holt a lot but I never cared for his rather uncouth father, who had not been proud of either of his sons, even calling them 'Nancy Boys' for joining the RAF. What kind of a father would speak that way about his sons fighting in a war, risking their lives? It made me understand Stan a little better. I know he idolized his mum, but he never talked a great deal about his father other than saying he had worked for the railway delivering goods by horse and cart, and demanded steak and chips for his dinner every night of the week. He visited the pub on the way home from work, most nights. That just about summed up my impression and opinion of his father. He died of cancer in 1958.

After the war was finally over Stan continued to fly with 610 Squadron, based at Hooton in Cheshire, for many years. When I met him he was still flying every weekend. It was his absolute passion in life. He lived and breathed planes. We had a church wedding and I wore the traditional white gown. I wanted to shop for it myself but my future mother-in-law suggested I borrow a gown from her niece (only worn once she said!) and I didn't like to refuse the offer.

You can gather by now that I was always doing things to please someone else, always afraid of hurting their feelings, rather than doing what I really wanted to do. It was a nice dress, made of lace, but not what I would have chosen. I purchased my own veil. It was a lovely day and Father paid for the wedding breakfast before we left for a two-week honeymoon in Minehead, Somerset. We travelled by train to London and stayed in the Railway Hotel, the proper name of which I cannot remember. I do recall it was large, old and very cold. Our bedroom was as big as a barn and I was thankful it would only be for one night.

It makes me smile now when I remember how terribly homesick I felt during that two weeks and how anxious I was to return home and see familiar faces, especially my mother's. Another matter which now is almost unbelievable when I think about that now all these years later! I realised when the honeymoon was coming to an end and getting ready to return home that I had no idea where 'home' was going to be. It was an incredible thought! It had never been discussed ahead of the marriage. I soon found that Stan hadn't given that important matter a thought either and certainly didn't have the money to buy a house. Renting was almost impossible after the war. Apartments were at a premium and many of them unfit to live in. Our only option was to live either with his parents – something I did not want to do – or live with mine.

If we had only discussed the matter before getting married I would have put up a good fight to stay working in the well-paid job I had loved. In spite of the fact we could not afford a home of our own for several years and lived in two rooms with my mother and father, he would not let me work. Apartments were still impossible to come by, though I searched the newspaper advertisements every night in the hope of finding something suitable. If I came across anything remotely interesting, I would jump on a tramcar, fervently hoping this time I would be lucky. Some of the flats were disgusting as well as very expensive. Most of them were grotty and didn't even have the basic requirements for cooking or washing, and finally I gave up chasing around, tired of returning home in disgust.

It took many years for Liverpool to recover from the war and the destruction of property, which increased an already existing problem. Months went by and in spite of the lack of housing and precious little hope of having enough money to buy accommodation, my husband still insisted he did not want me to work. His Victorian attitude was normal for the times. There wasn't an argument at all. I simply complied with his wishes. He worked at the Automatic Telephone Company as a signwriter through the week. I have no idea what kind of salary that occupation provided, but I don't imagine it was a great deal.

Two years later, my sister-in-law Hilda, engaged to John who was much older than her and worked at the Barracks of the Queen's Own Cameron Highlanders on Fraser Street in the City of Liverpool, told me there was a job vacant as Secretary to the Colonel in Chief. There were a hundred men at the barracks – most of them from Scotland! I was of course interested in being useful again and to my surprise, my husband agreed, probably because the offer of the job came from a member of his family!

I went for an interview and was engaged for the vacant position. One female and a large number of soldiers, mostly with accents I couldn't understand at all. Happily, my boss the Colonel spoke perfect English and we got along very well.

I had been there for a year when I became pregnant, and as soon as my very small bump became evident I left, mainly because of the number of males I was surrounded by much of the time. I wasn't unhappy about leaving because I was so excited about the coming baby. Even an unplanned one!

Ealing Film Distributors, Columbia Pictures and Phil Hamner's Enterprises were all part of my single, mostly happy existence from the age of eighteen until I was almost twenty-four, the age I was married.

Surprisingly, Stan and I were happy together. He still went to Hooton Aerodrome every weekend and eventually exchanged Spitfires and Wellington Bombers for Meteor jets. He wasn't too thrilled about the new faster planes at first, mainly because they had ejection seats, to be used if necessary, but he carried on doing it, in spite of the terrible loss of two pilots from the squadron, both in flying accidents on the new aircraft. I had met and liked both of them. They were relatively young and had survived being in action during the hostilities. Such a tragic way to end their young lives, though each of them had the same passion for flying.

Stan and I shared a love of music of many sorts and occasionally we would go to the Liverpool Philharmonic Hall and listen to several hours of classical music. He was also an avid fan of Frank Sinatra and collected every single record that came on the market and any literature he could find. I still have some of the books we bought him as gifts for Christmas and birthdays throughout many years. We were so lucky to grow up in an era which was rich with great movies and wonderful music, much of it still remembered all these years later.

Sometimes I search my brain for a favourite, and in doing so set myself thinking of years gone by, when I had a song connected to each and every boyfriend from my teenage years, all before meeting Gordon. We were all members of the Youth Club and knocked about together in a group, just as friends. We were also ardent ballroom dancers and most of us belonged to the Concert Party. We visited a couple of old folks' homes (as they were referred to then) to perform for them. We were never bored, either for something to do or lacking in ideas. They were a great bunch of friends to have.

One in particular I liked a lot as a good friend. Douglas had fair, crinkly hair and laughing blue/gray eyes and wanted to be a pilot. He loved Glenn Miller with a passion and his favourite piece of music was Moonlight Serenade. Doug did become a pilot and sadly was killed in a flying accident at the young age of twenty-two. Another tragedy.

Peggy Lee singing 'Bewitched' will always remind me of George, who often whistled it around the office. Of course he was much older than I was and I was forbidden to even mention his name at home, since it was assumed by my father that he could only want me for one thing. Guess what that was? Nothing could have been further from the truth – he was always a perfect gentleman. He had never married and he did propose to me, but I declined. However we did remain good friends though I never saw him again after I married in September, 1951. I still have the set of silver teaspoons that he and Mr Hanmer gave me as a wedding gift.

As a teenager, once a week I went skating with a boy who lived just around the corner from Hilary Avenue; his name was Bobby Bromley. We used to catch the bus into Liverpool City, then walk quite a distance to the Indoor Roller Rink. We enjoyed skating to music and always had a good time, though it was just another friendship. I wasn't attracted to him in any other way and of course it was great to have an escort on that long journey into town, otherwise I would not have gone on my own, especially during the winter months.

Returning home one night, as we neared Hilary Avenue, Bobby suddenly stopped and said to me in a very serious tone of voice "I really like you a lot Doreen, but my mother would never allow me to marry a Protestant, we have to just stay as we are, good friends." I wasn't at all hurt with that remark because, quite honestly, my father would never have allowed me to marry a Catholic! He would have even forbidden me to be friends with Bobby, whom he had never met – and never would.

There was such a divide between religions in those days. Hopefully, it has lessened, but I fear it isn't so. It always seemed odd to me and thankfully, when I grew into a mature adult, I had many friends who were of different religions and colour, and loved them for what they were as individuals and certainly nothing to do with their religious beliefs or their taste in music. I include Mormons, Jewish, Indian and Kenyan in that statement and I was always welcomed into their families.

Of course *Clair de Lune* was always one of my favourite pieces of music. It still has the power to fill me with emotion, reminding me of Gordon – tall, dark and very handsome, with brown eyes and a wonderful smile - my first real love. During my long life I have listened to all types of music and enjoyed so many fabulous musical stars. There was such a deluge to choose from and you didn't have to be rich to share it, you heard it by going to the movies or staying home with the record player or listening to the radio. We didn't have television in those days but entertainment could be had in abundance.

In fact, it was 1953 when I saw television for the very first time. It was for the very special occasion of the Coronation of Queen Elizabeth II. The daughter of our next door neighbour lived almost across the road on Hilary Avenue and she was the very first person to have a television. We were all very excited when she invited all the neighbours in the surrounding area to watch the very important ceremony. Of course it was a memorable occasion for everyone who managed to squeeze into their living room where this new-found technology, with its fourteen inch screen, proudly sat for all of us to ogle at.

It wasn't too long before everyone had a television, my parents included. A company called Radio Rentals began renting televisions at an affordable rate and for the rest of their lives, Mum and Dad took that route, along with most householders in those days. It did seem a good idea since, if anything went wrong, the company would either repair the television without charge or replace it with another set. The screens grew in size, just as they do today, but the rental fee was still affordable. When Stan and I finally had our own house, we decided to go the same route and we never did buy one, we found it very suitable just to rent from the same source – Radio Rentals.

CHAPTER FIFTEEN

STARTING A FAMILY

Stan and I didn't plan on having a family until we had our own home, but somehow it happened twice in spite of taking precautions, which obviously didn't work!

I have a small portrait of my two children which I really treasure. Christopher, who was thirteen months old at the time, is wearing a beige sweater and pants to match. His fair, straight hair is slightly askew, in spite of all my efforts to keep it tidy for the occasion, and Janice, my five-year-old daughter, wearing a short-sleeved pink dress, with a lacy top, and pink ribbons at the neck and sleeves. There is a matching ribbon in her dark brown, straight hair. I had knitted both of their outfits, every stitch a labour of love. Both children are smiling broadly, their lovely faces lit up in obedience to the photographer who had come to the house to take the picture.

As I look at them, my smile mirrors theirs and I let myself think back to the time of their births and the complete and utter happiness they each brought with them. I wanted so badly to be a mum from the time I was just a small girl myself, playing on the front step of my home in Liverpool with my friends and our dolls, imitating our parents as we undressed and dressed our babies, scolding and praising. It was the game of pretence that all kids like to play. Years later, when I was in my mid-twenties and married, I knitted constantly through the two pregnancies, making countless tiny white and pastel-coloured garments of every kind. When completed, each would be carefully placed between two pieces of thick brown paper and placed carefully beneath the large, heavy living-room carpet which covered most of the wooden floor. It was a good place to store them.

My husband - the soccer player and pilot - wanted a part in the making of the trousseau, and actually knitted a tiny white under-vest for our firstborn, a feat he was pretty proud of. From time to time we would unearth this collection of miniature clothes and look at each knitted piece, deriving immense pleasure just from taking a peep at the future.

My daughter arrived, one month early, on April 16 1954. It was a Good Friday and it took us all by surprise. I started with mild pains early that morning and thought it was just another stomach upset. My pregnancy had been a difficult one because of morning sickness which lasted all day, for months. However on that particular day my main concern was that I wouldn't be able to enjoy the precious small tin of red salmon I had hoarded for weeks to have for my dinner at Easter. I didn't have to share it with Stan, as he didn't like salmon and would only eat fish bought from the fish and chip shop! He was in fact a very fussy eater. Even though it was almost nine years after World War II, salmon was still one of the items in short supply.

I had craved fishy things right throughout the pregnancy, sometimes going to the corner shop to buy a tin of pilchards which I would consume entirely, as though my life depended on it! The salmon was to be my special treat on that holiday Friday. It is perhaps the reason my daughter doesn't care to eat fish! She gags at the smell of it. We have often laughed about it.

It became less important as the morning wore on and in the early afternoon my husband took me to the hospital, some thirty minutes away from home. The Ward Sister who examined me was, I think, a Sergeant Major in disguise! She asked me very sharply whether I was sure I was having pains. I was as scared of her as I was about giving birth. Even more so when she remarked "Well, I hope you won't need stitching, because there's no doctor on duty today, it being Good Friday".

Stitching? Whatever did she mean? She told my husband to go home. He could return at normal visiting time between 7 and 8 pm and, if this was a false alarm, I could go home with him. Her tone of voice conveyed that she thought it was. There wasn't a scrap of warmth or sympathy in her manner. I was just a nuisance taking up space and time on a Good Friday.

I was taken to a room containing a high, narrow bed, with a small bedside table, a large clock on the wall and off to the right a bathroom. The walls were painted a dull cream, the floor had green linoleum with black speckles in it. The whole place reeked of disinfectant, which turned my stomach, though I eventually got used to it.

Sister gave me a short hospital gown, the kind which robs you of all dignity, and pointed to the small bell on the bedside table and told me to ring if I needed anything.

I lay there having longer and more painful contractions. I felt terribly lonely and my mind was obsessed with the Sister's remarks about needing stitches. No one had explained that bit to me, in fact, no one had explained anything very much to me. Not my mother or the doctor I had visited each month for a checkup throughout my pregnancy. Again, ignorance was bliss! I had been completely in love with the idea of having a baby and now realised I knew very little about the actual birth process.

Now and then Sister popped in and finally agreed I was in labor. She didn't stay with me but instructed me to ring the bell when my water broke and when the contractions were two minutes apart. It was a lonely process, in those 'keep a stiff upper lip' days.

I didn't make a sound or ask for help until it was absolutely necessary. My daughter was born at 6.55 pm that Good Friday evening, the tiniest little thing I had ever seen, weighing 5lbs 3oz, and measuring 19 inches long, with a penny-whistle cry. Nothing could ever have prepared me for the overwhelming rush of love as I looked down at this tiny bundle - the absolute miracle of life. Gratitude welled up inside me, bringing tears of sheer joy and relief that all fingers and toes were present. She was perfect. All pain was instantly forgotten in the miraculous way that nature has, as I held my firstborn in my arms. And I didn't need stitches! That was definitely a big plus!

My husband, came into the room about 7.15 pm. He had not expected that the birth would be over - he was really just visiting me! I'm sure he looked in worse shape than I did. His face was as white as a sheet and he held a bunch of rather wilted red tulips in his hand. When he saw his firstborn I saw an expression on his face I will never forget. It was one of pure love and amazement that this had really happened. He had a daughter. We called her Janice Elaine.

Four years later we were waiting for our son to be born. This time I was determined to have the baby at home, and against doctor's advice because I had been terribly ill with morning sickness, spending two days in the hospital on a drip. I ignored the advice and with the help of a midwife who was gentle, caring, and very helpful, it was a totally different and wonderful experience for me. I gave birth to my son in my mother's home, with lots of encouragement from my husband and mum.

Most of the labour I spent downstairs with them, walking around and around the small living room, holding on to the furniture through each contraction, instead of lying alone on a hard bed in the hospital. Everyone but me was drinking tea and eating biscuits and time passed very quickly and when my water broke, all over my mother's living room carpet, it was time for me to go to bed. My father and youngest brother Raymond, were upstairs sleeping in the two adjacent bedrooms. Though I was in labour I hardly made a sound, very conscious of where I was giving birth, just feet away. In fact the midwife urged me to 'scream if I wanted to'. I didn't, I just groaned a bit every now and then when the pains got stronger.

Our son Christopher arrived at 1.40 am on January 4, 1958 and weighed 6lbs 8oz. He was perfect! Two completely different experiences, but the end results were the same, giving us our two beautiful children.

Nine months later we moved into a brand new three bedroom council house – our very first home – not too far away from my parents. It was such a happy time for us all. Stan decorated and painted while I sewed curtains and cushions and delighted in having a kitchen of my own to cook and bake in. We chose dark blue and white cupboards, and bought good furniture piece by piece, as we could afford it. We didn't want the traditional brown settee but chose instead a dark red suite, with gray and white cushions to tone it down a bit. Our carpet was in the same shades of black, gray and red. We loved how pristine it looked, so bright and cheerful. I was ecstatic that at last we had our own little palace.

Janice settled in her new school, just a short walk down the road, and Christopher was a good baby. I wouldn't have swapped my life for anything. It was 1959 and I was living my dream. I had a good husband, two beautiful children, a lovely house, good neighbours and lots of friends. Life was perfect.

I remember vividly the day it all changed, the day our long nightmare began. It was a bright, sunny morning. Stan had gone to work, Janice had just left for school and Christopher, who was fifteen months old, was holding on to the windowsill watching her walk down the road, with other children. It was his favourite thing, looking through the large picture window at the world outside. He wasn't quite at the walking stage. He divided his efforts between crawling and launching himself up holding on to the armchair close to the window, then make the short step that would take him there. He was a happy, bonnie little boy who amused himself and hardly needed attention. He would play for hours on the kitchen floor with my pots and pans, and apart from the clattering of the lids being taken on and off, you would hardly know he was there.

The exception to that remark was his discovery of a package of loose tea and a pot of strawberry jam and decided to mix the two items together on my kitchen floor and of course all over himself! What a mess that was to clean up, but my fault really for having them in arms reach at that particular time.

I glanced across at him still engrossed with the street, and noticed he was holding his right foot off the floor. I'd not seen him do that before and I watched him for a little while and each time he put the foot down, he would immediately lift it up again. I looked at his knee and saw it was red and swollen; he flinched when I touched it, but didn't cry. The left one looked a little puffy also. Strange I thought, I hadn't noticed it when he was bathed the night before.

I decided I had better have the doctor take a look at him. In England at that time, it wasn't necessary to make an appointment to see the doctor, you simply went round to his office, which was called a surgery, took a seat and saw the doctor when it was your turn. It was much like the walk-in clinics which have sprung up here, the difference being that you do have the same doctor on a regular basis. Ours was a very nice Jewish doctor called Dr Gore. He was a family man and had young children of his own. My two were not at all afraid of him.

Dr Gore held surgery twice a day, two hours in the morning and two in the early evening. He made house-calls during the afternoon for anyone too sick to attend the surgery. However, if you were in the hospital, as a patient, you never saw your family doctor. You would be looked after by a resident house doctor who would visit you each day, and once a week a consultant would come to see you, bringing with him a group of interns, along with a matron who did the rounds with them, and was always very respectful of the main doctor. A consultant had the title of 'Mr' instead of doctor. Interns and nursing staff alike were very much in awe and respectful of this important icon. They wouldn't dare speak unless he did so first.

The Ward Sister, who wore a navy blue uniform with starched white cuffs, and bonnet, topped with a bibbed apron, also white and starched, would follow the Consultant, holding the patient's medical records which she would hand to him when requested. It was a strange hierarchy and I believe it hasn't changed to this day. Doctors are still on a pedestal, regarded as next to God by a great deal of the population in the United Kingdom, including members of my own family.

That morning we sat and waited our turn to see Dr Gore. He examined Christopher's knees, after which he said he wanted me to take him to the hospital that afternoon. He would give me a letter for the doctor there. He confessed he didn't know what the problem was.

It was an awful shock to receive that news. I rushed home with Chris, gave him a bit of lunch and dashed a cup of instant coffee down as I scribbled a note for Stan, since I had no way of reaching him at work to explain. I ran next door to Bridgette and hurriedly told her what had happened, asking her to take Janice in until I got back home. Then I put Chris in the small stroller we called a Tansad and set off to catch the bus which would take us a short walk from Whiston Hospital, the familiar place I had spent a great deal of time in during my teenage years, as well as giving birth to my daughter Janice.

The journey took nearly an hour. I handed the letter to the receptionist, who took some particulars from me and told me to sit down and wait to be called. It was a large drab room with lots of long brown leather-backed benches in rows, which contained many other people waiting for one thing or another. We sat there for an hour before a nurse in green uniform appeared at the desk calling our name.

I was starting to feel anxious and as always when this happens, my stomach began churning and I tasted the bitter coffee in my mouth which I had drunk so quickly. My stomach was rumbling. I was hungry, but I couldn't have eaten a thing at that point. My son had fallen asleep on my knee and was blissfully unaware of the worry he was causing. I was wishing I knew what Dr Gore had written in the letter. He had not been his usual jovial self and I knew he was concerned. Why else had he sent us off so quickly to the hospital?

Our turn came. I carried Chris, who was still half asleep, and followed the nurse to an examination room where a tall, brown haired man about my own age, wearing a white coat and a stethoscope dangling around his neck, identified him as the doctor we had been waiting to see. He had Dr Gore's letter on a clipboard in his hand and had obviously read it. He pressed Christopher's knees, making him whimper, and asked me a few questions about his general health. He seemed interested when I told him Chris had recently had his first polio vaccination and made a note of it, though he didn't make any comment to me at that time.

Next stop was for X-Rays, something Christopher had never had before. Another long wait for our turn. A nurse came and took him off my knee and of course he immediately started crying and holding his hands out for me, but she disappeared into the X-Ray Room and closed the door. I could hear him crying, and then loud screaming.

Suddenly the door opened and the nurse re-appeared and explained I would have to hold him down while they took the pictures. The whole thing was an ordeal. As soon as Chris saw the X-Ray machine being lowered toward him he was completely terrified. I had never heard him scream like that before. It took two nurses and myself to hold him down while they took several X-Rays. I wasn't offered protective clothing. We both got the radiation on that day and on many, many more occasions in the future, always without protection.

We were waiting once more for the doctor. Christopher had been inconsolable and had finally fallen asleep in my arms, completely exhausted. I sat there watching the fingers on the wall clock slowly ticking by, showing me it was 4.30 pm. It was mesmerizing listening to the steady tick-tock, which sounded like the voice of doom as I waited for the verdict. I wanted to run with my son out of the hospital, but I sat there, glued to the bench. The waiting was hard. It left my brain free to think of a dozen scenarios and panic would wash over me, making my stomach jump.

The nurse in the green uniform appeared again and beckoned me to follow her. Another small office with a desk and two chairs.

The same doctor we had seen earlier. X-Rays on the back wall in a frame. I guessed they were my son's. I felt sick with anticipation. I heard the words I was dreading. They were going to admit Chris that day for further tests. They didn't know what was causing the inflammation in the knees; it could be one of several things.

I tried to be calm as I asked the doctor how long Chris would be in the hospital. He didn't know. I told myself that surely it would be just for a day or so and once they had done the tests - something I didn't want to think about - he would be back home again.

We were taken up to the third floor, to the Children's Ward. As we approached I could hear children crying. It was the usual long room with beds either side, something like twenty-four of them and three cots. One of them was empty. It was for Christopher.

The nursing sister-in-charge took Chris from me. He began sobbing. She told me briskly he would be all right. It would be best if I left now. I could visit him each night at six o'clock for thirty minutes and for one hour on a Sunday afternoon. I would see Chris for thirty minutes out of twenty-four hours - explain that to a fifteen-month-old child!

I could hear him screaming as I went down the stairs and out of the hospital.   It was dark as I waited for the bus to take me home and I went upstairs on the green double-decker and sat on the back seat. I was trying to hide from the rest of the passengers. I cried silently throughout the journey. My mind wouldn't function with rational thought. I could still hear the terrified screams of my son ringing in my ears.

The days, weeks and months to follow were full of anxiety. The doctors couldn't diagnose our son's illness. They had tested for tuberculosis several times with negative results and in spite of that, continued to inject him daily with an antibiotic called Streptomycin. His poor little bottom was like a pin cushion and I dare not let myself think of the fear and pain he was going through.

I visited every night, leaving Janice with my wonderful next-door neighbour Bridgette, with Stan's dinner in the oven for when he got home from work. He was just as upset and worried about Chris as I was, though he didn't have to endure the sound of his screaming every night when I had to leave him.

Each time I went to the hospital I would find Chris tied into the cot, even though he had wooden splints bandaged to both legs, eyes swollen, his voice hoarse from crying. He looked lost and bewildered at my desertion and clamoured for me to pick him up, but I wasn't allowed to take him out of the cot, I could only lean over and stroke him with my hands and repeat over and over "Mama's here". It was unbearable torture. The allotted half-hour visit would fly, and the pitiful crying would begin as I turned to go. It was a cruel and terrible punishment for a tiny child to endure.

I recall standing in the hallway outside the locked doors, waiting for them to be opened to admit the visitors for their thirty-minute stay. They were never a second early. Every minute was precious. The pungent odour of disinfectant would greet me, along with the sound of children crying. All too soon the bell would be rung for all visitors to leave immediately, no lingering was allowed. Visitors were just a nuisance, something to be tolerated. Once inside that children's ward, your child no longer belonged to you. The Ward Sister made that very clear to me when I gave Chris a small drink of orange juice because he seemed thirsty, and probably was. She saw me do it and flew into a rage, told me she would stop my visits if I ever again gave him anything to eat or drink. "He's not your child while he is my patient" she said. I remember those words. They are burned into my memory forever. She was a monster and I hated her, but I was scared she would take it out on Chris if I said anything. I was so typically English in those days, completely in awe of authority.

It is still difficult for me to think about it even fifty-odd years later, still so utterly painful to relive the feelings of loss and complete desperation and week after terrible week of not knowing what was going to happen to our son. I believed in my heart at that time that I would never see him grow up. I honestly thought we would lose him. I cried each night on the bus going home from the hospital, before facing my husband and my small daughter, who in her own way thought that she too had been deserted. The consequences of her childish thoughts were to last for many, many years. It was a never-ending battle to win back her love. She obviously thought she was second best and resented the time spent with my ailing son, being too young herself to really understand the reason for my absence.

Five agonizing months went by. Stan and I made appointments to talk with the Consultant. It was always the same news, no definite diagnosis. The knees were still swollen and inflamed. Chris was confined to his cot, tied in to stop him from trying to stand. He was potty-trained before he went into hospital, but now he was back in nappies (diapers). He looked pale and sickly. His lively spirit had vanished, and he looked lost and forlorn. I'm sure he felt we had deserted him as well.

Finally, at the end of six months, we were told they were going to operate and remove the lining from both knees. The doctors still had no idea what was wrong, and this was the only thing suggested which might help. Chris would then be in a body cast from waist to feet for another long period of up to six months. TB had finally been ruled out.

The surgery was done and Chris lay in his cot encased in plaster. A few weeks later the Consultant sent for us. I felt sick with anticipation, hoping he was going to give us good news, and at long last he did. He asked whether I could manage to take care of my son, if they sent him home, since there wasn't anything more they could do for him there. Still no diagnosis either.

What a question to ask a mother who had been to hell and back over the past six months! I would do anything to have my son home again. We eagerly agreed and brought Chris home by ambulance the next day. We had put a single bed by the window so he could watch the children playing outside. The whole family had a lot of recovering to do, but for the first time in six months I felt joy. I could hold my son in my arms, plaster cast and all. What a priceless gift that was for me.

One of the many legacies from the long hospital stay reared its ugly head that very first day home. Stan had decorated Christopher's small bedroom with wallpaper, while he was away. Animals on a pale blue background, cows, pigs, horses, hens etc. We thought he would love it and it would be something for him to look at from his bed at night, something which might help erase the past months.

After lunch I carried him upstairs to show him his new bedroom. He was heavy because of the plaster cast which covered him from waist to feet. I weighed 90 lbs and it was quite a challenge. We reached the bedroom and I was talking softly to him about the cows and the horses on his lovely new wallpaper. He started to struggle as soon as we walked through the door, crying, "Please don't put me in the little room." He was again completely terrified and I didn't understand why, but it was clear that his small bedroom scared him stiff. Needless to say he didn't sleep in that room for a long time. He slept in the living room on the small bed by the window and I slept on the chesterfield close by.

Determined to get to the root of his fear, I went back to the hospital ward one Sunday afternoon and talked to a few of the children I had got to know over the past months. They were all long-term patients. I asked a few questions of ten-year-old Michael, in the next bed to Chris, with whom we had become friendly on the many visits. He told me that each time Christopher dropped or threw one of his toys on the floor, he was shut in a very small room by himself as punishment. Another boy told me the same story. It had happened a lot. Now I knew why his own small bedroom had brought terror to his face; he thought he was being punished all over again.

We had years of problems ahead of us. Chris was petrified of loud noises, machinery and anyone in a white coat. Even the barber, who wore a white jacket, would have to remove it before I took Chris inside. Machinery and noise reminded him of the X-Rays which had traumatized him on that first visit. He had numerous X-Rays during that long stay in hospital and I was always called upon to hold him down, without protection.

I recall going into Lime Street Railway Station for some reason I cannot remember now. I was holding on to Christopher's hand when suddenly a train shunted nearby and he pulled his hand away and began running wildly down the platform, screaming in terror, probably because of the noise and association to it. I reached him and held him in my arms until he quietened down. Another lesson learned to add to the many. It was all part of the nightmare.

We never did receive a definite diagnosis from the doctors at Whiston Hospital, just a lot of maybes, septic arthritis being one of them. We hoped it was all in the past.

That hope lasted until Christopher was ten years old, then the same problem began again. Eventually the doctors in Vancouver, Canada, diagnosed his illness as juvenile rheumatoid arthritis. He was in hospital again for a long time, where they treated him with drugs and physiotherapy. From time to time he still has health problems but has managed to enjoy a fairly normal life. He has worked from the age of eighteen, married and has a son after many years of trying. The gift he thought he would never have.

I still feel anger when I think of the archaic rules and regulations which existed – and perhaps still exist – in some English hospitals. There was absolutely no regard or concern for the mental health of the family or the patient going through this kind of ordeal. The separation of small children from their parents and the harsh treatment inflicted terrible punishment. It is something I would never want to go through ever again. I would never tolerate it either, because I too have changed. Life eventually returned to normal except for the remnants of Christopher's long illness.

My being away from home each evening visiting Chris, although it had been necessary and I thought had been accepted by Janice, though she was still only six years old, started to have repercussions. It took me a while to catch on and at first made me cross until I understood what was happening. I would get both children ready to go somewhere and at the last minute, or even when we were on our way, Janice would say she needed the toilet. Of course everything was held up until that was accomplished. After a while I realised it was a cry for attention, as she was jealous of the time I had spent with Christopher and was now wanting her share.

Life eventually returned to normal. I was happy and busy again, sewing for my neighbours, usually frilly dresses for birthday parties or curtains, for which I just charged very nominal amounts in payment for my labor. We were friendly with Bridget and Bernard who lived next door to our left. He worked for the railway and Bridget was home most of the time before she took a part-time job with a photographer who visited homes, mainly to take pictures of their children, as we had done also.

Our little cluster of houses and the neighbours who occupied them were quite a mixed bunch and occasionally we would have a party night when we all got together to get to know each other better. I was happy and settled and thought we would be there for a very long time, just the way things were, watching the family grow and thrive. My sister and mum used to visit almost every day and we would walk to Huyton Village some distance away, pick up a few needed items, have a cup of tea, before we separated and said goodbye. It was a simple way of life but one I was completely happy with, no desire at that time to change it whatsoever.

Change though was just around the corner, something which was to alter our lives forever. It wasn't remotely foreseeable, had never ever been a topic for discussion between Stan and myself or any other members of the family, and if anyone had said I would be moving away from my present home, I would have scoffed at the very idea. In view of what did happen, I would now remark 'never say never'!

CHAPTER SIXTEEN

VOYAGE TO CANADA

I heard the warning blast from the funnel of the ship, followed by a voice announcing that all visitors must leave. We said our last tearful goodbyes, trying to hold back the tide of emotions we felt, the smiles painted stiffly on each face as we hugged and held each other, before they left. We stood at the rail, watching the figures on the dock below, getting smaller and smaller, standing in the cold November wind, still waving. In the background the familiar and much loved landmarks I had known all of my life, gradually fading out of sight.

With my two young children, Christopher, who was five, and nine-year-old Janice, I was on board the *Empress of Canada,* sailing up the River Mersey out of Liverpool to a country called Canada, about which I knew very little, other than that it was far away, a land of ice and snow - I'd seen a movie called *Rose Marie*, set in the Canadian Rockies, starring Nelson Eddie and Jeanette McDonald.

I remembered too that Canadian soldiers were liked and respected, as I was growing up in World War II. That was the extent of my knowledge of Canada at the time. I hadn't wanted to go. I prayed every night that something – anything - would stop me, but the days and weeks passed. The house and furniture were gone, and God wasn't listening to my prayers.

It seemed to have happened so suddenly. In the space of a few months our lives had been turned upside down. It all began when my brother Roy, who had roamed around the States and up to Canada, deciding to settle in Vancouver on the west coast, with his wife and baby daughter, came home to England for a visit early in 1963. He painted a glowing picture of life in his new surroundings. The streets were paved with gold, if you were willing to work hard. That wasn't a problem; the men in our family were all industrious and had reasonable jobs. All had strived to provide homes and raise children. Like most working class people in those days, I was completely content with my lot and so, I thought, was my husband. He had spent time in Canada long before I met him in 1950 and he never talked about it and certainly never expressed a desire to return. Then at forty years old, he had become enthused as we all listened to my brother telling us how good his life was there.

"Even the garbage man drives a car" he said. That was the yardstick, since 'bin men' or 'dustmen' as they are called in England, were at the bottom of the working-class pile, so for them to have a car to drive - something we couldn't afford - really impressed the men in the family.

Plans were made for Stan and my sister's husband John to go first, with the promise of temporary jobs in the window factory where my brother worked. He offered his home in North Surrey as a place to live until they sorted accommodation out for themselves. They accepted the help gladly. Mum and Dad, who were close to retirement, would follow along with my youngest brother Ray, his wife and baby son, sometime in the near future. Eventually, we would again be the close family we'd always been.

Everyone was swept up in the excitement, except me. There wasn't much discussion. I set aside my own reluctance to leave the country I loved so much, but I didn't verbalise it. I didn't think it would really happen. I thought it would fizzle out when Roy finished his trip home and returned to Canada.

That didn't happen. The following weeks were a whirl of activity. Visits to the Immigration Office in Liverpool; smallpox vaccinations; passports; forms to complete. We didn't have any problems being accepted. My brother was sponsoring us and we both had skills to offer. I had been a stenographer before marriage and babies. Apparently that was a plus. Little did I know how soon I would be brushing up those skills and using them again for many more years out of sheer necessity.

Early in July, Stan and John left for Canada, getting on a plane with only their clothes and toiletries in one small case. They were very excited, and promised to send for us as quickly as possible. Soon the letters started arriving, almost every day, containing mixed news, nothing negative, but a few red flags that all was not quite well. I knew Stan didn't care for his new job - punching holes in window frames on an assembly line was hardly a challenge to him - but at least he was working and on the day shift. This meant he could ride to and from work with my brother until he could afford wheels of some sort.

John hadn't fared so well, he was given the night shift. The factory was located on Annacis Island, not an easy place to reach from Newton, Surrey. I can now appreciate how difficult that must have been for him to travel back and forward at night, in a strange place, with little or no public transport available. His options were to walk or hitch a ride. Quite an impossible situation for anyone, but to a new immigrant, without a clue how he was going to get to the new job, it must have been very challenging.

Meantime, my sister and I proceeded with the daunting task of selling the contents of our homes - the furniture - and packing household goods into tea-chests which would accompany us on the voyage to Canada. They were the remnants of our lives in England, and for me it was very difficult to accept after waiting seven long years for my home and loving every brick of that small house. Each piece of furniture which had been carefully chosen piece by piece, as we could afford it, intending it to last our lifetime. Now it was all for sale. Buyers came like vultures to snatch up my beautiful walnut dining room suite, the dark crimson chesterfield and chairs and all the bedroom furniture. Buyers even returned to ask for the linoleum on the floors! Everything that couldn't be squeezed into a tea-chest had to go, according to my husband. Even our dog Kim, who was just a puppy, had to be given away because of the quarantine laws.

Six weeks later Brenda received a telegram from her husband telling her to hold off. She had already sold much of her furniture. We had notified the Council of our imminent departure sometime in the near future, which meant we would no longer need to rent our property. She arrived at my house, which was ten minutes' walk away from hers, distraught and bewildered by the turn of events. Miraculously, she managed to cancel the Rent Notice for her house, but had to replace all the furniture, which had sold quickly. A terrible expense, to say nothing of the trauma this news had caused us both.

In a nutshell, John was returning to England. Stan was staying. So much for plans. John's return took away my last vestige of desire to leave England. I was devastated, but didn't know what to do. In my heart I knew I would have to go and in spite of having two bouts of quinsy - abscesses in the throat - putting me into Walton hospital for two weeks, deathly ill, I found myself boarding the ship on a dismal November day, sick with misery. I loved my husband, we'd had almost twelve years together, many of them difficult at times, but I loved my family too. How was I going to live without seeing them almost every day? Why hadn't I had the courage to tell Stan I didn't want this new life that had been planned and was now in shreds?

All those thoughts crossed my mind as we stood at the rail of the ship, waving until our loved ones were tiny specks. The damp salty air blended with the tears rolling down my face, my heart so heavy and full of dread for the future.

Eventually, when there was nothing left to see, we went to our cabin. It was right at the front and deep down in the bowels of the ship and of course it was very small. Three bunk beds, a wash basin and toilet. Not even a port-hole. I felt so numb, I didn't really care. I suppose dinner was served, I don't recall anything about it, but I must have fed the children. I remember putting them to bed, tucking them in and telling them their usual favourite bedtime story - Goldilocks and the Three Bears – desperately not wanting them to know how I was feeling. They were too young to understand my anguish.

I wasn't ready to sleep and went up a few decks to the large lounge and found a seat against the wall and watched passengers playing Bingo. My mind still in another place and another time, trying to seek solace in the fact that I would soon be seeing my husband. We missed each other, his letters full of love, and a promise that we would return home if I didn't like it in Canada, making it impossible for me to tell him how I felt.

As I sat there that evening I could feel quite a lot of movement. The ship rolled a bit. It was getting rough, but I wasn't too concerned. I remembered the crossings I'd made to the Isle of Man as a child, in foul weather. They had been accepted as normal and I wasn't afraid.

At nine-thirty I made my way down to our cabin. The closer I got the worse the motion became. I opened the door and stepped inside. I heard the children crying "Help me Mummy, I'm sick, I'm sick". The stench of vomit in the small cabin was overwhelming and before I could reach the bunks to comfort them, the ship gave another mighty lurch, throwing me against the wall close to the wash basin, and I vomited up the contents of my stomach in one explosive gush. I hung on to the wash-basin for a long time, unable to do anything, feeling as though I was being spun around and around by my feet. I couldn't move, not even to reach the children across the small space. Hours later, the ship still lurching and rolling, I crawled on my hands and knees to my bunk still in my clothes and lay there, hoping to die, retching up bile. There was nothing else left to come up. The children had finally fallen asleep exhausted.

Morning finally arrived, though I had no idea of the time. I felt too ill to care. A tap on the door made me open my eyes. The Steward poked his head in, surveyed the scene and left quickly, promising to return with the doctor and someone to help clean us up. He said it had been a very rough night, and most of the passengers had been sick. We were in the worst possible spot for rough seas in the bowels of the ship, and at the forward end, feeling every lurching lunge as it rose and fell in the heavy seas. I hardly needed him to tell me that!

The doctor came and gave us injections which stopped the retching and helped us catch up on much needed sleep. Of course eventually we thankfully sailed into calmer waters. I felt sorry for whoever had to clean our cabin - it reeked of the night's events.

After that first horrible night, Janice would not sleep or even stay in the cabin, except to wash and dress. At bedtime I would take her up on deck, wrap her in blankets and leave her on one of the long wooden seats. I had asked my next door neighbour, who was one of the crew, to check on her through the night. It was fortunate he was on that particular ship because my daughter was traumatised by the events of the previous night.

The rough seas finally abated and almost a week later we sailed up the St. Lawrence River and docked in Montreal around 3 pm. All immigrants were told to wait for their baggage to arrive on the dock, where Customs Offices would check them and inspect their documents. I had to find my six plywood tea chests and one very large trunk among the mountain of boxes, cases and assorted bags of every kind, heaped on the dock. In the failing winter light and with the bitterly cold east wind blowing, it was a daunting task, but since there was no help in sight I began the search for my belongings, while Janice kept an eye on her little brother. It took me a while to locate them and when I did eventually have them all, I had to push them one at a time into a line for inspection. These boxes and the trunk were all I had to show for twelve years of married life. It was difficult to think about that standing beneath the gray clouds on that freezing cold dock.

As we waited huddling together for warmth, I contemplated the hotel room which I'd booked and paid for, prior to leaving England. Hopefully soon we would be having something hot to eat then off to bed as soon as possible in order to be up bright and early to board the Canadian Pacific Railway train, leaving at 11 am, which would take us from Montreal and deposit us in Coquitlam Station on the West Coast of British Columbia, our destination in the new country of Canada. My brother Roy, his wife June and my husband Stan would be waiting there to pick us up four days later to take us to our new home.

Finally the Customs Officer in his navy blue uniform and peaked cap trimmed with gold braid stopped at our pile of luggage, ticked each item off his list, then turned to me and tersely informed me in his fractured English that we were to go immediately to the adjacent Railway Station and have something to eat, since we were being put on a train leaving that same night at 7 pm. It was almost five o'clock when he issued those very unexpected orders. I tried to protest, explaining that we had a hotel reservation for that night, but it fell on deaf ears. Even the tears which sprang to my eyes, threatening to fall, had no effect whatsoever on this person, and I knew it was useless to go on trying. I barely spoke his French language and the same could be said about his understanding of my English.

He repeated that the baggage was now being loaded onto that train and we were to be on it also. He turned to move on to the next batch of cases, with one last warning, glancing at his fob watch which he pulled out of his vest pocket, and indicated there was no time to waste. I had no choice but to comply.

We trooped over to the nearby station and found a small café still open, and sat down at the nearest vacant gray-topped table. An unsmiling waitress in a black dress and small white frilly apron eventually came over and deposited a menu written in French in front of me and stood waiting for my order. My eyes raced through the sparse selection as I tried to decipher the items. By some miracle I recognized bacon and eggs. I couldn't fathom any other item. That would have to do, I decided. I didn't consult the children or give them a chance to argue with my choice. I did ask the waitress for toast and milk for all three of us, miming with my hands as I spoke.

The bored waitress took our order without comment, other than asking how we would like our eggs. At that time I wasn't acquainted with the variety of ways to cook eggs, other than boiled or scrambled, and I replied 'just fried'. The order came fairly quickly. She had probably understood every word but wasn't going to speak anything but French to this forlorn, travel-weary group. It was obvious even then that immigrants, especially English ones, were not welcome in this part of Canada.

The toast arrived and was accompanied by several miniature pots of peanut butter (something we had never eaten before) and jam and marmalade. They were a nice addition to our rather sparse meal and we ate everything in sight. Even my daughter, who was a very picky eater, demolished every bit, then asked for ice-cream. I didn't have the courage or the energy to engage in another conversation with the waitress. The children didn't whine or protest. I think they could read the look of desperation and misery on my face and decided not to pursue 'dessert' on that occasion. They knew when not to push their luck!

We left the station café' and joined the large group of weary passengers, mainly women and children, waiting to board the long train leaving to cross this land for Vancouver, British Columbia. At that time I couldn't imagine being on a train for four days but I knew that was how long it would take to cross this vast country to reach the West Coast. As for the hotel booking, I never did receive the money owing from the lost night at the Queen's Hotel in Montreal. No time to pursue it before we were herded, like cattle, on to the train. It was just one more thing which had gone wrong on this unwanted journey.

The crew were already on board, dressed in gray uniforms and peaked hats which they eventually removed. All were dark skinned and smiling warmly as they showed us our seats, which later would be made into bunks for us to sleep each night. Janice and Chris would have a lower bunk, while mine was overhead, accessed by a small ladder. We were offered milk or cocoa before making preparations to sleep in our new quarters.

A quick visit to the miniscule bathroom then with the help of the stewards, we retired to our bunks. The train pulled out of the station right on time. Lying close to the ceiling, cocooned in that small space, complete with heavy dark green curtains, now closed for privacy, was a strange sensation as the train journeyed on through the pitch darkness of that first night. The clickety-clack and the motion of the train actually put me to sleep quickly, though I woke many times, wondering for a few moments where I was, before realisation brought me back to the present. I finally woke up properly when the train stopped, just as dawn was breaking, and there was a clatter of metal and the sound of voices outside. We stayed about fifteen minutes before the train began to move again, slowly at first, then gathering speed.

Much later in the journey, I learned we had all been put on the 'Milk Run Train' which made many stops along the route to drop off supplies for Native Indian villages. We were not travelling on the normal train, originally booked. Of course, it became abundantly clear to us (the immigrants) why we had been rushed from ship to train that same night. Our journey now would take an extra day because of the change of plans. All accomplished without any consultation whatsoever, in spite of protests for an explanation why this was occurring. It certainly was not an auspicious start to life in this country of Canada.

The daytime hours though were fairly pleasant, spent in the Day Coach, with other mothers and their small children. I became friendly with a lady called Joyce who was a couple of years younger than I. She also had a daughter and son, around the same ages as Janice and Christopher. It was nice chatting to her though we didn't exchange a great deal of personal information since we had no idea of what lay ahead, especially where we would be living.

The only information I had received from my husband was the return address on the outside of his airmail envelopes – North Surrey, Vancouver, BC. No postal codes in those days. I knew also he had signed a six-month rental agreement on a bungalow (rancher) which would be home to us for the near future. I hadn't a clue where North Surrey was located but I assumed it would be a suburb of Vancouver, a city with department stores, near the sea and of course with transportation. That myth was soon to be dispelled!

During conversation with Joyce I learned that her spouse would be waiting in Calgary for her and I asked why they had chosen that particular city, thinking she was probably going to relatives, like most of the passengers we'd spoken to. She laughed when she told me they had each stuck a pin in the Canadian map, with eyes closed, and both had come up with the same province of Alberta, Calgary being the capital, and that was how it had become their destination. They had no relatives or friends in Canada. Over the years, I have occasionally thought about Joyce, wondering whether they settled in Calgary and established themselves happily and successfully. It seemed a strange way to find a new life with the point of a pin, blindfolded!

I now know more about the climate in that part of Canada, that often there is snow falling in June and winter can return for good as early as October. Needless to say their growing season is a brief one. There is compensation in those days when it is bitterly cold but very bright beneath the biggest blue sky you ever could imagine.

Early evenings on that long train ride were also made pleasant. Sometimes there would be music playing and 'Happy Hour' was observed. Another new event in our immigrant lives and very welcome too for those who enjoyed a pre-dinner drink. It had not been a part of my life before that time, apart from a gin and tonic now and then on special occasions. I was not a wine drinker in those days, and not at all familiar with it. That too has changed over the years!

Meals were taken in the dining car, which included starched white tablecloths on each of the tables and a menu to choose from. Many of the items were new to our English palates and shunned by some of us, especially my daughter who was difficult to please, much like my husband. It was fortunate he wasn't making this trip or he'd have starved to death, or at the very least been very hungry most of the way!

The first two days passed quickly. The crew were kind, always helpful and smiling. Each night they were around to help us climb into our bunks, making sure the dark curtains were closed. I was amazed how quiet the carriage was during the long night hours. The most difficult part was sharing the two small bathrooms. I showered or washed my children quickly before doing the same for myself. It was quite a job in such a tiny space and I sighed with relief when that particular part of our day was over and done with. Living out of a suitcase is never fun, even less on a very long train journey.

On the third morning we were no longer in Ontario. During the night we had travelled into the Province of Manitoba. Right after breakfast an announcement was made that we would be stopping in Winnipeg at 1.30 pm for three hours, during which time all passengers had to leave the train. This was to enable the scheduled crew change, and all that entailed, to take place.

Lunch was served early that day, amid a buzz of excitement at the happy prospect of getting off the train for a while to have some much needed exercise and a change of scenery. The journey so far had been pleasant but train travel is very confining, most of it spent sitting except for the short trips to other coaches. The three-hour break was a huge bonus we weren't expecting.

Directions were given for us to walk from Winnipeg Railway Station to the centre of the city. Apparently when we reached the crossroads of Portage and Main we had found it. The city was not a large one and there was a small shopping mall nearby, we were told. 'Dress warmly' was the last directive given. I was satisfied that I and the children were suitably dressed with knitted toques, gloves and scarves on top of winter coats. Little did we know at this point that standing on the corner of Portage and Main Streets waiting to cross the road, would feel like a visit to the North Pole!

It was very windy that day, an icy bitterly cold blast which cut through our clothes, making us feel almost naked. It was difficult for us to stay on our feet as we hurried as quickly as possible to what we hoped would be the warmth of the shopping centre. We spent the entire 'free time' waiting very anxiously to return to the comfort of the Canadian Pacific Railway coach we had earlier been so delighted and eager to leave!

At 4.30 pm darkness had already fallen. Most of the passengers, including us, were waiting for the moment to get back on the train. When we did so we were greeted warmly by the new crew, who were all Caucasian and just as kind and courteous as the previous staff. Once everyone was settled, we were on our way once more. That brief visit to Winnipeg is the only one I have ever made. I know now that winter in that particular province is very cold and I've no desire to visit it again, though I'm sure it must have many attributes which I'll never discover.

The early morning stops continued, dropping supplies off to the Native Indian population who must live in villages adjacent to the railway line. The tall milk canisters and large cardboard boxes, crates of other food items, were placed on the platform to be picked up by the waiting recipients. I couldn't help but think about the kind of existence they lived, so isolated and dependent on railway deliveries for their food and other supplies. It was all completely different from the life I had left behind in England and stayed on my mind with the fervent hope that I was going to live close to civilization where I could shop for groceries and the other amenities I was always used to having.

We were now heading across the flat snow-covered province of Saskatchewan and would eventually reach Alberta and the foothills of the Rocky Mountains. I had not been impressed with any of the landscape we had travelled through thus far, though in all fairness, much of it was during the long night hours. I did recall seeing lakes and trees throughout Ontario and small shopping centres, all of which seemed to boast a Loblaws Supermarket, a name which stayed in my memory, only because of the frequency with which it appeared during that first part of the journey.

We travelled for many miles that third and fourth day, eventually arriving in Calgary Station where Joyce and her two children, as well as a scattering of other passengers, alighted. This was the end of the journey for them and the beginning of their new lives. I pressed my face to the window, waving to them for a moment or two, before I saw a tall slim man in a navy-blue duffle coat grab hold of the two children, hugging and kissing them and Joyce. It was a heart-warming scene; the re-union of a happy family. My turn was yet to come and for the very first time since we'd left Liverpool, ten days ago, which seemed like ten years, I felt something stir inside me, a feeling of pleasure at the prospect of seeing my husband again after the long four months of separation, when he had left on a plane with just a suitcase for Canada. I had been to hell and back since that time and until now felt numb with misery, not wanting to leave my home or my family, especially my aging parents. We had always been a very close-knit family and the thought of not seeing them practically every day was almost too hard to think about. I'd had no choice under the circumstances. Wives in those days followed their husbands, with little to say about how they really felt. He was the provider in the family and in most cases, the dominant factor in the relationship. It was expected to be that way and I certainly never questioned it and didn't think it was anything but normal. Nevertheless, the misery that situation caused did certainly not make for a happy marriage. It was often just accepted and life went on as it always had before.

The foothills of the Rocky Mountains had appeared before our arrival in Calgary and I knew we would be travelling through them for the rest of the journey. I was looking forward to seeing them and of finally arriving at Coquitlam Station, which would be the end of our train trip. One more night to sleep in our bunks, which I had found unexpectedly comfortable. All three of us had slept well, which I put down to the motion of the train, like babies being rocked for hours on end, reminding me of doing the same for my daughter, who as a baby, had been a terribly difficult, sleepless child which lasted until she was two and a half years old. We'd spent countless hours rocking the pram in an effort to get her to close her eyes and sleep. The moment we stopped, she would wake up as lively as a cricket. She truly was a shocker!

Morning arrived as we journeyed on through the mountains. We were hoping and expecting to see animals – moose and bears – but we only saw a couple of moose, standing not far from the train, in fact not taking any notice of us at all, as they stood feeding on whatever they had found to eat, It was absolutely pouring with rain, gloomy and miserable with endless trees on both sides of the train. Occasionally we would slow down to get through very long tunnels and several hair-raising times the train crept slowly over very high trestle bridges, deep valleys of gaping space below. I found it quite nerve-wracking at times. I had learned from conversation with one of the crew members that we travelled over other many other more scary sections of the line during the night.

I thought many times of the countless men it must have taken to build this daunting part of the railway, battling the elements as well as driving through solid rocks to make tunnels and lay tracks. I know there must have been many lives lost in the building of that particular railway across Canada, many of them immigrants, lots of them from China. How hard it must have been for them. They are all heroes in my mind.

Finally, around mid-afternoon, one of the stewards came to tell me we were getting close to Coquitlam. We gathered our belongings, put coats and scarves back on in readiness and waited for the train to come to a stop. Apparently we were the only passengers to alight at this station. Our luggage did not disembark with us, apparently that would be later at the Port of Vancouver where we would have to pick them up when the Immigration Authority released them.

I looked around in surprise. We were still surrounded by trees and mountains, when I had been expecting to see tall buildings, streets and signs of it being the City of Vancouver. There wasn't a thing in sight, only more trees.

Then I saw my husband, accompanied by brother Roy and his wife June, coming towards us. Stan was almost in tears as he hugged us all at the same time. Janice and Christopher were of course delighted to see their father again. Hugs were exchanged with brother Roy and June.

I was now feeling curious about our new surroundings and eager to get into the car out of the rain for the drive to North Surrey. It was a long journey, more than an hour, mostly through roads with small dwellings, certainly nothing impressive. We crossed a bridge over the Fraser River, then onwards through more greenery, mainly trees, occasionally a few small stores. Apparently we were now in Surrey. It was all very uninspiring and unappealing to this weary traveller, as we drove on down a fairly wide road, which I learned later was the main artery through Surrey, called King George Highway, later changed to King George Boulevard. Our long journey ended as we turned off the Highway, along another paved road for a short distance then another right turn on to a short gravel road with a sign which told us it was 73a Avenue. We had arrived.

There was a small collection of ranchers and ours was next to last before reaching the scraggly bush ahead and also to the left of us. It was made up of birch trees, now bereft of foliage and stretching out of sight. This was going to be our home for the next twelve months. Apparently Stan had signed a lease to rent the property for that length of time. It was a complete shock to me and I knew even then it wasn't Vancouver City. I hadn't seen a single sign to Vancouver on that long journey to North Surrey.

I have never forgotten that voyage to Canada or the sickness that followed, of a very different kind. Homesickness, hard to describe if you haven't experienced the pain of longing for familiar things you've left behind. I once read something written by a wise person, that immigrants never truly settle. There is always a small part of you which misses something from each world, the country you left behind and the country you adopted. I heartily agree with that statement.

The first weeks I spent in Surrey were the most isolated I have ever experienced. I detested everything about this new life. Transportation was almost non-existent, as were human beings. I had been right about Vancouver, it was about fifty miles from where I was living. It should never have been included in the address on letters my husband had written to me. Each day I walked my children through the lonely bush, which didn't even have a proper path to follow, to school and pick them up at 3 pm to bring them home again.

That November it rained incessantly, and day after day the sky was leaden with low gray clouds. That was when I realised if didn't do something about the terrible loneliness, I would probably lose my sanity. For the first time in my life I began making bread from scratch, which I enjoyed doing, while half listening to the television which I turned on each morning just to have voices to break the silence. I hated the programs, which were usually soap operas, mostly American, something I had never watched before, generously littered with commercials. Most of the time I hadn't a clue what was going on. It was, however, better than the terrible silence, which increased my depression as the days wore on.

One particular day a couple of weeks after we arrived, the television was on as usual. I wasn't taking any notice of it until I heard the screaming of sirens. I glanced at the screen and thought it was just part of another soap opera plot, then I realised it wasn't that at all. I was looking at an open car with President Kennedy and his wife, on the back seat. She was cradling his head and there was shouting and crying and a voice broke in to announce 'the President's been shot'. I will never forget that day, November 22nd 1963, though it is now many years ago. I remember that Mrs Kennedy was wearing a pink outfit with her familiar pill-box hat perched on her head, holding her husband in her arms as he lay dying. It was awful to watch that scene and know it was actually true, and not another soap opera. An unforgettable event which would change the world. Taking the life of a man in his prime, all in the instant of a moment or two. That scene was seared into my brain forever, always easy to recall in complete detail, happening right before my eyes.

Of course, President Kennedy was only the first of several other assassinations in America; it wasn't too long after that his brother Robert was also shot and killed. However, that first experience was a terrible shock to me at that particular time, in my already very vulnerable state of mind.

The weeks passed and my solitary confinement in that small rancher was unbearable. Baking bread every few days did pass the time, but it couldn't solve my problems. I couldn't talk to my husband about it since I suspected he wasn't that happy with his job of punching holes in window frames. We did have an exchange of words every few weeks, when I would ask him whether he thought there might be a chance of him finding another kind of work, one perhaps he would enjoy. This conversation usually ended up with him banging out of the house in a terrible mood and me lying on the bed crying hopelessly. I had no idea where he went to on those occasions. I suspect he just sat outside smoking. It was a terrible situation for us both.

One night he came home from work and told me there would be two visitors from Prudential Insurance Company to interview him to see if he was suitable to sell insurance in North Surrey. He didn't have any other details at that time. We didn't have long to wait; they arrived the next evening when dinner was over. I stayed in the living room with them since there was no other place to go except the bedroom. I made them tea as they talked with Stan, asking him a lot of questions about his past experience and his education. He also had to complete a general knowledge paper. All this took about an hour and a half. At the end of the interview they told my husband he was very suitable for the work as a door-to-door insurance salesman and I could see Stan was looking very pleased.

Then the subject of salary came up, which apparently was just commission paid on each policy he sold. They left shortly afterwards and said they would phone in a couple of days to let us think the position over. I didn't need a couple of days to tell Stan we could starve to death if he took this job, or any other job which didn't pay even a small flat-rate salary to exist on. We had no savings at all to carry us through the first months and I knew in my heart my husband was not the pushy type and would never make a successful salesman, especially when it was something as nebulous as life insurance. For once in my life, I stood firm and told him to forget the whole idea, it would be a complete disaster.

Stan listened to me for once and I think he realised that I was right. It was insane to try and exist on commission only, for many reasons, especially in the area we were living. That was the end of it and we never mentioned it again. I did feel sorry for him because I knew he was wasted in his present job, but at least he was bringing home a pay packet, enough to keep us fed and warm and keep a roof over our heads.

The weeks went by. I was just as miserable as he was and wrote many letters to my father asking him for the fare home to England, but then I would picture them reading of my plight and getting upset and worried, so of course I never mailed them. I even got as far as the post box, which was outside a small corner store, about half a mile away, almost weekly, before turning back for home, letter still in my pocket.

A small car was now part of our possessions and although it was old and second-hand it was all we could possibly afford. I began to think about driving it, though in the past I'd never had any desire to do so. I asked Stan and he agreed to try and teach me. Little did I know what lay ahead, and what followed is described in the next section of this chapter. It makes me laugh as I read about my efforts but it wasn't funny at the time. It was out of absolute sheer desperation to have a change of scenery from the Friday night grocery shopping.

The first time I sat behind the wheel of a car was December,

1963 when I was thirty-five years old. Beside me in the car was my husband, who was going to be my teacher. That, I found, was my first mistake, one of many I would make in the weeks to come. Before this I had rarely been inside a car, let alone one which was almost the same age as I was! Growing up, I had walked, skated, cycled or used public transportation to reach my destination and on occasions, I rode pillion on a motor-cycle. I had never needed or wanted a car, which was just as well, since we couldn't afford one. Now, in my new life, stuck in the bush in the wilds of Surrey, a place I hated at first sight, I felt marooned and I was desperate to drive somewhere, anywhere, but where I was spending my days. There weren't any buses apart from one early in the morning to New Westminster, which would return home in the rush-hour around 5 pm and of no use to me with children to walk through the woods to and from school each day.

My isolation was something I couldn't imagine enduring through the twelve-month lease my husband had signed to rent the small rancher before we had joined him in Canada. The moment I saw it I named it 'the brown house' and brown had never been my favourite colour, except in a box of chocolates! The linoleum was brown, the carpet was a tweed mixture of browns and muddy white, and of course the awful furniture was brown. Soon I recognised it as being one of those inexpensive three-room groups from Wosks' Furniture Store in New Westminster, not really made of natural wood, more like hardboard or plywood. It was cheap and nasty rubbish and it looked it. It broke my heart when I thought about the beautiful furniture I had in our immaculate little house in England, with not a hint of brown anywhere, other than the beautiful walnut dining room suite and the bedroom furniture.

The ancient car I was now sitting in was a small black Austin with a hump-shaped sloping back, nicknamed the "Puddle-jumper" because of the numerous potholes in the gravel roads we travelled when we went shopping on Friday nights, and the car often appeared to leave the road entirely for a heart-stopping moment. That was my excitement for the week - going for groceries! Stan convinced Christopher that this magical relic could jump over puddles! The nickname stuck. Anyway, relic or not, it was the only means of transport to take Stan to Annacis Island where he worked, and the only car we could afford. He promised me that if I passed my Driver's License Examination he would try and get a ride with my brother and so leave the car for me. Another incentive for me to at least make an effort.

That first driving lesson started out OK. Stan carefully explained the different gears, how to shift, how to give signals, which for test purposes would have to be given with a hand stuck out of the window. Straight out meant you were turning left and bent at the elbow, hand upward, meant you were intending to turn right. Of course in Canada you drive on the right-hand side of the road. I tried to digest all this information. How could anyone do all those things at the same time, as well as steer the car, change the gears and keep it on one side of the narrow roads? I felt like a juggler with too many balls in the air at the same time!

Carefully, I started the car and gingerly drove at a snail's pace up the gravel lane to the long paved road and off we went, chugging and jerking along as I tried to keep it moving. My problems rose at every "Stop" sign when I stalled the car each and every time and I heard my normally mild-tempered spouse suck in his breath, becoming very frustrated at my continuous poor attempts to hold it on the clutch. Even worse, sometimes stalling this car meant it would not fire again at the turn of the key, but required my husband to get out and crank-start it by hand, something I'd only previously witnessed in old movies. Of course it was raining as usual!

All this didn't improve my performance. It only increased my anxiety, making it a dead certainty that I would stall out at the next 'Stop' sign. I arrived home after that first lesson feeling tense and exhausted. My neck felt as though it was in a vice, my jaw stiff from clenching my teeth, but I was determined that somehow I wouldn't let this monster of a car beat me.

Many times, through this whole experience of learning to drive, I felt like the comedy star Lucille Ball in 'I Love Lucy' which was a weekly television show with the lady in question always doing crazy things. I was much like her, completely out of control with the situation! There were several episodes which took place with me at the wheel which on reflection later, had me in fits of laughter at just how bizarre it would have looked to an outsider, certainly worthy of catching on camera, but at the time it was no laughing matter.

I recall one such time returning after a lesson with Stan. The stalling was still a problem to me - too many things to do and think about all at the same time and not enough limbs to accomplish everything together. Or was I so un-coordinated that I would never get it right? That seemed to be the case. This particular day I turned the corner of our road, thankful for once to set eyes on the small house. I relaxed as I made a right turn into the driveway, intending to come to a stop in the open carport attached to the rancher. I applied my foot to the brake but hit the gas by mistake. Suddenly we took off at quite a lick and careered through the back garden, my husband yelling at me "Dee, hit the brake"! Stupid man, that was what I'd been trying to do! The car hit the large plastic garbage can and sent it spinning through the yard, emptying its contents, before I ended up in the lane at the rear of the house, stalled again, but thankfully, this time!

I persevered and improved, or so I thought, until one Friday night after we'd finished grocery shopping, I said I'd like to drive home. The children were piled in the back, along with our $20 worth of groceries, which consisted of four large brown-paper sacks. You got a lot for your money in those days. The road was quite busy for Surrey, probably because it was pay day, and I was turning right on to the main artery which was King George Highway and suddenly spotted a big pot-hole in the road and instinctively swerved to avoid it. Apparently that was a very stupid thing to do. The air in the car was suddenly blue, tempers flared, heated words exchanged. I pulled to the side of the road, not caring about traffic behind me, got out and motioned Stan to change places. At that moment I made a vow never, ever to take lessons from anyone I knew, least of all my so-called better half. We drove home in total silence.

I have to admit until that evening, my husband had shown a lot of patience, but it appeared from the silent journey that he was finally losing it. I decided I was going to contact a driving school, hoping a few lessons with them would give me confidence. At least if I was paying for the desired instructions, they wouldn't dare yell at me, I thought.

I enrolled with a professional driver to take lessons. He was a chubby little man with red cheeks, probably caused by high blood pressure, perhaps because of women drivers like me, but he never showed any signs of frustration or fear even when he made me hold the car on the clutch at the top of an extremely steep hill in Cloverdale, without rolling back. That hill looked like Mount Everest to me! What a challenge that was, I hated being poised ready to slide out of control, until I'd accomplished it, but I did eventually. Strange though it seems, I never did stall his car at all!

It wasn't too long before he said I was ready to take my driving test. Miraculously and triumphantly I passed it first time, thanks to this darling, patient little man and I've been driving ever since. Passing my test didn't mean I now had a vehicle to go somewhere, because Stan still needed it to get to work. The plan for me to have the car occasionally never came to pass. However, it was the smart thing to do, because several years later I needed a car of my own, so it wasn't a wasted effort and it did give my flagging self-esteem a big lift, which I needed badly at that time.

CHAPTER SEVENTEEN

MADGE'S STORY

The first friend I made in Canada was a few months after I had been deposited into isolation on that small gravel road. My brother introduced Stan and me to Marjorie Powell, known as Madge. She too lived in North Surrey, about twenty-five minutes' walk away from our rancher, in a tiny house set back off the road on a large plot of land. It was the beginning of a long friendship, in spite of the thirty-year age gap between us.

It is difficult to tell Madge's story without including her husband Norman, for this story belongs to both of them. It is one of hardship, struggle, survival and courage. They were in their mid-sixties when we met. Madge was a tiny English lady, five feet or less, slightly plump, dressed in dark skirt, cream blouse, topped with a cardigan. She wore her gray hair in a short, straight bob, which did nothing to enhance her pale skin or her light blue eyes. It emphasized the sadness etched in her face. She seemed timid and quiet, there was a childlike quality about her, an impish look when she *did* smile, which made her face become almost girlish, but she didn't smile a lot.

Norman, by contrast, was a very handsome man, tall and lean, with a twinkle in his blue eyes and a complexion which spoke of an outdoor life. His hair and small, neat moustache had silvered. He always looked clean-cut in his long-sleeved shirt and fawn slacks, complete with tie. He smoked a pipe. He was every inch the English gentleman, in spite of the years spent in Canada which has a strong resemblance to America in many ways. They were both born at the turn of the twentieth century in Birmingham, England, of working class parents. Madge had one younger brother and they each had a few relatives living in the same area. They met and married and had a son who had died at three months old. Ten years later a second son arrived. They called him Brian. He was their pride and joy.

Madge ran the home and Norman worked as a bookkeeper in a manufacturing firm called Lucas which had branches across the UK, but when the Depression hit England in the 1930s Norman lost his job. Thousands were in the same boat at that time. They struggled to keep their rented home and provide for their son, then three years old, and when a letter arrived from Madge's elderly aunt in British Columbia offering them a job to work on her farm, a home and some land if they stayed for one year, it seemed like a golden opportunity. They had met on her only visit to England and had corresponded spasmodically since that time. She knew of their plight - the letter seemed heaven-sent, a chance to be taken.

They received assisted passage to Canada as immigrants, the cost to be paid back in instalments over a two-year period. Their relatives took their few pieces of furniture to store, in case life in Canada didn't work out, and they set sail on their long journey. When they finally arrived at their destination in North Surrey, they found to their dismay that the farm consisted of a small house on a couple of acres of trees and grassland, a few cows and a hen house with some chickens. It bore no resemblance to the kind of farm they had pictured it to be, like those in England.

From the start there was friction between Norman and the aunt. He was willing to do anything to earn their keep at that time, but he resented Madge being what he referred to as a household drudge, at the beck and call of the old lady, who constantly complained. She was impossible to please. She also hated having a three-year-old child around. It seemed they had made a terrible mistake.

The so-called farm was miles away from the closest town of New Westminster. North Surrey consisted mainly of homesteaders, a sparse population and very few amenities. The Powells had little money, no transportation, and a young son. World War II had started and returning to England was out of the question. They were stranded.

Several months went by, and eventually the friction between Norman and the aunt escalated into a blow-up. She told them to leave, knowing they had nowhere to go, but they packed their meagre belongings and left. The only shelter was the hen coop and that is where all three of them slept for the next few nights. On the other side of the road there was a neighbour with a large tract of land. On hearing of their plight, he offered to sell Norman three acres at $10 an acre, the debt to be paid back in small instalments, whenever it was possible to do so. Norman accepted and the deal was sealed with just a handshake. He helped Norman drag a small empty shack onto the property and this was to be their home for a long time. It had a dirt floor and the winters were much colder then than they are now, below zero and lots of snow.

They lived like gypsies. Norman gathered wood to make fires on which Madge cooked and boiled water for all their needs. His first task was to dig a well, by hand, and build a small outhouse and an area to house some hens. Often they went without food in order that Brian could have his fill – they would eat very slowly and wait for him to ask for more before finishing their own meal.

Once a week Norman would walk the eleven miles to the small village of Cloverdale and back following the railway lines, where he would peddle his eggs. He would also walk into New Westminster, at least the same distance, and for the same purpose, to buy food from the small market. The other essentials, such as shoes and items of clothing, were provided by the Salvation Army. Somehow they survived until eventually their luck changed and Norman found a job with a Seed company in New Westminster, where he worked until he retired. With his first pay packet he financed an old truck, with two seats in the small front cab. It provided them with much needed transportation.

Little by little, with no experience, he built the small, white frame house we frequently visited. It was almost hidden among the tall trees and grass. Every year he saved a little money and added to the house until it was finished. It took him ten years to do so. They had no electricity or indoor plumbing until 1955. The house was just 700 square feet in total, with a tiny front porch leading directly into the living room, through to the kitchen and the back steps down to the patch of vegetable garden. It had two small bedrooms and a bathroom. A cosy doll's house, sparsely furnished, an old brown leather chesterfield and a chair took up most of the space in the living room. The floors were covered with light brown linoleum with a few small scatter rugs here and there. The walls were painted cream. No frills, no pictures, just two lamps on side-tables with photos of son Brian. Madge had made sea-green curtains by hand for the small windows and cushions to match.

On Friday evenings, when we had done our weekly grocery shopping, we would visit them on our way home, always sitting around the silvery-gray formica topped table in the kitchen. We'd have tea, which was always served in English bone-china cups and saucers. I never once saw a mug in Madge's kitchen. Like me, she baked her own white bread and we would have a slice of it with our tea and finish up with a Peak-Freen biscuit.

Norman would sit in the corner near the wood-burning stove which heated the house, puffing away at his pipe, a contented look on his face. He was affectionate with us and our children and very soon we loved them too. We'd listen intently as Norman talked about their early days in Canada, the struggle to barely survive, and marvel at their courage. Madge would always have to reach in her pocket for her handkerchief, the memories never failing to bring tears. She had a perpetually sad look on her face and in her faded blue eyes. The rough years though had not changed her, she was polite and ladylike in everything she did. She gestured with her hands when she talked. They were her best feature - still smooth and white. She always wore shoes in the house. They had clunky heels, and she tip-toed around the kitchen on the highly polished linoleum, to avoid making it squeak. She always seemed slightly flustered when she was making the tea. To me, she looked so lovable, and so vulnerable, I wanted to hug her and make her smile.

Somehow the conversation would always turn to England. Madge still wanted badly to go home, just as I did. She was so very British in her ways, everything still done the English way. Tea had to be made by warming the pot first, milk in the cup before the tea was added, and so on. One of the many rituals of life before Canada.

Their daily menu never varied. Porridge for breakfast, a small mound of crisp lettuce, a slice of cheddar cheese and a piece of home-made bread for lunch. Suppers consisted of small portions of meat or chicken and home grown potatoes and vegetables. Theirs was a frugal existence, but one they had been moulded into with the events of their lives. They had been through so much that spending wisely became a way of life.

They did manage to make one trip to England to visit their remaining relatives before Norman became ill with lung cancer and died in 1972. It was probably caused by inhaling the dust in the seed factory he'd been so happy to be employed by. I don't think they wore masks or protective clothing in those days. Madge finally sold the property in 1974 and moved to Richmond to be closer to her son Brian and his family. She lived in an apartment, complete with new furniture, but it was never home to Madge. She was never truly happy. I too, was living and working in Richmond then and many times I would visit her to have my lunch, which predictably would always be the same - lettuce, a tomato, a piece of cheddar cheese and a slice of bread, followed by a Peak-Freen biscuit, the only brand she would buy, and a cup of Red Rose tea. The table would be set with a cloth and napkins and Madge would fluster around as though I was a visiting dignitary, instead of her very old friend.

Richmond wasn't her last stop. She followed her son Brian when he was transferred to Calgary, Alberta. He and his wife, Mary, built a small apartment for her in the basement of their home. Tragically Brian died in 1988 at the age of 51, of a sudden and massive heart attack at home. Madge stayed on with her daughter-in-law and two grandchildren, Mark and Lesley.

The death of her son was too much for her to take and she went downhill rapidly. I saw Madge only once after Brian's death. Mary put her on a plane in Calgary and we picked her up at Vancouver Airport. She stayed with us for a week and I realised during that time she had a dementia of some sort. She was confused and didn't seem to know us, though she was still the perfect lady - the polite guest - bewildered and sadder than ever. She died in a nursing home in 1991, in Calgary, after a long progressive illness.

There is no happy ending to this story, only fond memories of Madge and Norman and their wonderful, courageous spirit. I am still friends with daughter-in law Mary. She now lives in North Vancouver. She never married again and has a son and daughter and just recently she became a grandma for the first time to a lovely little boy named Tyler. Mary spends a lot of time with them, determined to enjoy being a Grandma.

CHAPTER EIGHTEEN

OUR MOVE TO NEW WESTMINSTER

I had been in Canada almost six months when Stan approached our landlord and made a request to cancel the twelve-month commitment to rent the rancher. I was still very unhappy, homesick as ever and desperately wanted to move to the nearest small town of New Westminster, known as the Royal City because of a visit by Queen Victoria in the distant past. This is where I hoped to find work, with the intention of saving enough money to return to England. While the subject was never discussed in depth, it was always there at the back of my mind. I knew I would never settle in Canada.

To my surprise, it was agreed to, and we packed up our few belongings after six months expired and went in search of an apartment in the town which boasted a main street containing shops and office buildings and a waterfront. There also appeared to be quite a lot of apartment buildings located on the nearby streets. The move would also make it easier for Stan to look for other work, since he still was not happy with the job in the window factory.

We tried to recapture some kind of happiness, but it wasn't easy. Most of the problem was again lack of discussion between us. I was willing to express my feelings now, but it always ended up in an argument and usually Stan leaving to avoid making it worse. I was hoping this much-wanted move and hopefully me finding work would help the situation. He knew what my intentions were for the future and agreed that we should return to England when that became possible.

The first accommodation we looked at was an apartment on Agnes Street, close to everything, where we saw a 'For Rent' sign outside a three-storey building which was not too large and looked quite presentable. We rang the bell which said 'Manager' and waited a few minutes for a response. Moments later the door was opened by a slim middle-aged man in his forties. He invited us inside to see it, telling us it was empty at the moment. It was on the second floor. After a quick look around we said it was suitable, since we had very little in the way of belongings and it was clean and bright with nice large windows.

We went with the manager to his office and made arrangements to move, choosing the earliest date possible. The landlord wanted us to sign a six-month lease but we declined after our experience in North Surrey. We actually told him we might be moving to Calgary some time in the future and didn't want to commit ourselves to a long lease. It was a lie of course.

He hesitated for a few minutes, then agreed to let us have the apartment on a month-to-month basis. We left feeling very happy and hopeful that this would be a better experience than living in the wilds of Surrey, especially for me.

My sister-in-law June, helped me move the small amount of furniture and belongings to the new address. I was so relieved to be leaving North Surrey behind and into what appeared to be a hint of normal civilization.

Our elation was very short-lived. We had a new nightmare to contend with in the form of our upstairs neighbours. From that very first night we listened to terrible thumping noises right over our heads, both during the day and evening and into the early morning hours, along with constant noise from the television. It was unbearable. It was obvious that whoever lived above us had a physical problem and wore heavy boots and used a cane to walk on the wooden floors. We bought ear-plugs, hoping to block some of the noise out so we could sleep, but nothing worked. We learned very soon why that apartment was vacant at a time when they were in demand. No wonder the manager had rushed us in and out of the empty apartment, back to his office!

We gave notice to the landlord that we were leaving at the end of the month. He didn't argue with us, or ask why, but we knew it was the reason he tried to tie us into a six-month lease. What a lucky escape!

I later spoke with a couple of other tenants about the problem and one lady did remark she wanted to warn us not to take that apartment when she saw us looking that particular weekend. Of course she didn't, and once more we were looking for yet another place to live. We were now more desperate than ever. During the next few weeks as our notice time ticked by, we looked at a few unsuitable apartments in the same area of this small town and finally had to settle on one in a four-plex building located right on the busy main thoroughfare of Royal Avenue. We guessed it wasn't going to be quiet in that location but hopefully the traffic would ease up once the rush-hour had passed. Of course we were almost beyond hope of finding a place by that time and decided this would have to do.

Once again, June came to our rescue and helped me move our furniture and belongings during the day to avoid the expense of a moving company and also to avoid Stan having to lose a day's pay from work. It was a gruelling process moving twice in that short space of time, but completely necessary. We could never have tolerated listening to the racket overhead for any longer than we had to.

The new apartment was satisfactory for our basic needs. It was fairly large and close to everything, including stores and offices, where I was hoping to find some kind of employment. My goal was to save enough money to pay for passage back to England for myself and the two children. Stan agreed he would stay behind and save enough to fly back as soon as possible. All this I knew would take time but now that we had at least begun the process, I felt at peace for the first time since I had set foot on Canadian soil.

Soon I found a part-time job, working for a lawyer located on the main street, three afternoons a week, from 1 pm until 4.30 pm typing divorce briefs which, after a while, was mind boggling; only the names were changed, since adultery was the usual, if not the only, grounds for divorce in 1964. Photographic evidence was provided by two men employed solely for that purpose. I realised very quickly that divorce was a sleazy business.

Once in a while the elderly secretary would make a cup of tea and offer me one. This was the only break I received during my working time, except for a trip to the toilet occasionally. The finished briefs would be checked, signed and put into pale blue folders and tied with thin white ribbon, ready to be taken to the courts.

I also managed to be taken on by the large Department Store on 6th Street, a few blocks up from Royal Avenue. It was Woodwards, an old established company with branches in Vancouver and New Westminster and probably other towns. Most of the staff were part-time workers and I was offered four hours on Thursday and Friday evenings, working in the Staples Department.

I spent those hours selling bathroom draperies, folding endless towels over and over again.

I now had two part-time jobs, both just a means to an end, providing much-needed income and hopefully, they would not be forever. I didn't get a break at the store unless I worked more than a four-hour shift. I didn't mind the arrangements, even though the work at both establishments was of the very boring kind. I was on a mission and nothing would deter me. I was saving every penny I could towards the time when I could purchase our tickets for the train journey back to Montreal and subsequently the ship back to Liverpool and home. I wasn't at all daunted at the thought of starting life for the third time and having to live again with my parents until we could save for another home.

One particular afternoon I stood looking out of the window of the apartment for a while, watching the busy Friday afternoon traffic, most of it heading over the nearby Pattulo Bridge into Surrey. I was waiting for my children to come home from school before leaving to work my four-hour shift at the store. Turning away from the window, I glanced at the clock and realised the children were late, but wasn't too concerned. Janice was a very sensible ten-year-old and took care making sure that six-year-old Christopher didn't dawdle too much. He was a bit of a dreamer at times and it was a very long walk to and from school, along the busy road. They had stop signs and traffic lights to negotiate which could make the journey slower. Still, anything was better than walking through the bush in Surrey, where we had lived previously. That had been a nightmare.

I set the table for their suppers and checked to see that all was ready for my husband to finish off the meal when he came home around four-thirty. It was now past three-thirty. I returned to the window to continue watching.

In just minutes Janice came in sight, walking quickly towards the house. No sign of Christopher with her. Anxiety bubbled up in my chest as I quickly went to the front door and ran the few steps to meet my daughter, trying to stay calm. I could see she'd been crying.

"What is the matter love? Where is Christopher" I asked all in one breath. Janice still close to tears, replied, "I waited ages for him Mum in the usual place but he didn't come, then I went to his classroom to see the teacher, in case he was being kept in. She said he had left with everyone else at the end of school, when the bell rang. I didn't know what to do."

Her words trailed off and tears ran down her cheeks. I ushered her into the house, telling her to stay inside until I returned, grabbing my jacket as I opened the front door and began running the seven blocks to the school at the far end of Royal Avenue, my eyes constantly scanning the busy road for signs of my son. Panic saturated my body with adrenaline as I ran and found myself chanting 'Christopher' over and over, like a mantra, until the school came in sight. Breathless and with the beginnings of a migraine headache in the back of my head, I raced up and down halls, looking in empty classrooms. The school was deserted, everyone, including the staff having left for the weekend.

Eventually I found the Janitor in the gymnasium and told him what had happened. He checked the school grounds and the washrooms and came back shaking his head. There was nowhere else to look. Where could Christopher be?

I ran back again along Royal Avenue, praying that a miracle had happened, that he would be home when I arrived there. It was hard to understand why this was happening. Christopher had always come straight home from school. It was something I had drummed into both of my children, over and over. That, and never to speak to strangers, or get into a car. Neither child had ever disobeyed the rules of the house.

There was still no sign of him at home. Thankfully Stan had arrived minutes before me. He already knew, but he listened to my frantic story, phoned the police, then got back in the car and took off to cruise around the streets of New Westminster. A middle-aged detective, accompanied by a younger one, arrived at the door about fifteen minutes later. They sat at the kitchen table and tried to calm me, assuring me that my young son was probably having fun in someone's yard. "No, No", I insisted, "we have only just moved here from Surrey and Christopher has no friends. Besides, he knows his sister waits in a particular spot every school day, before walking along the very busy road home together." I was absolutely adamant he would never have gone anywhere by himself, he knew he had to come home first. I was convinced something terrible had happened to him.

They took a detailed description of Christopher - scars, birthmarks, height, weight, colouring, the clothes he was wearing - and then requested the most recent photograph of him. They left, promising to return in a while, after they had searched Queens Park and the local neighbourhood. Meantime, they urged me again not to worry. "He will turn up" they said cheerfully as I closed the door behind them. I didn't believe them.

My husband returned, his face a white mask of worry, having driven up and down every street to the waterfront and back. We shared the awful fear now that Christopher had been kidnapped, perhaps picked up by a car and by now could be miles away in this massive country. We both knew he didn't have any friends as the police suggested and they had no idea where to look for him now.

The waiting was unbearable. We sat in mute silence, each lost in our own fears and thoughts, feeling totally helpless. This was a parent's worst nightmare and we couldn't believe it was happening to us. I began pacing the room and then returned to the window. It was now six-thirty and soon it would be dark. He'd been missing for over three hours. My head throbbed unbearably, I felt ill and queasy and needed to lie down, but I couldn't tear myself away from the window as the light faded, along with my hopes of ever seeing my son again.

Suddenly a small figure appeared, sauntering along, lunch bucket in his hand, coming towards the house. It was Christopher! I screamed "He's home!" and we all rushed into the street. He looked quite unconcerned and hadn't a clue anything was wrong, until he noticed the tears of relief on our faces. I wanted to hug him and strangle him at the same time for the agony he had put us through.

The police had been right. Someone in his class asked him to go his house, not far from the school, to play, and he had gone. All the dire warnings to come straight home had gone right out of the window and he hadn't even given a thought to Janice waiting for him.

Stan took over, and sent me to bed to recover from my savage migraine, then fed a rather sheepish son his supper. Later, Stan sat down with Christopher and explained how much worry and trouble he had caused with his thoughtless actions, how he had made his mother ill and the police were still searching for him. They would probably be calling again any minute. He wanted his son to learn a lesson and hoped the police would scare the living daylights out of him. That he would never do it again.

The nightmare had only lasted three hours or so but it had seemed like a lifetime. A terrible ordeal we would remember for a very long time. Of course I missed my shift at the store, but after Stan phoned and spoke to the Department Head, explaining the ordeal we'd gone through that evening, they understood. I still had my part-time job for as long as I wanted it. At the time I hadn't even given it a thought.

CHAPTER NINETEEN

THE GREEN GREEN GRASS OF HOME

Everything eventually returned to normal after that terrible scare. I continued with my two part-time jobs and saved every penny until I finally had enough to pay for the journey home to England. I never changed my mind about the decision, even though it was a stressful situation. My health had suffered because of it and in spite of the joy I felt and the anticipation of finally being back where I belonged, it wasn't easy to leave my husband behind. However, he promised to join us as soon as it was possible to do so. It was just a question of saving enough to fly back and that shouldn't take too long.

I didn't ask for any money to keep us back in England because I intended to look for work as soon as possible. We would stay once again with my parents and Mum would help with the children. Stan would only have himself to feed, leaving him with all his salary. I was completely sure and very optimistic about the future and ecstatic at the thought of being back in the place I loved with all my heart.

We left New Westminster early in May 1965 on the train for Montreal, once again taking as many belongings as possible, which amounted to the same as our journey from England almost eighteen months previously. One large travelling trunk and six tea-chests filled with bedding, towels, clothes and most of the kitchen utensils, the remnants of our second home. Then onwards to the ship, the SS *Empress of Canada*, heading for Liverpool, England.

I was soon on that ship with my two children, returning home for good after my miserable experience in Canada. I had never told my parents how unhappy I had been during that time; the pleading letters for help had been written but never mailed. Miserable though I was to the depths of my soul, I couldn't bear to worry them. None of it mattered any more. I didn't care about belongings on that glorious morning in May as we steamed up the River Mersey, the familiar buildings coming into sight. My heart was bursting with happiness and my head was filled with the voice of Tom Jones singing 'The Green, Green Grass of Home', one of my favourite songs at that time. It was the most wonderful feeling, and at that moment I wouldn't have changed places with anyone in the whole wide world.

How true those words were for me and what a contrast of emotions to those I had felt leaving this exact spot eighteen months earlier on my outward journey, as Canada's most reluctant immigrant, watching the Liver Buildings disappear taking me further and further away from everything and everyone I loved.

As the boat slipped into the dockside I looked down and spotted two small people – my parents – standing waiting for us. I was overwhelmed with emotion. Quickly we made our way down the gangplank, then I was running towards them, having for a moment completely forgotten my children, in the absolute joy and excitement of being home. I was almost run down by a taxi driver who honked his horn very loudly and brought me back to my senses. I was back where I belonged and vowed silently I would never leave my beloved England again.

We lived with my parents and soon I was working in the School Board Offices as a Secretary, in Huyton Village not far from home, the children back in school and settling down well. Janice won a scholarship to a grammar school, which would eventually pave the way for her to attend university. The green grass of home was looking greener every minute.

Unfortunately my health was still fragile and many days I could not stomach solid food, existing on milk and mashed potatoes. My heart though was mending quickly, and each morning I woke and looked forward to the day. I liked the new job and the staff were very kind and sympathetic towards me and full of encouragement that everything was going to work out for our new life. I even managed to buy a little old Austin car from my sister's son-in-law, out of my earnings which took me to and from home, avoiding long waiting time for buses.

Stan wrote me loving letters telling me how much he missed us all and that he was coming soon. I was happy and looking forward to that time; even the struggle of getting a third home together didn't worry me at all. I planned to stay working and save the deposit for a house. I felt my new job was a good place to start and hopefully would be permanent. Canada would eventually be a distant memory.

The weeks went by and things went wrong again. Stan broke his ankle and was off work. We knew his return would be delayed until it healed. He was living in a small apartment on Agnes Street again, and at times I sensed he was depressed and missing the family, just as we missed him. His intention to return was the same and we looked forward to that time. I honestly didn't give it much thought, I was so utterly happy with my old life back in the place I totally wanted to be.

Seven months passed and there was no hint that all wasn't well, no clue of what was to come, until one Saturday morning in December, around 1.30 am when the phone rang in the downstairs hall. In those days my parents' phone was rarely used, certainly never without good cause, so that ringing phone, in the early hours of the morning made us all quickly tumble out of bed and run down the stairs to answer it.

My father reached it first, then handed it to me, his face like thunder at having been wakened from his sleep at such an ungodly hour. Mother stood behind him, looking frightened, wondering what was coming and certain it was bad news.

My heart was beating like a hammer in my chest and I tried to stay calm as I took the phone. It was my husband's voice on the other end and our conversation was brief and one-sided. I was too stunned to reply to the words which will be etched on my heart forever. He said "Dee, I'm not coming home, there is nothing there for me".

There was complete silence. He didn't offer any further explanation or words of any kind. I put the phone back on its cradle, giving my parents the news before going upstairs to lie on my bed in the dark for the rest of the night - my world upside down.

For two days I cried myself into a stupor, while listening constantly to Father's words of wisdom that if I wanted to keep my marriage intact and have a father for my children, I had to return to Canada. I couldn't bear the thought of that, but in the end I knew there was no alternative.

I think if my father had shown a different attitude, perhaps offered me and the children a permanent home until a time in the future when I could put my life in order, I would have refused to return, but that of course wasn't going to happen. He told me constantly my children needed a father, and it was my duty to be with him. I had no choice.

CHAPTER TWENTY

RETURN TO CANADA

A week after that phone call we were on a plane returning to Canada to start life there yet again. Father had taken charge completely. He had booked the flights and visited my School Board employers to explain what had occurred. He said he would make arrangements to ship our belongings once more back to Canada.

I knew I was very close to having a nervous breakdown, and I dreaded the future. I felt so ill on that long journey. I had not heard again from my husband, but he knew we were returning on a flight into Vancouver Airport. He was there waiting for us, all smiles, delighted to see us as we made our way to his car, the little black Puddle Jumper I had learned to drive in, which now seemed a very long time ago.

We were actually starting over again a third time. Needless to say I had no idea what to expect, but I knew it would be anything but easy. I don't think I was even capable of rational thought at that time, not even of asking why he had changed his mind and had broken his promise to me. I was numb with misery having to return to a country I had no desire to live in.

It was a very long, hard road back to any kind of happiness. I only stayed for the sake of the children; I no longer had any normal feelings of closeness for the man I married. He had no idea what he had put me through with his decision not to return home. I didn't hate him, I just felt totally devoid of emotions, a blank space filled my head and heart.

I knew I was in a deep depression during those early months. I managed somehow to get through each day, only because I knew I had to try for the sake of the children, to make another home for them. They too had been moved from place to place in Canada before returning to England. They never once asked why or complained. Like me, they didn't show any emotions and I didn't know whether they were happy or unhappy with their fractured lives.

The first three weeks back in Canada were spent in a very modest motel on busy Kingsway in Vancouver. Not exactly an auspicious address. We needed a place to live, schools for Janice and Christopher and somewhere where I could work as a stenographer. We again rented several apartments for a couple of months in various areas, close to New Westminster, none of them really suitable Moving had again become a way of life. It was fruitless to unpack really but we had to.

Finally, at my insistence, we settled on Richmond, a rural area but quite close to Vancouver. I told my husband I would never, ever live in North Surrey again. We rented a three bedroom rancher on Montego Street, off No. 5 Road, opposite to an Evangelical Church which we began to attend spasmodically, mainly because our daughter had become friendly with the Pastor's children who lived next door to the church.

Mitchell Elementary School was within walking distance for the children without depending on transportation. They were both enrolled and I began another search for a job. I had never wanted to be a stenographer, but it really came to my rescue at that time.

I had several good jobs over the years, starting with the Department of Transport at Vancouver Airport. At the interview I was told the position required the taking of Minutes from the meetings held frequently concerning the proposed Third Runway. The staff were mainly from Ottawa, mostly men, half a dozen of them. They journeyed back and forth each week, leaving Friday afternoon and returning on Monday morning. The man who interviewed me for the job was so desperate for someone with shorthand skills and able to take Minutes at the numerous discussions that he offered to hire me on the spot. I had to confess right away to him that I was not a Canadian citizen, a requirement of this particular position, but he said that wouldn't be a problem, he would take care of it. Short of having no hands, he wanted me for the job!

Eventually, I agreed to give this rather unwanted position a try. Taking minutes and working for a bunch of civil servants wasn't my choice but under the circumstances, I accepted and soon was receiving praise for my minutes, usually presented the day following a meeting. I didn't like the task or the men I worked for, and apart from a Chinese girl called Angie who had been employed to take the minutes in the first place, but was hopeless at it, we were the only female staff members.

I stuck it for a couple of months then resigned. My next job was an eighteen-month stint at Canadian Pacific Airlines, again close to the airport on Sea Island and difficult to get to. I had been one of many applicants and was given typing and shorthand tests, answered pages of general knowledge questions and finally told I was accepted.

I had no way of getting there by public transportation so first requirement was another old car, a small blue Austin Sunbeam, financed through Richmond Credit Union. I first worked in the typing pool. It was there I made my first new friend, June, also an immigrant, from London. We liked each other from the start and the friendship remains intact years later. Much water has gone under the bridge for both of us since that first meeting in 1967.

After a while with the airlines, I bid on another job, and was successful in getting it. I found my new work quite interesting. It was keeping records for the pilots and air crew who are required to undergo various medical and other tests on a regular basis.

Along the way we bought our first house, on No. 4 Road in Richmond. It was on almost an acre of woodland and scrubby brush, and it was unfinished upstairs and down, but at least it would be ours, although it was in a sorry state. There were thick spiders' webs around the windows in the basement, which looked as though they had been there for years, and I didn't look forward to the removal of them, but that would definitely be the first task.

The rest of the basement was just an empty space - nothing had been done to it. The main floor upstairs required a lot of work also, starting with a staircase, which had never been put in, but it was at least livable and reasonably clean.

The rented house on Montego Street had been sold, though there had been no indication that it was up for sale, and we were forced to buy before we were ready, borrowing the $500 required for the down payment, again from the Credit Union. However, it turned out to be a good decision. We lived in that house for 17 years, providing Janice and Christopher with a stable environment to grow up in.

My misery had now diminished but I still had terrible bouts of homesickness, longing to see anything familiar from home, especially my parents. My husband did an amazing amount of work and became a jack of all trades and made a great job of everything he did. First he built a staircase to enable us to access the basement without going down a flight of wooden steps from the balcony to the open carport. That was a difficult task and he made it just a little too narrow. Not noticeable at the time, but in later years when we bought new larger furniture, it had to be brought upstairs using the balcony entrance again. He installed new windows, turned a bedroom into a small dining room and even put a new roof on this large building, without any help and also without any previous experience. In England he had decorated and wallpapered but that had been the extent of his efforts.

We did have an experience I would never want to repeat. Even writing about it makes my flesh creep and brings back the memories of one warm August day in 1975. I was about to enter our house through the basement from the carport after work one Friday when I heard my husband shouting to me over the upstairs balcony, not to come in that way but to use the outside steps up to the living quarters. Of course, my curiosity was immediately aroused and I did open the downstairs door and walk through to the front hallway.

A horrifying sight met my eyes. The wall, which was normally a nice shade of pale green, was now a black, seething mass of ants of all sizes. There were tiny ones, large ones, some with wings – thousands of them. It was like something out of a science fiction horror movie. The hair on the back of my neck stood up with horror and fear, as I stood there and looked at this moving mass of insects.

By this time my husband had joined me and we looked at each other in disbelief, made worse by the realisation that it was Friday evening, the start of a weekend and probably the pest exterminators would not respond to our frantic phone calls. That was, in fact, the case, and we left messages all over the Lower Mainland, trying to get help. Meantime, Stan had dashed to the corner grocery store and picked up several canisters of Raid, and without any thought for our health or consequences, we emptied the insecticide into the black mass of ants. After that we shovelled up the now dead insects and cleaned up the hall, trying to convince ourselves we had got them all, but we were still paranoid.

We walked around and around the rest of the house, searching for more, and even though that night we didn't find a single ant anywhere in the house, we never stopped looking. Finally we went to bed in the early hours, completely exhausted. We had packed our son off to stay with a friend and Janice was not at home that weekend. I don't think either of us slept a wink that night, and as soon as it got light, I gathered up a bundle of clothes to be washed – one of my usual weekend chores – and gingerly headed down the stairs to the front hall and the rest of the basement. To my intense relief there was nothing to be seen in the hall, but as I turned the corner to the washing machine and dryer, at the far end of the basement, I saw a seething black mound of ants, about eight inches in diameter, on the step leading into the utility room and another one, even larger, huddled close to the water heater. I really felt close to losing my sanity as I screamed for my husband to come downstairs. I know we both cried, partially from the sleepless night and partly because this was a nightmare of a situation we didn't know how to cope with. I had always hated creepy crawlies of any kind outside, never mind in my home in enormous quantities.

More Raid was purchased and again we emptied the canisters into each moving mound. The chemical smell was awful, but we foolishly didn't care at that time, breathing it in without taking any precautions. The whole weekend was spent looking and looking for signs of the insects. We had to wait until Monday to receive a response to our urgent telephone calls and the first exterminator appeared at the house on Tuesday morning. We had kept a few of the insects in a glass jar for inspection. He gave us some very interesting information about ants. He identified our particular species as cornfield ants and said we were lucky they weren't carpenter ants, which are much more destructive. We tried to count our blessings at this bit of news but it was hard to feel lucky after the weekend we had just lived through.

The most surprising bit of information was that ants form their colonies and settle in to breed and live, but every August they choose a new queen and move to a new location. We had usually been away in August in previous years, when the children were on holiday from school, so this could have been happening then, without us knowing anything about it. He believed me when I told him that we had never seen a single ant inside the house, just a couple out on the paths in the garden where you would expect to see them, but not enough for us to do anything about it. He also assured us that they would not move upstairs and that was a comfort, though we still kept looking just in case. We were hard to convince!

He also found the source of the problem, which was something my husband, in his ignorance, was responsible for when fixing up the basement. He had channeled the moist heat from the clothes drier underneath the floors, to take advantage of the heat emanating from it, creating the perfect breeding ground for ants to multiply. I had no idea he had done that because I might have questioned it, even though I didn't know a lot about fixing up houses and basements at that point.

We had the exterminator do his work, not once but twice, just to make sure we were free of ants, and although we never did see any more, I don't think we ever stopped looking for them, especially when August came around. We never did feel quite the same about that particular house. It was a hard memory to erase, and even now, if I close my eyes, I can still picture that seething black army of ants and the nightmare of that long weekend. To this day I cannot look at ants, not even on television, without a feeling of absolute panic and revulsion.

For weeks after this episode, every time I came home from work I would come in the back way, searching the whole basement for signs of further invasion of the hated insects before going upstairs. To say I was obsessed about them would be perfectly true. I don't kill spiders, I get them into a jar and put them outside but if I see an ant I stamp on it before I can help myself!

In the job world I eventually left Canadian Pacific Airlines to be School Secretary at two elementary schools, Mitchell and Hamilton. My reason for doing so was the advantage of having the school holidays to spend with my children, which seemed like another good idea at the time. In my new life I had to make sure they were secure until I returned, and of course I wanted to be with them as much as possible. It was a difficult decision to make, because I loved the work I'd been doing and got on well with staff and management.

At both schools I was the only secretarial staff, which kept me very busy. I found several of the teachers at Mitchell to be very demanding, always wanting their work to be done first. One teacher was putting on a school concert and asked me to type one of Gilbert and Sullivan's operettas, *The Pirates of Penzance*. She wanted it 'yesterday'! Not only was it an awful lot of typing, it was difficult to do. Anyone who is familiar with this particular operetta would agree it has a lot of 'Yo Ho Hos' in it. I detested that kind of work.

I finally finished it, then had the daunting task of running many copies off using an old Gestetner, the only kind of copying machine available those days, requiring me to turn the handle hundreds of times before finishing this mammoth job. I finally completed it and the next day I woke up and couldn't move my head or my right arm and the pain was awful. I was off work for several weeks with terrible headaches and having physiotherapy. Even then I was not really fit, and in fact it has left me with a problem neck which has followed me through the rest of my life. All this convinced me that school secretarial work was not for me, and I resigned at the end of the school year without a single regret.

Finally to my last job in the Clerk's Department, again as a stenographer, at Richmond City Hall. I was fortunate enough to be chosen for that particular position over twelve other applicants, including those already working for the Municipality. All jobs had to be posted internally before advertising any position. That was a Union Rule. I was delighted when I received the good news. City Hall was only five minutes away from home, right in the heart of the main shopping area and close to Minoru Park nearby.

My first day there was early in January, 1969 and just as I was getting ready to go that morning, I received a phone call from my brother Raymond in North Wales. My stomach flipped with anxiety and I knew before he spoke something bad had happened. We didn't exchange telephone calls at that time unless there was something really wrong, because of the expense.

He gave me the awful news that Mum was in hospital after having a stroke and wasn't expected to recover. I didn't know what to do about the much needed, much wanted, new job. Every fibre in my body wanted to be on a plane going to England to see my mother. I went to work and tried to act as though everything was all right, but I made many trips to the washroom that day trying to stem the tears, pull myself together, all the time trying to make a decision about going back to England.

Mercifully that decision was made for me. One of the staff, a girl called Nelly, found me in the washroom and could see I'd been crying. Wanting to confide in someone, I told her about the news I'd received that morning. I asked her not to say anything to anyone, especially the boss, Mr Youngberg, but of course she did, though I didn't know it at that particular time.

I went back to my desk and tried to concentrate on what I had been given to do, though it was impossible for me to think straight. At four o'clock Mr Youngberg sent for me and I walked into his office with trembling knees, wondering what was coming. He was a big man in every way, intimidating in manner and in looks, but as I sat down in his large office, there was softness in his eyes as he looked at me and said "I understand you have had bad news from home today?"

Nodding my head I replied, trying hard to control the tears which threatened again. Then he asked me what I wanted to do. Without hesitation I blurted out "I want to go home". He looked hard at me for a few moments, without speaking, then said "I'll give you three weeks' leave. Either you are back at your desk then or your job will be gone. Do you understand?"

I again nodded my head, stuttered my thanks and in tears I left his office, packed up the desk, where I had spent just one day, and went home.

There was much to be done as quickly as possible. The next afternoon my brother Roy and I flew out of Vancouver, leaving three feet of snow behind, and landed in a blizzard at Toronto Airport, skidding off the runway and across the grass in hair-raising fashion before we finally came to a stop. It was the last plane allowed to land at Toronto that afternoon. That was quite an ordeal in itself, but there was worse news to follow. No planes would be leaving for the rest of the day. We, along with hundreds of other travellers, were stranded, waiting for onward flights, in the Departures Lounge. It was packed, with nowhere for us to sit.

Our next flight was to Manchester, with very little hope of getting there any time soon, though we had spoken with the staff to tell them of our plight and the urgency for us to fly as soon as possible. We stood around not knowing whether to try and find a hotel for the night, but we decided against it just in case the weather abated enough to start operations once more.

To our immense relief we were called to the desk at midnight. Swissair had decided to put a plane out going to Zurich and we managed to get on the flight, then another onward flight to Manchester Airport. By then we had been travelling twenty-seven hours, but we went straight to the hospital where my mother lay dying. She was unconscious, strapped into an armchair, her head hanging forward on to her chest. She looked terribly uncomfortable. To this day I can't fathom out why she wouldn't have been in a bed.

She passed away at 3.30 am without knowing we were there. In spite of that, I felt it had been the right thing to do and who knows perhaps she *did* know we were there. I like to think that could be true. I couldn't have sat at home waiting for news, as it would have created unbearable stress and I couldn't have forgiven myself if I hadn't made that one last visit to see my lovely Mum.

Roy and I went back to stay with my father until the funeral could be arranged. Of course I had the rest of my three weeks leave before returning to my new job with City Hall, but I was too preoccupied to even think about it.

I found my old home to be terribly cold, in spite of the fire burning brightly in the grate. In fact, the whole house felt like an ice-box. I'd never noticed it before, though I had lived in that house as a child, as a teenager and for seven years as a married woman. Now

I was back after listening to that phone call which all immigrants dread receiving, and Mum was dead at the age of sixty-six.

For the next three days she lay at peace in her coffin in the sitting room of her home, dressed in a new pink nightgown and matching bed jacket which I had hurriedly brought with me from Canada. I suppose I was still hoping for a miracle recovery, that I would see her sitting up in bed wearing it. The curtains (drapes) were closed in all of the rooms to keep evil spirits out. They would remain that way until the funeral was over, along with all the neighbours' curtains.

Mrs Henderson, who lived directly across the road, took charge of opening our curtains at the appropriate time and also providing refreshments for the mourners to have on their return. This was the custom in those days in our part of the world. In the meantime I took care of my father, who spent most of his day staring into the fire. He looked so lost and forlorn, not at all like the strong man who had dominated our lives, made all the decisions, in total control of the rest of the family. He seemed quite helpless and frail.

I knew there was much to be done in the three weeks ahead before my return to Canada, including what to do with my father. This was my first trip to England in winter since moving back to Canada, and I realised quickly that I had changed into a hothouse plant. I felt horribly cold and shivered my way through each miserable day. It was a huge challenge each morning to gather the courage to get out from under the mountain of blankets I had piled on the bed where I lay each night curled up in a tight ball with only my nose and forehead exposed to the freezing air. I was reluctant to take off the woollen bed-socks and flannel nightdress to use that icy bathroom, teeth chattering until I was finally dressed.

Sitting on the cold toilet seat first thing in the morning was like receiving an electric shock, the jolt reminding me I was still alive! The only time I thawed out slightly was when I sat with my feet in the fireplace, knees almost up the chimney, shins getting burned, while my back was still chilled. The constant shout of "shut the door!" could be heard daily from my brother Roy and me to avoid letting any more cool air into the living room. The irony was this modern house boasted four fireplaces, two upstairs and two downstairs, but only one was ever used – the room we lived in.

Roy was quite amusing at times. He would wear his heavy outdoor Canadian jacket in the house and my Dad would look up from his reverie and ask "Are you going out son?" Roy would reply, with a wry smile, "No Dad, I'm just bloody frozen". Somehow the words went over my father's head, because he didn't approve of anyone cursing. He didn't feel the cold as we did. It wasn't as if there was a howling gale or even rain. It was quite mild outside, much better than the three feet of snow we had left behind in Vancouver and the terrible blizzard in Toronto.

Weather is always a topic of conversation in England and many of the neighbours who dropped by to pay their last respects to Mother remarked how lucky we were to have the current weather. They weren't bundled up as we were, so it had to be something which had changed us. Looking back, I do recall how suffocated Stan and I felt when we moved to Canada, especially when we were in stores and apartments. Everyone seemed to have their homes so hot and stifling that we couldn't wait to leave. The usual comments as we got outside were "wasn't it hot in there?" We must have acclimatised to the Canadian way of life without knowing it, and each time over the years we returned to see family – and it was always during the summer months – we would feel cold in their homes. They all have central heating now, but only seem to use it for short periods in the morning and perhaps in the evening, just for a while, mainly because of the cost. My father did not have central heating in his house, nor did he have any windows which would open. He had them all sealed with wide tape and tightly shut. The three weeks spent with him were the coldest I can ever recall.

Just before it was time for me to fly back to Canada I talked with my father, asking what he wanted to do when he was ready to think about the future. The once close family was scattered around the globe like leaves in a wind. No family around, the nearest being Raymond who lived in North Wales, several hours away by car. My sister Brenda and her family had eventually emigrated to South Africa after her husband John returned from his short stay in Canada where my brother Roy and I were of course living. It was so difficult to settle anything at that particular time, but I did assure my father he would be welcome if he wished to come and live with us.

I knew I had to return to my desk at Municipal Hall at the end of the three weeks' leave granted to me. It was terribly hard for me to say goodbye to this frail, rather befuddled man, who didn't seem able to come to terms with Mum's death. It was much too soon to expect anything different. I felt as though I was deserting him, but had no choice except to reassure him I would stay in close touch.

Of course I was back at my desk at Municipal Hall on time and spent the next twenty-three years with the Municipality of Richmond. I had finally found my niche. I also made some good friends. One was a lovely lady known as Sunny, though her proper name was Sonia. We became inseparable and shared years of friendship and many events, both joyful and otherwise. I learned to laugh again and my life was very happy because of our close relationship. I owe her a great deal.

She showed me all the wonderful beauty spots in Vancouver and its suburbs and we spent time sunning ourselves on the many beaches, Spanish Banks being the favourite choice. It was an education I'll always be grateful for, since I had no idea such places existed until then. It is a vast and beautiful area of Canada, commonly referred to as 'Beautiful British Columbia'.

We shared a love for the same kind of music, particularly a recording with music by Anita Kerr and Rod Stewart reading poetry, called 'The Sea', which will always remind me of Sunny, who sadly has recently passed away.

The years went by, and along the way I became Election Supervisor. In 1981 the Provincial Government established their first Vital Statistics Office in City Hall. I was appointed Deputy District Registrar for Births, Deaths and Marriages, a job I loved very much and never got tired of doing. Civil marriages were performed in the Council Chambers at that time, much to the chagrin of the Mayor, and eventually Marriage Commissioners were appointed to perform Civil Ceremonies anywhere in the Province. Many ceremonies were performed in the office, shared with another Deputy District Registrar who had joined the Clerk's Department. Rod Drennan had turned many female heads, but eventually he got married a second time to Ruth, who came from Germany. They asked me to do the honours and I was delighted and privileged to do so. It was performed at a Vancouver Golf Club, and hopefully it was as wonderful a day for them as it was for me.

Rod and I were very busy in the days before the income tax cut-off date was close, when couples decided to marry in order to claim back the tax amount paid the whole of the previous year. We took turns going into the Council Chambers to those wanting to beat the deadline. They came one after the other, especially as the last day arrived and the clock ticked away the last chances to beat the tax man!

I really loved my time with the Municipality and Glynn Morris, the new Municipal Clerk who replaced Mr Youngberg when he retired, was the nicest man to work for. I never heard him raise his voice in anger the whole time I knew him. He was an absolute gentleman. Originally from Wales, he spent a lot of years living in Rhodesia – as it was then called – and married a minister's daughter. He retired and moved up-country, where he lived with his wife in the peaceful surroundings of the Shuswap Lakes. Sadly, he became ill with kidney cancer and died not long after. I was always touched by the fact that during his last week of life, he phoned to thank me for all I had done, as one of his valued employees.

At the end of 1989 I decided to retire from Richmond Municipality and freelance as a Marriage Commissioner, which I did until the end of 1993 when my husband's worsening health problems forced me to make the decision to resign. A very sad day for me. I had by then married over a thousand couples. To me, each wedding ceremony was special, as were the bride and groom. I would meet with them ahead of time in an office I had in my home at Ocean Park, and go over what they really wanted included in their particular ceremony. Poetry, special music, something important they wished to say - whatever they wished to do, I would help them accomplish it.

There were some special venues where I loved to perform the marriage ceremony. One in particular was my favourite in South Surrey, an imposing manor house built specially for the purpose of arranging every aspect of the perfect wedding. It had a large seating capacity, beautiful chandeliers hanging from a very high ceiling and a balcony around the entire auditorium with changing rooms for the bridal groups. Most stunning of all was the long wide staircase for them to slowly walk down, while the organ played the appropriate music.

I did so many memorable weddings at the Manor and many

times was invited to stay for the wedding reception, which was catered for in the same beautiful manor house. I always declined so I could return home because of kitchen duties for my husband's dinner!

I performed weddings at White Rock, sometimes along the pier itself and a few on the actual beach. One busy Saturday afternoon I went to marry a young couple. The tiny bridesmaid was their daughter! When I arrived the groom was in the pub opposite where the wedding was to take place, having a drink before getting married! I was puzzled when the bride started looking around the rather stony beach and finally she laughed and told me she was looking for the actual spot where their baby had been conceived three years earlier. It takes all sorts to make a world!

I have many happy memories from those days, meeting lovely people, doing something I never dreamed of being able to do, and occasionally on a dreary wet day I pull out my large box of 'Thank You' cards from many of my satisfied brides and grooms and read them again and usually finish up with tears in my eyes at the lovely compliments they included with their thanks. They take up a lot of space, but I can't bring myself to throw them away.

I never in my wildest dreams thought I would have the opportunity to be part of so many people's lives, creating happiness which in turn, gave me enormous pleasure. Sometimes you couldn't write the script for your life and mine has been one of those lives, full of unexpected surprises – not all of them happy of course, but I suppose it all balances out in the end.

CHAPTER TWENTY-ONE

LUCKY THE POODLE

A few months after Mum died my father decided to sell his house and join Stan and me, which was such a relief. I had been receiving letters from his neighbours telling me in no uncertain terms that he was not looking after himself. One neighbour actually wrote in very plain terms that if I didn't do something about the situation very soon, he would be joining my mother.

Stan built a one bedroom, one living room flat for him in the basement of our home and we looked forward to having him with us. We arranged for my brother Raymond to escort Dad and booked a flight for both of them. The date had to be changed several times because apparently Father would change his mind about living in Canada, but eventually it happened. He and my brother arrived, along with his seven-year-old white poodle, Lucky.

We could never have imagined the chaos one small dog was about to heap on us. This poodle had a psychotic personality and right from the start we had terrible problems with him. He constantly guarded my father and wouldn't let any of us near him, sitting tightly hunched against Dad's leg. He would snarl and snap

206

at us and viciously bare his teeth. He was like a jealous, besotted lover, guarding his possession. It was frightening at times. I had to warn the children not to go near Granddad since I was so afraid Lucky would attack and bite them, as he surely would have done.

At night the dog slept on Dad's bed. Stan and I lived with the worry that should Father become ill and need help, no one would be able to get near him. We just hoped and prayed that situation wouldn't arise while the dog was alive! It was a constant concern. Anything dropped on the floor – and I do mean anything – would be pounced upon instantly by this perverted poodle and immediately swallowed whole. Stan and I sometimes entertained thoughts of "accidentally" dropping something which would remove him from our lives, but it was only thoughts; we could never have actually done it. The dog survived in spite of many items it ingested: aspirins, blood pressure medication, any food dropped on the floor and on one occasion, a man's full-size white cotton handkerchief, which reappeared intact several days later through the normal channels. Amazing! We hardly needed a vacuum cleaner in our house! Dogs must have amazing digestive powers, for I felt sure Lucky would have a blockage with the handkerchief episode, but I was wrong.

After months of putting up with all this, we eventually told Father he had to keep the dog in his bedroom at all times. We were honestly worried about our children and frankly, we were scared of the dog ourselves. Father never settled in Canada. It was an ordeal at times and I would return from work knowing his red swollen eyes meant he had been crying most of the day and was terribly unhappy. I understood how he felt since I'd been in that situation without any resolution to my problem. I learned later he had scrawled a letter to my sister in South Africa with one line on it, 'HELP ME GET AWAY FROM THIS PRISON'!

Strange words, because my father was a free agent and had chosen to live with us. We made him and his dog as welcome as possible. I did understand how he felt, so homesick it destroys any kind of logical feelings. I know at times I felt I could swim back to England, given the freedom to do so!

Anyway, after two years of chopping and changing his mind, he returned to England and after a few wrong choices he found the Garden Hotel in Southport, a very nice seaside resort on the North West Coast, some twenty-eight miles north of Liverpool. At that time the owner catered to senior citizens. He was very happy there, being waited on hand and foot, no meals to worry about. Because of the six month quarantine laws there, applicable to animals, Lucky, the mad dog had to remain with us. It was strange, when on my visits back to see my father, he never mentioned Lucky. Neither did I!

I spent most of my holidays from work visiting my father, staying with him in the Garden Hotel where he was living. Each morning we would walk along Lord Street, the main shopping area with the vast array of stores displaying beautiful merchandise in every window. I always returned to Canada with a case full of beautiful clothes. In those days I wore dresses or suits. Women were not allowed to wear pants at Municipal Hall. We would have coffee at the same café in one of the expensive stores, along with several other lady friends he introduced to me. He was always dressed immaculately in suit, shirt and tie, topped with a brown Melton overcoat, complete with trilby, which he doffed many times to passing ladies He had completely changed and seemed content in his new surroundings.

I chuckle now when I think of the letters I received when he was in his early eighties, telling me he was thinking of asking a certain lady to marry him and seeking my permission to do so!

Apparently he asked every member of the family the same question. In any case he never did marry again, though from all accounts he had a few near misses!

He spent his last couple of years in a care home in Colwyn Bay not far away from my brother Raymond, where he appeared to be happy and well cared for. My husband and I visited him several times but sadly during the last two years of his life he didn't seem to recognise me at all, perhaps because my hair was now several shades of gray instead of the dark brown I had until my mid-fifties. It had happened quite suddenly - just one silvery streak appeared in the front of my hair, which everyone at the office thought I'd had put there professionally by the hairdresser and urged me not to remove it, because it looked so good! Before I could make up my mind, the whole front of my head joined the silvery streak and I let it stay there.

On one occasion Dad turned to Stan and said "Is she going home with you?" He obviously didn't realise I was his daughter! It hurt a bit but I knew then he had a dementia of sorts which had only started after he'd had prostate surgery when he was eighty-five years old. I had always thought that was a big mistake at his age. He was never the same after that stay in the hospital.

In spite of the changes to his sharp mind, he still enjoyed his food. I remember one visit to North Wales. We picked him up and took him out to lunch in the lovely small town of Bettws-y-Coed, where he asked for fish and chips. It came with the usual generous helping of peas, which seems the only vegetable that a lot of restaurants serve with everything on the menu. He tucked into the fish and chips then we watched with amusement, as he speared the peas one at a time with the fork, concentrating on his task without looking up, until every single one had gone. It took forever! He never liked to see food left on a plate which I think was a throwback to his poverty-stricken childhood.

One of the strangest things I thought about many times over the years was that I never heard Father speak about my mother after she died in 1969, and that was long before he lost some of his memory. It seemed as though she had never existed and it used to puzzle me. He sold his home and its contents and eventually made a completely new, seemingly happy life and never looked back, even though they had been married more than fifty years. As for the Lucky, we dared to hope he would turn into a normal animal but quickly he transferred his protective affections to me, creating the same situation. Stan could no longer sit close to me or touch me without Lucky snarling and baring his teeth. He followed me everywhere and mercifully each night I managed to coax him into Dad's old bedroom on to the bed where he slept overnight, with the door tightly shut. It's just as well, because without a doubt there would have been a divorce in our house. Stan threatened many times to have Lucky put to sleep, knowing he'd never do it. Killing anything – except ants - was against both our natures and my father had loved his dog and I loved my father. Lucky remained with us.

Several months later his luck finally ran out. He was with me in the front garden. I was weeding, Lucky sitting on the path close to me. Suddenly he got up and walked straight on to the road and was hit by a car. It happened so fast and it was very unusual for him to leave my side, especially for the busy road. We rushed him to the vet just five minutes' drive away, but he was too badly hurt and was put to sleep. He had led us a dance for two and a half years and for a while turned us off wanting another dog, but we surrendered to the charms of a Bassett Hound we adopted called Morgan, who showered us with affection and adoration as well as an abundance of her white and brown coat which she shed on our green carpet each and every hour of the day.

We had to be interviewed to adopt Morgan, going first to the owners' house, then having them visit our home to see if it was suitable for her. Apparently it was! I soon wondered whether they had given her away because of the amount of fur she shed, though the reason given was that their pet guinea pig was 'mean' to Morgan. We swallowed the story hook, line and sinker. I guess there's one born every minute! Morgan was advertised as "free to the right home" but she cost us thousands of dollars in vet bills. We discovered she had glaucoma and went blind at eight years old. Later on she was in such pain that we couldn't bear to see her suffering and had her put to sleep. I held her in my arms and it was quick and peaceful for her, but a terrible loss to us.

Morgan was the last of an assortment of dogs and definitely our favourite. She was such a character and so very easy to love. Our lives began to be much better, though we still had a lot of fixing up to do with the unfinished house. Knowing that we no longer had the uncertainty of rented property being sold over our heads without a lot of notice helped us feel much more settled.

Occasionally on Sunday morning we would attend the Evangelical Church opposite which we had lived when we first rented in Richmond. It wasn't the denomination we had attended in England for many years, but Janice seemed to enjoy going to the new one and certainly the congregation had seemed very friendly and welcoming.

1966 was our fourth Christmas in Canada and living in the first house we were now buying. Even though it was a bit of a mess at that time, we could see the potential, even the acre of birch trees and brush offered hope for the future. We had managed to pay off the down-payment we had borrowed and our twenty-five year mortgage was manageable, now that I had full permission – even his blessing - from my husband to work! We had made five moves in a short time and it was so hard on the two children, to say nothing of their parents, who before moving to Canada were barely on nodding terms with removal vans.

Christmas morning dawned bright and sunny with that crispness in the air which always lifts the spirits, and we were looking forward to spending our Christmas Day in our new house alone. First though, I thought it would be a great idea to attend the morning church service. The children for once didn't protest and neither did my husband, which made a welcome change. He was never enthusiastic about participating in religious matters, especially this new and different denomination, which bore no resemblance to the Anglican Church we were familiar with.

The Pastor was a tall charismatic man with striking good looks, dark hair, piercing brown velvet eyes and a warm inviting smile. I liked Pastor Taetz a lot, even when he was preaching hellfire and brimstone in order to save my soul! His wife by contrast, was small and plain, a no-nonsense type of woman, but she was polite and very pleasant on the few brief occasions we had met. They had four children, aged three to thirteen, and lived next door to the church in a large house. The service over, we drove back home, feeling pleased that the rest of the day was ours to enjoy.

I remember I was in the kitchen when the phone rang just after we had arrived back. It was the Pastor's wife. She had never called me before and I hadn't a clue why she would be calling now. Seconds later I knew. We were invited over for Christmas Dinner that evening. She took me completely by surprise!

My brain went into a tailspin. I stammered both refusal and thanks in the same breath and tried to explain that my husband was a very fussy eater, that he didn't like turkey, something which I stupidly assumed would be served. "Oh, don't worry", she replied "We are not having turkey, we are having goose. We don't want you spending your Christmas Day alone. Come about four o'clock." In short, this lady was not going to take no for an answer!

I should explain that soon after Stan and I married in 1951, I realised he was a terribly fussy eater. It was to cause a lot of problems in the years ahead. During our six-month engagement we occasionally had a meal in a restaurant and he always ordered the same food – steak and chips – something which should have clued me in, but didn't! To be honest I don't remember discussing food, our likes or dislikes. Of course in those days we didn't share a home until after the marriage and really knew very little about each other's habits or idiosyncrasies. Three months after the wedding bells had chimed, the words "I don't eat that" had grown very familiar to my ears. By then I had learned not to serve chicken, turkey, pork, pasta, casseroles of any kind and Chinese food – heaven forbid that I would be so foolish!

Cheese was OK as long as it was orange cheddar and alone on a sandwich of white bread, never melted or cooked in any way. Fish in greasy batter bought from a fish and chip shop would be tolerated only because of the chips which accompanied it. The list was long and growing. My friends would jokingly remark that I had grounds for divorce. I think some of them were serious!

I do admit that he never complained when I made roast beef and he ended up eating leftovers five days in a row, by which time it resembled a piece of worn shoe leather. Clearly his passion for food did not equal his immense passion for flying!

I'm sure by now you get the picture, that eating out was never much of an adventure or pleasure with him, which brings me back to Christmas Day 1966. I had murmured my thanks to the Pastor's wife and put the phone down, my heart sinking at the thought of Christmas dinner with virtual strangers and all the ramifications of my husband's refusal to eat anything he didn't like. By this time I had an audience of three in the kitchen, staring at me in horror, having listened to my one-sided conversation and put two and two together. Not only did my husband not eat turkey, he didn't eat goose! Nor had the children ever eaten it and to be honest, it wasn't my favourite either, though I knew I would at least eat a little of whatever was served to avoid hurting the hostess.

It was like World War III in the kitchen! I was bombarded with protests, as though I was an enemy and a traitor. The questions flew at me. "Why did you say yes?" cried my eleven-year-old daughter and "Why didn't you say we were having company?" asked my better half. I guess they were willing to lie although they'd just come back from church! Seven-year-old Christopher decided to stay silent.

It was absolute pandemonium for a while but I remained firm that we had to go, though it was the last thing I wanted to do now and I certainly wasn't going to lie about it. They went off to sulk. The Christmas spirit which had filled our house early that morning had vanished. I ended up in tears and still at my wits' end over the dilemma of the goose dinner. I had in fact, planned steak and onions for husband's Christmas meal, and bought a turkey breast for myself and the two children. It was the usual kind of Christmas dinner which I had become familiar with and never tried to change.

Eventually I pulled myself together, screwed up all my courage and phoned the Pastor's wife to ask whether she would be offended if I took the dish of steak and onions, ready cooked, for Stan. I didn't push my luck with the mention of goose for fear she would come up with yet another alternative that he still would not have eaten. There was a brief, pregnant silence while she digested this latest bit of news, then she said "That's all right, bring it along." By now I was sure this poor woman was totally regretting the impulsive invitation.

We left home at the given time for our drive of fifteen minutes or so. The short journey to their house was made in silence you could have cut with a knife. I think by now they were ashamed of their behaviour, but I wasn't going to make it easier for them. The only words I uttered as we got close, directed at all three, were "Put a smile on your face and be grateful, this is supposed to be a happy Christmas day".

Somehow we got through that memorable meal, Stan eating his steak and probably enjoying it, the children eating the tiniest amount of the greasy goose meat which I could see they didn't care for. I dared them with my eyes not to make a fuss. "Just eat it", my look said. I was going to even if it choked me.

I wish I could tell you that it was a happy and successful Christmas dinner; it wasn't. Conversation was sparse and strained. At times it seemed the meal would last forever. Apart from the food fiasco we were almost strangers and had very little in common at that point, and on top of everything in this strange mix, our host was the Pastor of a church. It was difficult to view him as an ordinary acquaintance, to chat with him freely, as we did with our friends. I felt 'on guard' throughout that evening, unable to relax.

Of course the meal did eventually end, and with it some of my embarrassment and anxiety evaporated, but it was a never-to-be forgotten meal. The whole episode had ruined Christmas Day and the plans to spend it in our first real home in Canada.

Later the children went off to play and I went with Mrs T. to help with the clearing up of dishes and kitchen. She suddenly put her hand on my arm and said "It must be so difficult for you". At that point I didn't trust myself to speak. I just nodded my head in agreement as I carried on drying the dishes. The rest of the evening was less tense and thankfully we parted at ten o'clock, on smiling terms, but still very happy and relieved to be going home.

Remarkably, we remained firm friends with the Pastor for the seventeen years we lived in our Richmond home. He dropped in on us many times, always by himself – but we never shared dinner ever again. I really don't have to wonder why!

I haven't seen Pastor Taetz for over twenty years now, but I'm willing to bet he will still be charismatic and handsome, still preaching the Gospel to anyone who will listen. Like all of us he will have aged. His piercing eyes, which always reminded me of dark brown velvet, might have faded a little, his honey-coloured complexion less vibrant and the black hair is probably that shade of gray which makes most men look even more attractive, while it sometimes has the opposite effect on women. Perhaps his six foot two, slim frame stoops a little with the passing of the years, but I know for certain he will still have that magnetic quality which drew a large flock of faithful congregation to his church, Sunday after Sunday. He was a spellbinding preacher but always warm and welcoming. A man's man and definitely an attractive one to the opposite sex. He was the personification of "tall, dark and handsome" and a lot more, he was amusing, intelligent and very charming. He came to our home many times, not just as a Pastor, but as a real friend, someone we enjoyed as a person, not just a preacher.

We saw him spasmodically after we moved from Richmond to Vancouver, then we lost touch when we moved further out to White Rock, close to the United States Border. I like to think of him as he was then, sitting in one of our shabby living room chairs with his long legs stretched out, completely at ease with us as we were with him, having a visit from someone we liked enormously. He had a wonderful smile which lit up his whole face. He was hard to resist and so likeable as a true friend. He could have been in the movies and made millions! He certainly met all the requirements needed to make a star.

I have often over the years, especially when I've been having one of my "Doubting Thomas" spells, wondered whether priests, ministers etc. have any doubts of their own, or if they are all blessed with that unshakeable faith that most of us long for. Is it just another job, another profession, a way of earning a living, especially if you have the gift of the gab, as Pastor Taetz did, plus all the charm needed to succeed? I like to think there is someone at the helm in this violent world we live in, but if so, why doesn't He or She do something about the mess? So many lives have been lost in the name of religion and it still continues and will go on long after we've all found the answer to the burning question, is there a Heaven? Another life, a better place than this? Or is it just myth and hope that keeps some of us on the straight and narrow? A need to believe that we do survive death and go into another dimension?

It won't be too long before I can answer that age-old question, but I doubt very much I'll be back to tell anyone. I like to think I'll be so ecstatically happy to see all those loved ones who have gone before me, that I just won't have the time! And of course it would be nice to see Pastor Taetz again!

Do you believe in miracles? I always tried to keep an open mind about it, but I'm not a true Doubting Thomas any more. While I'm on the subject of religion and Pastor Taetz I thought I would relate the following true story. Our son Christopher, who had been so sick when he was just a toddler and hospitalised for a long time with a mystery illness, never diagnosed in England but finally identified at the UBC Hospital as juvenile rheumatoid arthritis. By this time he had undergone several surgeries to remove the lining of both knees in an attempt to slow the disease down and put it into remission. He was then encased in a plaster cast to rest the areas. This painful and debilitating illness affected his whole body, making every joint hot and swollen. He took twelve aspirins daily and was under the care of the Vancouver Arthritis Centre, several times as an 'In-Patient' at their facility on Ash Street, for intensive therapy and to help him learn how to cope with his disabilities. Although he was in constant pain, Christopher seldom complained. He did his best not to miss too much school, and in spite of the obstacles in his life, he graduated from Vancouver College right on schedule.

Where is all this leading, I can hear you ask. It is leading to what I know was a miracle. Christopher had a long re-occurrence of his illness when he was in his early teens. He could only walk with the aid of crutches and he wasn't sleeping because he couldn't stand bodily contact with the bed or even the bed clothes. Watching him trying to cope each day tore my heart out, I felt so helpless, and this particular week, he looked even worse than usual. He was white and exhausted and unable to walk without holding on to the walls as he made his way from bedroom to bathroom. A really sick boy, whom I loved so very much, but couldn't help. I was at my wits' end.

I thought if only he could sleep, he would at least be able to cope better, until the disease decided to go into remission and this could be anywhere from one to six months – or never. I read everything published on the disease, as well as endless health and vitamin books. I was a walking encyclopedia, but nothing seemed to help. I constantly prayed for help though I wasn't really a deeply religious person, just a very desperate mother. I didn't get down on my knees and ask the Almighty properly, I just asked Him over and over as I was doing my day's work, to please tell me what to do to help my son.

One Saturday night I fell into bed exhausted with worry and misery and I had a vivid dream. I was looking at my son lying in his bed and heard a voice telling me to get him a waterbed. I woke up, the dream still very much with me, and I thought I could sense a presence in the bedroom. Of course it could have been my imagination. I couldn't go back to sleep. I just turned the vivid dream over and over in my mind and knew I had been given the answer I was searching for - I never doubted it for an instant.

At that time I had never seen a waterbed. I believe they were just coming on to the market, but I really don't think I knew anything about them, certainly it wasn't in my thoughts. I was totally convinced my dream was a message from whoever we perceive as God.

That Sunday morning I told my husband about my strange experience. He didn't laugh at me and like me, didn't question why I'd had the dream. As soon as the stores were open, we went through the yellow pages in the phone book to start the mission of finding a waterbed. We phoned many furniture stores and mattress outlets without any luck, but eventually we were directed to a newly opened store which was not listed in the phone book. It was Pacific Waterbeds on Georgia Street in downtown area of Vancouver, quite a distance from where we lived in Richmond. We drove into town that afternoon and eventually bought a water-bed, the first of its kind. Just a brown vinyl mattress in a plain dark wooden frame, which you filled with water, plus a heater to warm it. The water sloshed about, especially when you moved on it and it made me feel a bit queasy when I tried it in the store, but I kept my thoughts to myself. I knew I'd been given an answer to my prayers.

The bed was delivered to our house the following Tuesday morning and we filled it with water right away and waited. Christopher tried it on the Wednesday night when the water had warmed sufficiently. I watched him sink into the mattress, without wincing with pain, and covered him with just a sheet and a lightweight blanket. For the first time in many weeks he slept through the night. No pressure on the painful joints to keep him awake. It was something to rejoice and be very thankful for.

Soon his energy improved and eventually, many weeks later, his illness once more went into remission. I am happy to relate this story to anyone who will listen, as it proves to me there are still miracles happening. Perhaps not in the way we look for them, but in the most unexpected circumstances, we find them. I know for sure that I found my miracle in my dream that Saturday night.

Christopher stayed with the water-bed until he reached working age and eventually married. He finally had to part with it since he wasn't allowed to have it in the apartment building they had chosen to live in when that occurred. I don't think his wife ever cared for the bed either, and not everyone does. Stan and I did and we had them for many years. It was only when we started having to move from place to place because of his long illness, and emptying and filling the beds became a real problem for me, that we switched back to the normal type beds. I haven't seen a water-bed in the stores for a long time and probably they are now out of fashion. I however, will never forget how wonderful it was to discover them and how much they helped a very sick young person sleep without pain, after months of trying.

CHAPTER TWENTY-TWO

PLEASE DON'T TALK ABOUT THE WAR!

In his late teens, Christopher acquired an old, pale-blue Volkswagen Beetle which was his pride and joy, his first car, and more important to him than anything else in his life at that time. I swear if he could have taken it to bed with him, he would have done so! Endless hours were spent washing and waxing it. Every penny he earned washing cars at a dealership on Saturdays bought a new gadget for his beloved Beetle. I would often be annoyed when I thought of the hours he spent keeping this object in immaculate condition while I had to beg, threaten and bribe to make him tidy his bedroom which looked like a tip most of the time.

He didn't seem interested in girls, but suddenly all that changed when he was 21 years old and met Aileen. Right from the start I knew this was a serious romance, since he had brought her home to meet us. He'd never done that before. She was just out of high school, very shy, with braces on her teeth. She blushed very easily. I guessed this was definitely the one, as it was easy to see Chris was absolutely smitten.

She told us her parents were from Germany and although it honestly didn't matter to me, I knew that could be a bit of a problem. My husband had been a pilot in the Royal Air Force during the latter years of the Second World War, flying Spitfires and later a Lancaster bomber, dropping bombs over Germany, maybe on their hometown. Even though it was now 1979, people have long memories. He still loved to talk about flying whenever the opportunity arose. It was in his blood, no doubt about it. I was nervous about meeting them, but I knew that sooner or later we would have to do so, because it was pretty obvious there was going to be a wedding - and a fairly big one at that, some time in the next couple of years.

The months went by and a wedding date was set for August 15th 1981 in the Lutheran Church in Richmond. I invited the bride's parents, Ed and Margaret Becker, over for an evening to at least become acquainted and to show each other we had our children's well-being at heart. It was a long evening but somehow we got through it, though it was filled with long awkward silences from both sides. My husband didn't help one jot and contributed little to the conversation, while I chattered like a magpie, trying to fill the silence and hating every minute of the time. I was *so* afraid that somehow we would get on to the subject of the war. Here we were English entertaining Germans who would ever have thought it possible.

It was a strained evening and a relief to us all when it was time for them to leave. I didn't like or dislike them and I'm sure they probably felt exactly the same. Fate had thrown us together and time would take care of some of the raw spots. I consoled myself with that thought. At that moment in time we didn't have anything in common, except their daughter and my son getting married.

As the date of the wedding drew closer, I became more and

more apprehensive. The wedding reception was going to be long, the hall booked until midnight, complete with band so we could all dance. All those hours to get through. There was a bar, and alcohol makes people lose inhibitions. All these thoughts added to my nervousness.

We invited the Beckers over again for a casual dinner just prior to the big day. The weather was warm and sunny and we held it in the garden, hoping it would create a more relaxing atmosphere. My brother Roy and his wife June, also from England, joined us and in spite of her trying to engage in conversation with the Beckers, it didn't change the stiff climate between us, in spite of valiant efforts again on my part and my talkative and friendly sister-in-law, who tried very hard to draw them into conversation.

I wanted to be a good hostess that night and my stomach seemed to be in a permanent knot. I passed food around but couldn't manage to eat anything myself. It was hard work and that dinner certainly was not the social event of the year!

My biggest fear still was that Stan would make reference to the war. He wasn't well endowed with tact and still had such a passion for his flying days, and I found myself saying "please don't talk about the war," every chance I got. Eventually in those weeks leading up to the wedding, this became a catchphrase and part of my daily life. At work, where I had confided my fears to several of my colleagues, they would murmur, loud enough for me to hear, as they passed my desk, "please don't talk about the war!' Of course it was a joke to them and in their company I could join in the laughter.

It was a different matter as we drove to the church on the big day. I was a nervous wreck, hoping my nightmare would not come true. I felt like a parrot repeating the now familiar words over and over to my spouse, as we drove to the big wedding, and then hoped for the best as we arrived at the church. I had tried very hard to keep peace between us and the family we would now be part of. Happily all went off without a hitch. The two sides didn't integrate very well, but it wasn't too apparent and everyone seemed to enjoy themselves.

All that was a long time ago and since that time we, the parents, were thrown together on all those special days throughout each year, such as Mother's Day, Father's Day etc, and gradually we have become friends with each other. Not close friends, but enough to include each other for barbecues once a year and the occasional spontaneous event They made us very welcome, as did members of their family we've met over the years. The silences are no longer painful and awkward and there is normal conversation. We realise perhaps that we are all just ordinary people whose paths have crossed through marriage – we are no better or worse than they are and just want the best for our children. But we still don't talk about the war!

CHAPTER TWENTY-THREE

ON THE MOVE

After living in Richmond for seventeen years, Stan and I began to think about moving to something smaller and to a new location. The large garden was becoming too much for us to keep up. We began to spend Sundays looking at properties in an area called Champlain Heights, not too far from Central Park in Burnaby, which borders Vancouver. We came across a small cul-de-sac with fairly new town houses with nice gardens. They were Bare-Land Strata homes, which meant we would not be responsible for exterior house repairs, such as the roof, which is always a big item in cost to replace. The garden however, was ours to do with it as we wished.

This house had a living room, kitchen, two large bedrooms, two bathrooms and a nice family room with a big patio window leading onto the back garden. We liked it and made an offer on it, successfully. We moved in 1980 to our new home and settled in quite happily. Our neighbours on both sides were lovely....a couple in their thirties from New Zealand adjoining our place and an older couple from Holland on the other side.

We hadn't been there very long before BC Hydro installed solar panels on all our homes as part of an experiment. It was free of charge and we were very pleased to have them. Even on dull days – and there are always many of them, not only in the winter – they provided us with all our hot water.

I was really happy with our new location and the smaller house, but there was one drawback I didn't catch on to for a while. The windows were quite small compared to our previous ones, with the exception of the patio window. We had a bigger one installed, but on the days when I spent time alone, I would feel very depressed, without any real reason. I finally came to the conclusion that I was missing the sun and the lack of light.

I was always happy to be back at Richmond Municipal Hall on workdays. I worked a nine-day fortnight which had been introduced at the office, and it was good to have an extra day off work which gave me a three-day weekend. Most of the staff opted for either Friday or Monday, giving us that long weekend.

One Sunday afternoon I suggested to my husband that we take a drive to White Rock, a nice seaside town close to the United States border, and have 'afternoon tea' at a new restaurant I'd seen advertised in the newspaper. Apparently it was quite a hit with the public since it was a replica of a typical English restaurant, serving tea and scones and all manner of English dishes. We found it easily and enjoyed our visit. It was just like being home in England for a while. The waitresses were attired in long old-fashioned dresses with white starched aprons and frilly bonnets on their heads, serving tea in English beautiful patterned bone china. It was a delightful afternoon and we promised ourselves to go back again soon.

It was a lovely day for a drive and we decided to return home via Ocean Park, which was a small area on the way to Crescent Beach, another pretty small village right on the water. On our journey we passed a billboard at Ocean Park advertising a small gated development being built just up the road. We decided to take a look at it just for curiosity's sake. No intention of living out there. It had big black iron gates leading into the crescent shaped courtyard, with trees, shrubs and flowers scattered around the area of two different types of houses, a small bungalow type and larger three-storey homes on either side.

We looked at the show houses for both styles and while the bungalow would obviously have been sufficient for our needs, I fell in love with the larger house. This development was called San Juan Gate and had a Spanish look about it. They were really unique, like nothing I had ever seen. Seven different levels, forty-three stairs from top to bottom, three full-size bathrooms which included a jacuzzi in the master bathroom, which was very large, complete with a window. That was a real plus in my opinion.

I was smitten, very vocal and full of praise, but as usual my spouse just nodded and didn't become as enthused as I did. If I'd have had my way, I would have immediately put our names on one of the larger homes. However, Stan said we needed to think about it. "What is there to think about, they are absolutely beautiful!" I replied.

The subject was closed for that afternoon, but we did walk around the area and I knew, without a single doubt, I wanted to live there. The new place stayed on my mind. I even drove back there a second and third time on my day off from work and each visit only confirmed my desire to move there.

Finally, Stan agreed and we signed papers to buy the one facing the quiet street. It wouldn't be finished for six months, which suited us because we had the present house to sell. I hoped it would do so quickly. I was so excited!

We immediately put our house on the market for what we

perceived to be a good price. It was much less than we had paid for it, but we knew the market had dropped considerably in the past two years, and it was still practically new and had the added attraction of the solar panels.

The weeks went by and we held open house each weekend, leaving at mid-day and returning home at 4 pm, always hoping there had been an interested party, but nothing happened. We had signed up with the realtor for a six month period, thinking that would be more than sufficient. However, time passed and soon the very last open house was to take place that Sunday. As usual, I had done as the realtor advised, made a batch of scones and a pot of coffee giving off lovely aromas – with zero results.

We returned home just after 4 pm only to be told that no one had left an offer on the table. I was terribly disappointed and quite truthfully, we didn't feel enthusiastic about putting it on the market again, having to go out every Sunday afternoon in order to leave the house free. Of course the constant task of making sure there wasn't a thing out of place gets to you after a while, to say nothing of the scones and coffee I made during that last period. I just wanted to take a short break before we signed on again, perhaps with a different realtor.

That Sunday evening after dinner was over I was lying on the chesterfield watching television, feeling a bit down, when the phone rang. I didn't move to answer it because it was nine o'clock and I was tired, then I heard Stan having a conversation. "Hold on a moment" he said and put his hand over the mouthpiece. "Dee, it's the realtor, he wants to bring a couple round to see the house". I replied "What a time to come! Tell them 'yes' but I'm not leaving the house while they do it, in fact, I'm not moving from the chesterfield!"

Ten minutes later the doorbell rang. It was the realtor with two small Asian men, who nodded briefly to us, then proceeded to make a very hasty and cursory tour of our house, then nodded again and left. I looked at Stan and said "What a waste of time that was, they didn't even have a proper look at the place." I went back to watching the screen and completely forgot the recent visitors.

The phone rang again about fifteen minutes later. It was the realtor to say he needed to come back because the two Asian men, who apparently were chemists, wanted to buy the house. No haggling or bargaining – they wanted it! Unbelievable!

Needless to say, we accepted and moved to our new home in Ocean Park. It was a beautiful place to live and I hoped it would be for the rest of our lives. We chose royal blue and white for the main theme, which complemented the stunning white fireplace in the living room. I not only loved the house, I loved the whole area and liked the fact it was close to the United States, where we shopped frequently. I had of course given myself a very long drive in busy traffic to Richmond where I still worked and for a long time, didn't mind it.

Life was perfect for a while, but not for too long. Our lives were to change drastically and suddenly.

CHAPTER TWENTY-FOUR

THE BLACK PIT
OF DESPAIR

I visited the black pit of despair many times during the years in my role as caregiver to my husband, Stan. He began a long, complicated, roller-coaster illness in March 1993, which stole a great deal of his memory. It started with flu-like symptoms and trouble breathing and he spent a week in hospital recovering and then returned home. He was quite normal in every way, just a bit under the weather after a week off his feet. He was prescribed one tablet daily of Digoxin. The dose was increased quite a lot, until Stan became very ill and slept most of the time.

In 2008, this memory loss was still not officially diagnosed, though it was thought to be Alzheimer's disease in the first three years when we attended UBC Hospital for testing, without reaching any real conclusions. No one would consider that it could have been caused by the overdose of Digoxin and the doctor who prescribed the overdose of medication never admitted negligence in doing so.

In the first year, when Stan became so ill, I decided I would have to sell the large house we were living in at Ocean Park. We both loved this home a great deal. I had to make this agonizing decision without being able to discuss it with Stan. He wasn't functioning at all on a normal level; he was in a zombie-like state at that time. I was worried about him plunging head first over the banister and down the stairs, and I knew that in spite of our attachment to this home, it had to be sold.

It did so very easily. It was a wrench to do it but I felt at that time, I had no other choice. I bought a brand new rancher in another new gated community, Twin Lakes, in Walnut Grove, Langley, to be close to Christopher and Aileen, who lived and worked there, and for three years this was a great help. In the meantime, Stan saw a heart specialist, who was shocked by the large amount of medication he had been prescribed. It helped the zombie-like situation but he was far from being his old self. His memory was impaired and it gradually worsened. He was diagnosed with atrial fibrillation and the doctor eventually did a cardio version which worked for about fourteen months before it reversed itself. That procedure was never repeated. Stan was prescribed Warfarin to thin his blood to avoid stroke or heart attack.

Just having my son and his wife drop by for short periods was reassuring at that time. I knew they were just a phone call away and five minutes by car. That came to an end in November 1996 when Christopher's company closed the Langley Branch and transferred him to Seattle, USA.

The new rancher, however, was perfect in every way for Stan and me, with heated floors, lots of windows, two large bedrooms, a lovely living room with a white fireplace and a large kitchen and family room which led out to a small patio. We settled down very quickly and hoped again that it would be the place we would live in for the rest of our lives. The development also had an outdoor pool and a very attractive clubhouse for meetings and functions. It was set in beautiful grounds with lots of greenery and paths to walk, and of course, as the name suggests, there were two lakes, which eventually had ducks and visiting birds taking up residence.

Being a gated community was wonderful for Stan, who could walk around and stop to get his breath, pretending to look at the flowers in the gardens. He appeared to be very contented. I really was convinced it was the right decision to buy this new house, which of course did not have any stairs.

As the months passed the rancher gradually became my prison, albeit a nice one. Our only outings would be to the local shops and to the doctor's office. I was too nervous to leave Stan alone because he now fell frequently without warning and could be so unpredictable at that time.

One hair-raising day Aileen and I returned from a short shopping trip and found him cooking his favourite food, left-over potatoes. The kitchen reeked of disinfectant, and we were puzzled until we discovered he was frying his potatoes in Pinesol Disinfectant, which he had mistaken for oil, perhaps because it is a similar colour.

As the end of that year drew close I decided I would have to give up my job as a Marriage Commissioner which had given me so much joy for the last eleven years. The official black robe hung in the closet for a long time, a reminder of those happy days, along with countless photographs of smiling brides and grooms. Stan and I continued to spend our days watching the numerous birds feeding on our patio which overlooked a ravine. The blue Stellar Jays were our favourite visitors. They would sit on the fence and screech, demanding the peanuts we used to buy in large quantities. It was a pleasant way to pass the time. We learned to identify so many species of birds and it became our hobby. The squirrels and chipmunks also helped themselves from our feeders and we loved to see them all. They were company for us, in what had become a very solitary life.

Christopher had been transferred back to the United States again, still working for Kenworth Trucks and hoping this time it would be a permanent move and that his Green Card would be obtained fairly soon. The lawyers had promised it would be so. They bought a house and settled down for the second time in America. We missed having our son and his wife close by and at this time, friends seemed to be rather scarce. Mental illness will do that; it is a reality and something that a lot of people are uncomfortable with.

We stayed in touch with Ann and Hans, who lived in Abbotsford, and they would visit us every now and then and we would drive out there and have some lunch with them. They were our only visitors at that time.

This was before Stan's health began a very steady decline and going anywhere at all became more difficult. One morning I thought he was in the bathroom, as he seemed to be a long time. I found him lying unconscious in the hallway and phoned for an ambulance. They took him to hospital and I jumped in the car to follow. He was kept for a few hours then I was told he could return home.

This episode was just the first of many. He would crumble to the ground without warning, and we had numerous visits to the Emergency Department at Langley Hospital, where he would see a different doctor on every occasion. Each time he was taken to hospital we would have to go through all the lengthy business of giving the same details over again, even if he was at the Emergency two days in a row.

I thought computers were to help store information and make things easy, but it certainly didn't work in Langley Hospital. It was a complete puzzle why they had to ask for the same information each visit. On every occasion, Stan would eventually recover from his episode and be discharged, without treatment. He was never admitted as an in-patient. Several times the physician on duty would tell me he needed more exercise to strengthen his legs. I knew this was rubbish because he would be white and sweating and his heart-rate would be very low. I used to watch the monitor as he lay on the bed in the Emergency. In fact, the doctor concerned actually arranged for Stan to attend the hospital and have a regime of walking on a treadmill, something which made him gasp for breath and definitely made him feel worse. I stopped taking him for this treatment which obviously didn't help him one bit.

Eventually I requested that he see a heart specialist in a different hospital. By now I knew he had a leaking heart valve, but a new one was out of the question because of his ever-increasing memory loss. This was the verdict given at UBC Hospital, where he spent a week having more tests, after my request to our new family doctor.

Nothing further was done to help Stan's heart problem, except giving him more and more medication. At one time he was taking nineteen different pills each day and I had to wake him during the night to administer some of them. I was terribly lonely and at the end of the summer in 1997, I decided once again to move, this time to be closer to my daughter Janice, who lived and worked in North Vancouver. She kept insisting it was difficult for her to drive to Langley to visit. I knew it was a problem.

Once again the house was put on the market. It was an agonising decision for me, because we loved the rancher, had spent a lot of money making it into our special place and I wasn't quite ready to let go of it, but commonsense kept telling me that I would be better off if I made the move, especially if I needed any kind of help. Finally, I put the rancher up for sale and once again began looking for a place to live in North Vancouver, not knowing where to start since it was a place I'd seldom visited, an area which neither Stan or I ever wanted to live.

I was guided mainly by my daughter, who had lived most of her adult life in the area. I would make the long drive on the busy motorway back and forth from Langley, looking at apartments which were much more expensive than Fraser Valley, which seemed the only solution to an ever-shrinking bank balance, and finally I settled on an apartment close to Parkgate, not too far from Deep Cove. It was on the eighth floor of a striking looking building opposite the golf course. It was a concrete structure and it met my basic requirements because I was hearing horror stories about numerous leaky condos, which scared me to death. I also had a desire to have some space around me knowing I would still be a shut-in most of the time. It was set in nice grounds which I hoped would give Stan a safe place for him to walk.

We moved there in the spring of 1998 and quickly I nicknamed it 'My Ivory Tower' because this life-style was more isolating than ever. I hardly ever saw a living soul, except the close neighbours who used the elevator as I did, to pick up my daily mail. Much of the time I would bury myself in the kitchen, baking endless batches of muffins and bread, finding some consolation in the wonderful aromas wafting from the oven.

Stan got used to it quite quickly, though at first he asked me 'are we on holiday?' and 'when are we going home?' Then in time he forgot about it and stopped asking questions. He would sit on the chesterfield with his beloved books and was very contented, though he didn't seem to get further than the first few pages. He never complained as long as he had me around and although there wouldn't be a great deal of conversation between us, he appeared to be happy. It was a lonely existence, but somehow the days would pass and I could go to bed, hopefully to sleep and shut out the world and my problems with it.

With me always was the huge, constant array of emotions:

anxiety, anger at the doctor who had administered a toxic dose of medication which had started his illness, grief and a terrible sense of loss and most of all, terrible guilt that I could – and should – cope better and should be more patient, but sometimes at the end of a particularly trying day, I would scream my frustration silently in my mind and hate myself for it.

That year I began writing my daily thoughts in a journal. Scary words to me now as I read again my innermost thoughts of the desperation I felt sometimes. I had changed from a happy, outgoing person, who loved to sing and dance and be with other people to this exhausted being who couldn't wait each night to bury her head under the bedclothes.

All this was nothing compared to what I felt when my husband's name came to the top of the Nursing Home list which the visiting Health Worker insisted on doing, after she had assessed Stan in a short visit to the apartment. A phone call came telling me a bed was available and I had three days to claim it. There was no going back to the bottom of the list - it was now or never. I felt devastated with grief, and consumed with guilt. I told myself I would just take a break, then resume taking care of him. I thought of the countless times I had listened to marriage vows being exchanged, the promises to love and cherish, for better for worse, in sickness and in health. My own vows almost forty-nine years ago, and I was breaking them. It was the darkest period in my life.

Those three days passed quickly. I thought of nothing else but the coming ordeal. I ironed labels on my husband's clothes and packed them in a suitcase, my silent tears dripping on each garment as I did so. My husband would sometimes glance at my endeavours, but his curiosity was never aroused. However, I couldn't bring myself to just spring the news on him on the crucial morning. I typed a loving letter of explanation and gave it to him the day before. He read it in stunned silence, the tears falling down both of our faces unheeded. I knew, because of his memory loss, I would face this whole scene again tomorrow, but in my selfish agony, I wanted to cry and comfort myself by sharing it.

Admitting day came all too soon and we made the short journey to the Home. Aileen and Christopher had travelled up from Seattle for support, along with daughter Janice. I will never forget my first impressions as we entered the unit through the floor-to-ceiling heavy doors, closed off from the rest of the facility. I saw a sea of faces, mostly female, many asleep with mouths open wide, some in wheelchairs, some pushing walkers, the rest of them staring at us, the newcomers, as we made the journey down the hall to the room which would be home for Stan. At that moment in time, all those poor souls looked alike to me and I was horrified at the thought of leaving my loved one in this place, which reminded me of a long-forgotten movie portraying mentally ill patients in an institution. I think it was called *The Snake Pit*.

Again, I told myself I would just take a break, get my energy back and go on as before. The next few weeks were difficult as I tried to adjust to living alone for the first time since I married. I cried incessantly, couldn't sleep, didn't eat, couldn't even sit still. I was beside myself with grief and guilt and many times decided I would bring my husband home. Stan, however, settled down very well and the weeks turned into months and I realised that I was coping better and coming to terms with the situation. I got to know many of the patients. I stopped each time I visited Stan, to wave a hand, help someone find their room, give a hug or touch an arm, as I passed, always with a smile on my face and their name on my lips. They no longer melded into a mass of faces. I could see each one as the individuals they truly were. Life had dealt them a terrible illness which diminished their capacity to live normally –

it can happen to each and every one of us. I very much wanted to reach out to them and with a little effort, bring some sunshine into their lives with a smile and a few words. I knew a lot about Alzheimer's by that time and became totally convinced my husband was not afflicted with the awful disease.

Six months later, I finally emerged to reclaim my life, my sanity, my energy and most of all, a little joy. My first step was joining a creative writing class and I blossomed from that first reluctant decision to do something - anything - to kick-start my life. Since that time, I've met so many great women; interesting, friendly people, willing to share their experiences, and I've enjoyed every moment of it - it makes me feel alive again and part of the universe.

It has been a very long journey and I still wrestled with the guilt I felt that my husband was no longer sharing our home, but the time I spent with him was truly quality time and the burden of his illness was shared with the wonderful staff at the nursing home. They were true angels of mercy and Stan was happy there.

I brought him home for a few hours each day and he stayed with me at the weekends. I still hated being separated from the man I had shared my life with - I never truly came to terms with it. We lived in the moment, each one precious, something I looked forward to and treasured, and as I look back on this whole care-giving experience, I realise with surprise, that I gained something from it and think I am a better person because of it. A more compassionate, more understanding, patient individual with something yet to give my fellow human beings and a heart that was still brimming with love and pity for the man I married.

As summer turned to fall I saw another decline in Stan's health. His efforts to breathe became even more difficult and his appetite diminished drastically. His thin, frail body looked as though he had been in one of the concentration camps which were revealed to the world in the last days of World War II, where millions of people had been starved and massacred. I remember those pictures very vividly, even now all these year later, one in particular showing a death's-head grin of naked skeletal frames, barely alive, discovered in Belsen, only one of many in Europe to be discovered. Man's inhumanity to man... the slaughter of six million Jews. My husband's body now looked like one of those suffering souls, the flesh had dissolved away, his energy gone - he just wanted to sleep.

Occasionally in the evening he rallied for a while and you became aware that in spite of everything, his wry English humour was still intact. The family will remember him for his wise-cracks, his funny little songs, his sick jokes, his love of French fries, roast beef and steak in an otherwise faddy diet, and his Walter Mitty approach to life. I will remember him best for his flying days and how passionate and happy he was in those years, still flying long after the war ended, with the Auxiliary 610 Squadron based out of Hooton in Cheshire, England, with whom he flew every weekend and any other chance he got. He lived and breathed flying, nothing else was important until he met and fell in love with me.

We had some great parties with that handsome group of pilots who shared his passion to the full. They were a crazy, daredevil bunch of men who lived life to the fullest and sometimes lost their lives doing what they loved the most. Just after Stan and I were married in September of 1951, he was posted with the Squadron on a three month course for Meteor Jets, to East Anglia in Norfolk. Most of the wives stayed at home but I was a newly-wed and we were inseparable and I went with him. In the evenings we would meet up with the air crews at some inn or other and have a riotous time. They were a noisy, friendly bunch who shared their laughter and their jokes with me. I never felt like an outsider. They were happy, never-to-be forgotten times and like all young people, we felt immortal and life was absolutely perfect.

Now it was the autumn of the year and of Stan's life, and I made the decision to bring him out of the nursing home where he had been for a year, and have him with me for a little while. In the words of one of his favourite Sinatra songs, I will savour the precious days I'll spend with him.

He was home with me from Wednesday afternoon, 13th September. I'd rented an oxygen tank and a lightweight wheelchair to transport him from the Home to the apartment. We had a few hours of warm pleasure sitting on the balcony in the autumn sunshine which felt more like mid-summer. It was lovely just looking at the pots of flowers still blooming and the tomatoes he loved to grow but wouldn't eat, which were finally turning red.

Friday the 15th was the start of the 2000 Olympic Games in Australia, which Stan would have dearly loved to have watched, but he was too exhausted that particular day to open his eyes. He was resting comfortably. He was not in pain or distressed at that time, just a bit befuddled when he wakened and didn't seem to know where he was, but he was all right once he recognised me. Then he took a turn for the worse and couldn't urinate. I had to take him back to the nursing home so he could see a doctor.

Janice came over for supper that evening to visit her father. She told me each time she visited she sat in the car afterwards and cried. I'm sure Christopher in Seattle was doing the same thing. It was hard for him to be so far away and hear via the phone the daily bulletin of mostly bad news. My heart ached for both of them. They were having their first experience of losing a parent and of course I knew what that was like. We all have to do it sooner or later, there's no escape and the more we care, the harder it is to part with them.

I had promised them only the truth about Stan's condition, no pretending. We all knew the end was close. There was no way back, only peace for one tortured soul of a man who had suffered greatly for so many years. I prayed every night for that peace to come, that God would gently, silently, steal him away and my beloved pilot would once again fly in the blue yonder of his youth, free from his earthly body.

That happened on November 12th 2000 at ten minutes past two in the afternoon. He left when Janice and Chris had stepped outside for a few moments while I had gone home to shower, after spending the night in the hospital. We all felt he couldn't bear to leave us until there was no one around. Silly thoughts I suppose, but it did seem strange that after the long vigil we had just gone through, making sure there was one of us there with him always, that he left when he was alone.

I grieved for a long time and in my solitude I would think back to the early years and the dreams we had for the future then. Girlish dreams, white wedding gown and confetti, to play house, have children, a home of our own, to make into the special place where we would live happily ever after. Fairy-tale romance, my prince not on a white horse, but flying a plane. Happiness was seeing him flying over the house and later striding up the avenue to home, the smell and feel of his blue serge uniform, the love on his face as he hugged me, blue eyes soft on my face. Happiness was curling up on his knee to share the big armchair while we listened to the Saturday night play on the radio. He called me 'Monkey' and he was my tree - my safe place.

Our idea of luxury was one day to be able to afford to eat a leg of lamb, straight from the oven, slicing it up on the carving board and devouring it, or to drink a whole can of evaporated milk for no other reason than we loved the taste of it. Or more sanely, to sit down to a plate of thick pink boiled ham, carved off the bone, with home-made chips, peas and crusty white bread, our Saturday night treat. What children we were, playing house in our make-believe world that nothing could ever go wrong. We had nothing – and everything. Two rooms and our hearts filled with love and expectations which we shared. Nothing ambitious – a home and children where we would grow old together. Vacations to the seaside not far away. Walks in the countryside each Sunday, very close to home. No car, no plans to have one. We had each other, and that was enough then. Later it was to change so drastically, but the first ten years of life together was idyllic. Nothing and everything, a paradox and a lesson that the best things in life are truly free. You cannot buy happiness. Happiness is a state of mind created by giving of yourself. In the true act of giving, you are actually receiving much more in return.

Life has taught me many harsh lessons and if I could retrace my steps there is little that I would do over again. Only the early years would remain the same. Our simple life was all I ever needed, I managed to convey that to him, with words and loving deeds, during the last years when he needed me more than ever before.

CHAPTER TWENTY-FIVE

MY NEW ROLE

During the past few months in my present solitary state, I seem to have acquired some new faults and habits, changing my daily life. They have crept in without me noticing, making my life less busy and more flexible, but nevertheless making me ignore those things which used to seem important. I have learned to leave unwashed dishes in the sink overnight and that they will still be there in the morning – quite unharmed – which in my previous existence as one of the 'Stepford wives' would have been quite unthinkable! I can look at dust gathering on my tables, very noticeable on sunny days, and completely ignore it, without guilt, until the mood strikes or I am eventually shamed into reaching for a duster, instead of just trailing my finger through it each time I pass by.

My vacuum cleaner and I are not too well acquainted at the moment since I am waiting for replacement carpet to arrive after my flood in March of this year. Apparently it is on its way from Georgia in the USA, so the cleaner and I might be idle for a while longer! I'm in no hurry, there's not much point in cleaning the old carpet, which will be heading to the scrap heap eventually.

On those days when I don't want to face the world or do anything useful, I lie in a warm scented bath in the dark until the water grows cold. It is my escape and my form of meditation, the penalty for which is that I emerge resembling the prunes which sometimes occupy a bowl in my fridge. My body parts now seem hell-bent on going in a southerly direction, much like the snowbirds which go south for the winter. It would appear, however, that my bits and pieces intend to take up permanent residence in that direction and not return north in the spring!

No more is dinner on the table at 5.30 pm each night. I eat when I feel the need, at odd times, and I go to bed and get up when I wish. I drift through the flying days and weeks without accomplishing too much of anything, but not really caring whether I do or not. What does she do with herself, I can hear you ask? Well, I do try to scribble a few pages each day and walk a few kilometers every other day. I lie on the chesterfield and read, sometimes the most appalling rubbish which might spur me on to writing better things. I hope I never stop wanting to read or write, I cannot imagine my life without it.

Of course there's always the washing and ironing. I'm probably the only female on the planet who still gets pleasure from watching laundry swirling around in the suds in the front loader washing machine – the one possession I absolutely wouldn't part with. I'm also still into ironing almost everything, something which makes my daughter shake her head in wonder at this ancient, almost extinct, practice!

On Wednesdays I now go to the nursing home again to help in any way I can, even if it is just serving tea and cakes with a smile on my face and my hand reaching out to touch those in need of it. Touching is so very important to all of us, something I don't have much of right now. Just being there in those familiar surroundings makes me feel useful for a while and thankful for the faculties I still have, especially my brain, though that's debatable at times!

It is indeed very hard to realise that I now have only myself to please, that I no longer have to do anything, go anywhere, watch a clock or have a drummer to march to, if I don't so wish. Do I like my new existence as this rebel who is learning to say 'No'? Only now and then. The rest of the time I struggle with the yearning for the old life, the old me, the woman who always wanted approval and usually earned it; something which began in childhood as Daddy's little girl and never really stopped.

For me, life has gone full circle. I have been wife, mother and in my working life, several satisfying things, before becoming caregiver to my husband Stan, and in the end back to being like a mother to him in the latter years of his illness when he became like a child to me and I was just as fiercely protective of him as I had tried to be with my two children.

My solitary existence after nearly fifty years with him is sometimes unbearable but I don't want to change that – or anything else at this time – it is too soon. I need to heal my shattered spirit first, slowly and cautiously, and it is a good feeling just having the courage to change and to say 'no' sometimes. It is the only compensation I can think of in my new role as a single woman living in the ivory tower where I spend most of my days.

I remember returning home on a mid-March afternoon in 2001. It had been an emotional day. I had left my apartment at 9.30 am to keep appointments to deal with Stan's final income tax return and to have a new will drawn up for myself. Seeing the word 'widow' for the first time, as my new title, brought the tears which were never far away.

It was 3.30 pm as I turned the car into the underground apartment block where I lived. I felt totally exhausted. I needed a cup of tea and a lie down on the chesterfield for a while to recover. It had been a brutal day.

But the gods had other plans for me. I opened the door of my apartment to find it awash with water and large footprints in the soggy carpet leading up the hallway to the bedrooms. My first thoughts were that I had been burgled, but where was the water coming from?

I looked in the master bedroom. It was inches under water, which was coming through the closet ceiling, soaking everything in there. Water was in everywhere except the living room. I had been badly flooded from the apartment above me.

I turned tail out of my front door and almost collided with two large men dressed in navy blue sweats with Cromwell Restorations written across their chests. They were looking for me and took charge of the chaos and damage, which was considerable and took many weeks to deal with. I had several drying machines working constantly, so noisy I had to stay with my daughter to avoid the terrible racket. It was all so distressing. My clothes, some of them brand new for a planned visit to the UK some time later in the year, were taken away to be dry-cleaned. I had very little left to wear until it was all accomplished. The carpet was to be replaced some time before the end of the year.

Everything stayed the same until the day when it finally arrived from the United States. It had taken months for that to be accomplished. Finally, I received word that installation was imminent. Once again chaos reigned again, but this time it was planned chaos. I had been collecting cardboard boxes for weeks and spent most of Monday stuffing all the loose items into some of them. All those things which adorn sideboards, dressing tables and furniture located in every room. I dismantled my computer and disconnected the printer, sewing machine and serger (an automated sewing machine). I emptied the closet floors of their shoes, handbags and a variety of items too numerous to mention. I thought I'd done a good job and the carpet installers would just lift the drawers out of the furniture, with contents intact to ease the weight for moving. That wasn't my concern, but that was the way I thought it would be done.

Cromwell Restorations, the company still in charge, had promised me help to pack china and fragile objects from the living room cabinets and on Tuesday morning at 8.45 am two ladies arrived at my home. They were loaded up with supplies – cardboard boxes, rolls of wide adhesive tape, bright orange 'Fragile' stickers on a huge roll and a similar green one with 'Storage only' written on it. My first thoughts were "why do I need two ladies to pack one china cabinet and two other pieces of furniture containing my good dishes and other treasures. And why the huge wads of flattened cardboard boxes for my amount of breakables?"

I walked them through the rooms, proudly telling them I had packed the two bedrooms. There was nothing loose in sight, nothing really for them to do. The bedroom breakables had been stowed among my underwear in the drawers – they weren't going anywhere.

Well, instead of a pat on the back for trying to help, I was quickly informed that every single item, from every drawer, cupboard or piece of furniture, had to be packed and listed. It appeared the carpet installers would only move empty furniture. I was absolutely amazed to hear that bit of news.

The two ladies began the task and worked tirelessly from 9 am to 5 pm to build a mountain of packed cardboard boxes measuring sixteen inches by twelve and ten larger boxes, a total of fifty-eight boxes in all. Later in the week, one lady would be back to help me unpack and return each item to its original place. What a daunting thought that was. It was exactly like moving, except I wasn't going anywhere!

I sat there in stunned silence and watched them work. Just as they were finishing up, I had a frantic thought rush through my head. I had no clean underwear and no outdoor shoes and I had several days yet to get through. Mercifully, I hadn't joined the seemingly huge band of women belonging to the 'Depends Brigade'! I had to have my underwear!

I conjured up the courage to tell them and I felt so guilty as they consulted pages and pages of lists before they located the much-needed items – in two separate boxes of course! During this whole procedure I vowed, yet again, to do something about my possessions, to reduce the quantity of things I have acquired over the years, a promise I have made in the past many times. I did tackle the kitchen a year or so ago and filled six boxes which I gave to an organisation which helps battered women to re-establish their lives, and early this year I parted with most of my husband's belongings. It was a painful and emotional process which took many attempts, many hours and endless tears before it was accomplished. After that I no longer had the desire or energy to continue my quest to reduce the clutter, but now, after seeing the massive assortment of belongings I was still giving house room to, I really had to do something about it and definitely before my next move to who-knows where.

One thing I did know for sure, I would think very hard before ever deciding again to have new carpet installed. It had been another incredible experience I never wanted to repeat and this was only the preparation to install the new stuff and when that is finally over, every item had to find its home again. Definitely the new carpet would be here to stay!

I wasn't exactly looking forward to what lay ahead and even less so when I got up that particular morning and saw it was raining heavily and not a good day to have new carpet installed. I was even more dismayed when the two workmen who had turned up to do the installation piled some of my living room furniture outside on the balcony, which was only partially covered. It often gets wet when the rain blows in certain directions and being located on the 8th floor makes that happen frequently. After I had expressed my concern, they agreed to cover it with a roll of underlay and I heaved a sigh of relief.

They were going to re-carpet the living room first and I left to take refuge in my bedroom, grabbing a jug of water and an apple to take with me. I lay on the bed writing, it was the only thing I could do and that was only a temporary refuge until they decided to dismantle it sometime later in the day. I still had access to my bathrooms, though they too, had stuff piled in them; perhaps I could sit on the throne there when the bed was no longer available. They could hardly take that away!

A while later there was a tap on my front door. It was my next door neighbour, Walter, wondering what was going on. He'd been away in Montreal and had only just returned. I invited him in, rather than let him stand in the hallway and when he saw the mountain of boxes, he asked in a very surprised voice, was I leaving? I assured him that I wasn't and explained it was all because of getting new carpet after the flood earlier in the year. I told him all my belongings were packed in the fifty-eight boxes he could see everywhere. He was totally amazed at the amount of work involved and echoed my own thoughts that his next move would probably be in a pine box!

He left still shaking his head, returning to the sanity of his orderly bachelor apartment, not at all envious of my new carpet and the chaos it was causing. I had to admit that it was worse than I had expected, but I knew I had to get through it, telling myself that time takes care of every unpleasant event, something my father taught me years ago when I was going to have my first tooth pulled by the School Dentist.

My jug of water was eventually empty, the apple eaten long ago. Hopefully space in the kitchen would be returned to me soon so I could have a cup of tea. It was still pouring with rain outside, but thoughts of going for some real food kept entering my head. It seemed like a good idea, if only I could access my purse, which was buried inside the dishwasher where I had put it for safely, thinking I would retain dominion over my kitchen. That illusion was soon shattered and the small kitchen was filled to capacity with the left over furniture and other items from the living and dining room, which couldn't make it on the balcony.

I peered cautiously out of my bedroom door to investigate and realised that unless I was Mary Poppins, I couldn't even make it to the kitchen. The men were now working in the hallway and thoughts of retrieving my purse would have to be put on hold, along with my ever-growing hunger.

By 1.30 pm I was hoping the workmen would go and have some lunch and leave me to explore the possibilities of accessing the fridge. I thought they must be hungry too as they hadn't stopped since they arrived over four hours earlier. At two o'clock they finally stopped work and began eating their lunch, which they obviously had bought with them. They ate it sitting on my new living room carpet with a radio blaring out music I was not at all familiar with.

I took this opportunity to explore the kitchen, but only made it as far as the doorway. It was entirely blocked with furniture, making it impossible to get into the fridge or the dishwasher. I was stumped. Then I took a second look and decided I could just about reach the small freezer section of the fridge by stretching across the top of the big chair wedged in front of it.

It worked! I retrieved a small package of something from the front, which turned out to be several slices of frozen fruit bread. So far, so good. Feeling like an explorer on an important expedition, I crawled and squeezed between the legs of my dining room table, which had been turned on its side in the middle of my small kitchen. Giving thanks that I was small and skinny, I successfully reached the far side, which gave me access to the glass jars on the counter-top, containing tea-bags and instant dried milk which I use when baking bread, and most importantly, the kettle, plus a mug sitting in the sink waiting to be washed. I managed to free the toaster from beneath a mound of cushions and soon I was back on my bed, feeling very triumphant with my success and enjoying a feast of dry toasted fruit bread and a mug of tea. It tasted pretty darned wonderful! Who was it that said "necessity is the mother of invention"? I guess he or she was right.

The workmen did not finish that night. They had dismantled my bed, but at least they put it back up for me so I could have my much-needed sleep.

Of course the work is now finished, and all my belongings are back in place - in a fashion - but I have all winter to worry about it. I'm just relieved this entire event is now over. I am wondering what the gods will have in store for me next. I hope and pray it is not another flood. I couldn't bear the thought of having more new carpet installed!

CHAPTER TWENTY-SIX

THE LAKE DISTRICT

In my early teens I had a favourite poem, "I Wandered Lonely as a Cloud", written by William Wordsworth, familiar to poetry lovers the world over. It is probably his best known work. His vivid word-picture of golden daffodils, fluttering and dancing in the breeze, always delighted my senses and stirred my imagination. Some thirty years later, I visited the Lake District in the North of England, the place of Wordsworth's birth, and the inspiration for this poetry and much of his life's work, and thus began for me a love affair and a passion for walking in that beautiful, gentle green countryside, which has never diminished and remains with me to this day.

Many years have passed since that first visit and I love it more each time I manage to spend precious time there. The Lake District is an area covering some 850 square miles. A cornucopia of lakes, mountains, forests, quaint villages and much, much more, it offers walking, hiking and climbing to suit everyone's taste. To enjoy this paradise, all you need is a pair of good boots, a waterproof jacket and a walking stick, preferably one with a pointed metal end to help you over any difficult spots. The rest is free and yours for the taking.

My first visit was almost accidental. I was staying with my youngest brother Raymond and his wife Barbara for a few days on my yearly visit to my father in Southport. He mentioned that they enjoyed hiking in the Lake District and asked me to join them for a couple of days. I never could have imagined the impact this was to have on my life or the joy it has given me, including the close bond forged between my brother and myself, something which really didn't exist before, because of our eight-year age difference. It is something we no longer notice.

Whenever we can, we spend precious time together sharing our love of walking in this idyllic place. Barbara and my husband Stan also shared this passion for these green hills. There are easy walks over the gentle green fells, covered with heather and ferns in the spring and summer months, and there are more challenging walks which take you to higher places, requiring steady nerves and a love of heights. We have sampled both kinds, but my very favourite walk is a gentle one, over Sale Fell – about five miles in distance and it begins at the ancient Church in the hamlet of Wythop. Our path is mainly on sheep tracks which rise steeply on that first leg of our hike and then levels out as you reach the first bend to the right, giving you a bird's eye view as you walk of woods, farms, valleys and lakes. A breathtaking panorama which urges you to stop and stare.

It gives me an unbelievable sense of peace and wholeness to be there. It restores my soul and at that particular moment in time, I know, without a single doubt, that I wouldn't trade places with anyone in the world. The solitude is wonderful. You can walk for miles and meet only other hikers going in the opposite direction.

Halfway through the walk, we stop at a favourite spot which looks out over the green valley and Bassenthwaite Lake far, far below. We avoid the sheep droppings and find a place to spread our plastic sheets and then devour our packed lunch, a simple affair of sandwiches, fruit, a few nuts and a cold drink.   We eat and gaze at a view which never ceases to make us exclaim at its sheer beauty, though we have seen it many times before. The sheep and lambs are all around us, usually oblivious to everything but the quest for moist green grass. They seem to spend their entire day just eating and fertilising the ground with their prolific poop!

The silence is broken only by the bleating of sheep as they caution their offspring to stay close. Occasionally the quiet will be shattered unexpectedly by a different sound, as a fighter plane, probably from RAF Valley, doing exercises, will swoop out of the sky and fly over the lake below, before pointing its nose upwards to gain height and disappear into the clouds. It grabs your attention because it is actually flying beneath your line of sight, giving you an odd feeling that your world is slightly topsy-turvy.

After lunch we continue to climb, through leafy woods which smell damp and earthy, to our highest point, some 1600 feet, on this particular walk, and look once more at the stunning view before heading downwards on our walk back to our starting place, where we usually amble through the churchyard looking at the headstones on the graves – some of them dating back to the fourteen hundreds. Our walk is over for that day and we are full of joy and satisfaction as we return to our holiday home for a shower and some hot tea, satiated with the sights and sounds we love so much.

Our day usually ends with a visit to the Sun Inn located in the small village of Bassenthwaite, where they still light not one but two fires in the main parlour, when the evening is chilly – a welcome sight to the fell walkers who frequent the inn to have supper. The atmosphere is warm and cosy, filled with the quiet babble of voices relating their day's hike, the aromas of hot food, mingling with the smoky smell of the fires; a perfect end to a perfect day. I have a much loved picture of this inn, done by a local artist, hanging in my bedroom – a gift from my brother several years ago – and one I treasure.

Over many years we stayed at Keskadale Farmhouse overlooking the Newlands Valley located on a long winding path from Braithwaite Village and eventually reaching Buttermere Lake, another fairly long walk we like to do when visiting the Lake District. Margaret, the farmer's wife, used to cater for visitors and provided full board, serving delicious meals. Then over the years, as health problems cropped up, she switched to bed and breakfast only. We still made this our very happy base, though the drive at night began to be something we no longer relished and nowadays we choose to stay in a hotel or other accommodation, providing dinner.

We still have wonderful memories from the early days of sitting in Margaret's warm and welcoming sitting room with a blazing fire in the grate on cool evenings. The black beams which adorned the ceiling were generously hung with brass ornaments which gleamed in the firelight, creating an atmosphere of contentment and peace. Our hostess would provide us with a tray of tea or cocoa and a plate of biscuits or scones, always asking "How was your day?" We would then give her the details of yet another idyllic walk which had filled our hours. We didn't care about the weather, though of course it was always nice to have sunshine. Over the years we have walked in all the elements nature saw fit to send that particular day, even the rarity of a blizzard didn't deter us. We were equipped for any eventuality. Our visit would inevitably come to an end and as we said goodbye to our lovely hostess, it was always with the hope of yet another chance to walk those green hills. 'Maybe next year' was always in our hearts and thoughts.

It was October 5th, near the end of my visit to the UK, as I packed my case once more, this time with hiking togs and a tiny precious parcel of my husband Stan's ashes which I had carried on the flight from Canada. My brother Ray and his wife Barbara and I were heading once more to the Lake District. The sunshine which had followed me from Vancouver and stayed with me throughout my three-week visit was still with us that morning as we drove the three hundred miles north from Wales to our destination of Braithwaite Village, not the usual Keskadale Farm of the many previous visits.

This time we decided to stay right in the village, making it more convenient to have our evening meal as age was now catching up on us all. Our mission on this visit was to scatter some of Stan's ashes at his favourite spot overlooking Bassenthwaite Lake, where the fighter planes swooped and dived. Braithwaite is a pretty hamlet with narrow streets, tiny cottages and small houses, a general store, post office and several small country hotels, a mix of old and modern buildings. It also has a holiday camp site containing six cabins and a number of caravans on a large green space. Running through the village is a beck or river giving off the lovely sound of water running over stones, with small rustic bridges scattered here and there.

In spite of the lateness of the season, my brother had encountered problems with accommodation and had to settle for a caravan. I wasn't thrilled with that at all, but since I had sprung the news of my visit on him as a complete surprise, I could hardly complain if the only affordable accommodation was the last thing I wanted. I still had unpleasant memories of almost freezing to death during my last stay in a caravan.

It wasn't just the cold I dreaded. Anyone who is familiar with a holiday caravan will agree that when they advertise a four-berth accommodation, it means there is one double bed in a fairly small room and a second minuscule bedroom, measuring approximately ten feet by six feet, which contains two narrow benches only fit for a couple of small children. Of course this room was to be mine for six days!

I wasn't looking forward to retrieving the bedclothes from the floor every couple of hours, which is what happens each time you attempt to turn over or even move in that narrow space. In fact, I was not looking forward to bedtime at all and thought longingly of the warm, comfortable bed I had left behind in my Ivory Tower in Canada - the only thing I missed, I should add.

We unpacked the food and our belongings and in spite of everything, I was excited and happy to be back in the Lakes under any circumstances. I vowed to enjoy every moment - except the bed, which I knew from past experience, was going to be a real challenge to my aching bones.

On Sunday the 6th we took a four-mile walk on the Miners Road through leafy woods to the next village of Thornthwaite, where we sat outside the old church of St Mary's in the sunshine before returning. It was a fairly flat walk but I was aching all over and not feeling my best on that day. I had not slept well the previous night and as predicted, woke many times to find the bedclothes on the floor. In spite of dressing warmly to go to bed - in fact I wore more items than during the day - I was stiff and cold when it was time to get up.

The weather forecast on Sunday night promised us yet another dry, sunny day and we had tentatively planned to walk the five miles over Sale Fell at Wythop Mill to scatter Stan's ashes at his favourite spot overlooking Bassenthwaite Lake far below, where he used to love watching the fighter planes diving across the lake between the mountains and then swooping back up into the sky. It never failed to give him pleasure. His love of flying never diminished, and even to be an observer obviously brought reminders of the past and renewed the thrill of being part of it.

I woke before five o'clock on the Monday morning, again feeling terribly chilled in the cold mountain air. I had battled with the bedclothes many times during the night and I was stiff and hurting, especially my right hip, which was aching right down to the toes. I groaned as I got out of bed. Not a good start to my day, that's for sure. I wondered whether I would be able to walk at all that day, never mind five miles up and down hills!

At 7.30 am I stood under a hot shower for ten minutes, letting the water run down my sore hip to soothe the pain. Ray and Babs were still in bed. I made them and myself some hot tea, limping around the tiny kitchen and making our simple breakfast of cereal and toast. I added an extra-strength Tylenol tablet to mine and said a prayer that the pain in my hip would diminish enough to allow me to hike over the Fell to fulfill my promise to Stan and to myself.

The weatherman had been right. It looked as though it was going to be a sunny day. The sky was a clear blue with just the odd white puffy cloud. It was too good a day to waste and I decided it was going to be the special day, pain or no pain. Breakfast over, I packed the lunch, while Barbara cleared up the breakfast dishes and soon we were on our way. The discomfort in my hip and leg had miraculously gone, perhaps due to the Tylenol and/or my prayers, but I tucked another pill in my pocket, just in case it returned.

This particular walk we were about to undertake was very familiar to us all. We had walked it so many times. The Wythop Valley never ceases to reward all our senses in so many ways, and this day was no exception.

It was warm, yet not too warm, perfect for a hike. It was just a short drive from Braithwaite Village to Wythop Mill and we parked, as always, in the farmyard. We sat on the wooden seat at the side of the lane to change our shoes for hiking boots, fastened packs on our backs and began our journey past the church built in the 1400s and onwards through the uphill walk under a canopy of tall trees, through which the sun shone, looking like green lace and scattering sunbeams at our feet as we walked. The hills around us were emerald green, many still bright with yellow gorse. Away to our right in the fields below, the sheep were grazing contentedly.

We continued on the path and after about a forty-five minute walk we arrived at one of our favourite stopping places, a place where we had sat so many times to eat lunch, perched high on the hill, looking down on Bassenthwaite Lake to our left, surrounded by woods and hills and dominated by Skiddaw Mountain, the highest in the area.

In spite of knowing every inch of this fell, it looked different this time. The large grassy areas were heavily covered with waist-high fern and sheep were not as abundant. We knew the changes had been caused by the foot and mouth outbreak, which had closed off these fells to animals and humans for well over a year. We had noticed the difference in the scenery around us as soon as we set off on the wooded path from the farmhouse.

I looked around for a marker of some sort and found three large rocks among the still-grassy verge. It was here that I placed Stan's photograph on one of the rocks, and slowly scattered half of his ashes around it. It was emotional of course, yet I had a strong sense of peace in the knowledge that I had succeeded in my quest and I felt very close to him in those moments. We took pictures and finally I dried my eyes, said my last goodbye and then we continued on our walk upwards to the top of Sale Fell.

As usual, we sat and ate our simple lunch of sandwiches, yogurt, fruit and water, then went on our way, stopping as we always did to drink in the stunning beauty all around us. This passion for the Lake District was something the four of us had shared for over thirty years. It had never diminished, it never ceased to delight and we were always overawed with the beauty, the silence and the peace which filled each one of us. Now we were three instead of four and Stan would always be missed and never forgotten. In a sense, he was with us still as we walked and recalled some of our past visits.

Our walk took us five hours, every moment enjoyed, a day which will be treasured forever. I was so thankful I had accomplished that simple act. My heart was lighter for having kept my promise, with the help of my brother and his wife. It was so fitting that they shared this day, for they had been our walking partners through the years and were responsible for kindling the passion in Stan and me for walking on those beloved green hills of the Lake District. I am so grateful for every moment I can still spend there. The following is the much loved piece of poetry which I connect to this part of the world, which I learned as a child at school. I hope the reader enjoys it too.

I Wandered Lonely as a Cloud

I wandered lonely as a cloud
That floats on high o'er vales and hills,
When all at once I saw a crowd,
A host, of golden daffodils;
Beside the lake, beneath the trees,
Fluttering and dancing in the breeze.

Continuous as the stars that shine
And twinkle on the milky way,
They stretched in never-ending line
Along the margin of a bay:
Ten thousand saw I at a glance,
Tossing their heads in sprightly dance.

The waves beside them danced; but they
Out-did the sparkling waves in glee:
A poet could not but be gay,
In such a jocund company:
I gazed - and gazed - but little thought
What wealth the show to me had brought:

For oft, when on my couch I lie
In vacant or in pensive mood,
They flash upon that inward eye
Which is the bliss of solitude;
And then my heart with pleasure fills,
And dances with the daffodils.

William Wordsworth

CHAPTER TWENTY-SEVEN

MOTHERS AND DAUGHTERS

My mother was important in my life, but not as important as my father, who was very much in charge of everything in the household. She was such a quiet, accepting person, raising a family in the shadow of a domineering husband who eclipsed her personality totally. There were glimpses of her sense of humour at odd moments. I do know that I still think of my mother a great deal even though she has now been dead over forty years. I still see her image in my mind and I sometimes struggle to understand some of the childhood things which had me puzzled then. Some of them were to do with the superstitious beliefs she held on to all her life.

I think perhaps we take our mothers for granted and only picture them in the kitchen making dinner. Because she's always there, you forget to understand that she is an individual with feelings all her own.

The ongoing relationship between mothers and daughters is a complex one. My thoughts sometimes run from the less than fulfilling relationship I had with my own mother to the long, rocky road which has been travelled in my role as mother to Janice, who was a much wanted and loved child. Normal until the mid-teen years, she evolved into a flower-child of the sixties & seventies with everything that phrase conjures up. The all-knowing, all-loving generation, with the long straight hair and shapeless clothes worn down to the ankles. The delight in being as different as possible from every adult on the planet, and in particular, from me. I was 'just a housewife' who didn't know anything, according to her.

Janice was an extremely smart child who excelled at school when she wished to, but during the last of her high school years, she clearly didn't wish to. She had two burning ambitions. One was to graduate and leave school and the second was to move out of the house and lead her own life. Although she was blessed with the brains to achieve anything she wished, she chose commercial college and took courses there to become a secretary. She moved into a communal house on 7th Avenue in Vancouver just as soon as she graduated from the college. I was beyond understanding what made her tick, but I never gave up. I was always determined not to lose my daughter no matter how thin the line we walked.

As a mother I could not come up with answers to puzzling questions. Why would an eighteen-year-old want to leave a nice bedroom, decorated exactly as she had wanted, in a loving home, to share heaven knows what in a run-down house, in a room where the only furniture was made of orange boxes, apart from a rocking chair which had been a birthday gift to her when she lived at home? The kitchen was shared by all of the eleven assorted occupants of the house. It surely would never have passed health standards in a million years, and it gave me the shudders to even think about food. I never saw the bathroom, which is probably just as well.

On the couple of visits we made to 7th Avenue, mainly to check where she was, Stan and I found her sitting in the rocking chair, a deep pink crocheted shawl over her shoulders, like some aging Grandma, reading or just rocking. She did eventually move to a basement suite in North Vancouver and lived there for quite a few years. We were never invited to see this apartment, but she liked it and stayed quite a long time there.

Her first boyfriend was a tall, quiet lad with a lot of ginger fuzzy hair. His name was John and apparently he was a poet, or a poetry lover. We met him for the first time at the Lulu Belle Restaurant on Broadway, in Vancouver. Stan's mother and sister and her husband Ron were visiting us from England to celebrate her 75th birthday. We chose that particular restaurant because it was a lively place where they had a sing-a-long of some of the old English songs. We thought she would enjoy it, rather than just dining out close to home in Richmond.

We had also invited two old friends we'd met from Yorkshire. Fred and Ruth were quite a bit older than us; we'd met them on a trip to Reno several years earlier. They became almost like parents to Stan and me. He had been gardener and chauffeur to a lord of the manor in Yorkshire and very old fashioned in his ways. Still the English gentleman, he always wore a suit and tie. His wife Ruth had been a nurse before marriage and she was equally fussy about her clothes and always looked immaculate.

The night of the birthday party, all the ladies were attired in beautiful evening dresses, hair washed and set. My mother-in-law had managed to get into a long white dress of mine and she looked absolutely lovely for her party. She had been a redhead in younger days and still had an abundance of reddish locks – even at seventy-five she hadn't gone really gray. She still looked great in a swimsuit at that time!

I had invited Janice and her poet John out of courtesy but never imagined they would want to go to this particular venue, so it was a surprise when part-way through the festivities, they turned up, looking to me like a couple of hippies. Janice wore a long, shapeless dress which looked more like a nightdress and her hair was now very long and straight, parted in the middle like a curtain. John wore old brown corduroy trousers and sported a red scruffy beard. They looked terribly out of place and I was utterly embarrassed for the rest of the evening. I wondered what Fred and Ruth were thinking about my daughter, whom they had not met before, and I felt the same about the Holt relatives, who had not seen her since she was a beautiful nine-year-old before we came to Canada and as normal as can be. It was so difficult for us to understand the whole enigma.

Of course this was just a phase which had come from nowhere and which, with the passing time, disappeared, but while it lasted, it created a vast no-man's land between us. It led her to a first unsuccessful and unhappy marriage, not to John but to his friend Gary, to which we did at least receive an invitation. I as the bride's mother probably looked overdressed! Janice wore a simple white home-made dress with blue flowers scattered throughout the material and carried a bunch of blue cornflowers purchased from the corner store. The groom was attired in brown checked shirt and brown pants. No tuxedos at this wedding!

It was a brief civil ceremony which took place in North Vancouver, at which the elderly registrar who conducted the ceremony was wearing a pair of shabby brown house slippers on his feet. The sight of these almost had me choking with suppressed laughter. It was the worst wedding ceremony you could ever imagine, memorable only for the awful brown slippers. Thankfully the whole thing was very brief and soon we were out of his dingy office, breathing sighs of relief.

We had a nice meal at Capilano Canyon Restaurant with

Christopher, who was just a teenager then, and Janice and her new husband Gary, along with his parents, brother and sister, who we were meeting for the first time. They were nice, ordinary people and we got along well, right from the start. They lived in North Vancouver.

The marriage was fine for the first few years, and they appeared to be quite happy. Both had jobs and worked in Calgary, Toronto and then back to Vancouver, saving all the while for a piece of land they wanted to buy up in the BC interior to homestead. Their dream of living away from the rat-race and society, was eventually realised. They purchased five acres sixty miles north of Williams Lake in a tiny place called Likely – 'Not Bloody Likely' as my brother always referred to it! Apparently it was a haven for Americans avoiding the Vietnam conflict. Gary built a tiny house and they had a large vegetable garden, and when we made our one and only visit to Likely, they appeared to be settled and getting along fine.

Sadly the marriage fell apart after a couple of years and Janice phoned to ask whether she could come home until she got back on her feet. Apparently Likely was not the paradise she thought it would be, and married life had not lived up to expectations either. She was working three part-time jobs to keep body and soul together, the only contributor to the business of living. He spent a lot of time playing baseball with the local yokels.

I was so thankful we had hung in and could be there for her, weathering the storm of those terrible years when we were poles apart, when it would have been so easy to wash our hands off her. I had told my children many times that while I didn't always approve of their choices in life, my love is unconditional and they can always ask for my help. My husband shared these sentiments.

Janice went to work at the Toronto and Dominion Bank in downtown Vancouver, dressed appropriately and I fervently hoped this was going to continue and she would find whatever she was searching for. However, six months later she went off to England and lived there for four years, working for a lawyer in London, commuting from Romford in Essex each day. It was during the time when the IRA was setting off bombs in and around London. It was an anxious time, and she had friends in Canada who would let me know she was safe, when there had been a bombing.

Looking back, it has been a long journey to establish a loving relationship with my daughter, a child who was wanted and loved and of whom we were so proud. What went wrong? I asked myself that question so many times and realise I still don't know all the answers to those puzzling questions.

Now she is in her fifties and happily, the last few years have been really good between us. She works in North Vancouver and has a very responsible job and has married for the second time. She never had children, nor did she want any. She has had several cats which she is devoted to. The current one, a ginger cat called Max whom she rescued, spends most of his time going from room to room to catch the sun, which he loves. He sunbathes on the two beds and a white canvas chair he is fond of, depending where the sun is shining, and only appears when it is time to eat. What a life he has!

Janice is a beautiful artist and has produced many stunning pictures, some of which grace the walls of my home. She doesn't have a great deal of free time in her busy life, but hopefully she will in the future. She is a talented painter. The time we spend together now is enjoyable and she is supportive of what I'm trying to achieve when putting my thoughts on paper, something I find therapeutic. She wants me to have a life. She often tells me the magical words I waited such a long time to hear again: "I love you Mum." Those three words make it all seem worthwhile.

CHAPTER TWENTY-EIGHT

THE VAUGHANS

The smiling face in the photograph on the table beside me belongs to Jane Vaughan. It was taken in October 2002. Jane is almost the same age as my daughter Janice, and I remember her being born. I saw her regularly until the age of nine, when we left England for Canada. She is the eldest of three sisters, Kate and Helen being the other two, the daughters of Eileen and Arthur Vaughan. Arthur and Stan worked together, were friends and also best man at each other's weddings, only a year apart. Eileen was a lovely blue-eyed, fair-haired girl with skin like porcelain and a lovely smile. We all became very close friends and visited each other often at the weekends. My daughter, Janice was born just a few months ahead of Jane. We kept in touch with them over the years mainly by letter and occasionally met them for dinner when we visited England.

In 1991 a letter arrived giving us the news that they were coming to Vancouver to visit us. We were very excited at the prospect of sharing some precious time with them, catching up with our lives, and news of our offspring, now all grown up, as well as showing them the various beauty spots in and around British Columbia.

But then early one morning came a phone call from Arthur. It was shocking news, unbelievable at the time. Eileen had gone into the bathroom to get ready for a doctor's appointment. She had been having a few nasty headaches and decided to get checked prior to travelling to Canada. Arthur heard a loud bump and tried to open the bathroom door, but couldn't because Eileen was wedged behind it and not answering his frantic questions. He dialed 999, England's Emergency number. The firemen came, smashed the bathroom window and found Eileen unconscious on the floor. She was rushed to the hospital and died that evening of an aneurysm to the brain. She was 65 years old.

We were in shock for a while. We kept in touch with Arthur, mostly by mail, feeling his terrible loss. It must have been awful for him and his daughters.

Two years later in April, 1993, Arthur decided to take that planned trip to Vancouver alone, and again, fate stepped in. He arrived on April 9th, just after the start of Stan's long illness, and was shocked to see him in a zombie-like state, the cause of which I didn't know at the time, but discovered later, was due to an overdose of medication. Sadly, Stan was never aware of Arthur's visit and never awake long enough to know his old friend was there. Arthur insisted on cutting short his visit. I protested, but Arthur said he didn't want to burden me further. The visit ended on such a sad note for us.

A few years later he married for a second time, another Eileen. She had a stroke six weeks after the wedding and died eighteen months later. Tragedy had struck our old friend again.

We still exchanged letters spasmodically, at Christmas and a couple of times through the year. We both became computer literate in a fashion, and shared our extreme frustrations and occasionally a tidbit of knowledge of this new and strange technology of which we were striving to be a part of, and we enjoyed this exchange. Eventually we both went on line and learned that every dot and every space is important in an e-mail address and after a while we actually got it right!

When I visited the United Kingdom in May 2002, Arthur arranged a hotel for me in Southport, since he lives just a short drive away. It was a rewarding six days. Bridgette, my first next-door neighbour, came to see me. In fact most of my old friends turned up on that trip, Arthur included. We had a couple of enjoyable days together and a memorable dinner at a restaurant called the Cloisters, as a thank you from me for his kindness. That night as I was getting ready, I was as excited as a teenager on a first date. I took ages deciding what to wear, wishing I was at least three inches taller, that I could look more glamorous, that my hair was any colour other than silvery gray. I spent hours curling it and looking in the mirror, making sure I looked my best.

Suddenly I looked at the image in the glass. "You are crazy!" I said out loud. "You are acting like a sixteen-year-old. This is just Arthur for goodness sake. You've known him for years! It's just a dinner!"

But somehow it didn't feel just like a dinner, it felt like a date, and it was a wonderful feeling. It was the first time since Stan's long illness and death that I had felt that kind of excitement and emotion. It felt strange and it felt good.

I took a last long look in the mirror as I left and felt fairly satisfied that I looked all right in my black skirt, matching velvet jacket and a new expensive cream blouse I'd bought that same day from a dress store a few doors away from my hotel. I did notice that my cheeks were very flushed. All this nonsense had probably raised my blood pressure, but I wasn't going to worry about that either!

Arthur had also taken some care with his appearance, though he always looks nice. He wore dark pants, a Harris Tweed jacket, a pale mauve shirt and matching tie. We had a delicious and leisurely meal and talked of many things, never stuck for words. No awkward silences to fill. Comfortable with each other, like the very old friends we are.

During that evening, I felt there was a subtle change in our relationship. There was a little electricity in the air which had never been there before. He had made me feel like a woman again – and I liked the feeling. I liked having an arm to get hold of as we walked along Lord Street, back to my hotel and saw me to my room, before saying goodnight. Even to have the basic contact with another human being was so good. In my solitary life now, I go for weeks without the ordinary touch of a hand, something we take for granted, until we no longer have it. It was a perfect evening in every way and I didn't want it to end.

There was to be another invitation before that evening was over. His daughter Jane had asked me over for dinner the following night, at her home. I would see him again! What a nice surprise that was and I was delighted at the thought of seeing one of his daughters, after all this time.

As soon as I met Jane, I felt connected to her. She was such a warm and gracious person and I felt very much at home with her and the family. Phil, her husband, and her son Matthew were pleasant and welcoming. We had a delicious meal of chicken, followed by home-made apple pie – all washed down with wine. Then we had a couple of happy hours talking, taking pictures and it all went by very quickly.

Then came the time for me to leave. Not only Jane, but Arthur too – it was my last day in Southport. I was going to visit my sister not far away from Arthur's home, but I would not be seeing him again on this trip to England.

Now I am back home in Canada, the weeks have passed, and

it all seems like a dream and I wonder whether I imagined that electricity which seemed to be there that night. Did I read more into the warm looks from those green/gray eyes and the longer than usual goodbye kiss on the lips as I left him for the last time? Did I also imagine that I could feel Stan's approval of the whole thing, or was it all wishful thinking and my lively imagination?

Whatever it was, it made me feel alive again, just for a little while, and who knows what will happen in the future. It is written that in the spring a young man's fancy turns to thoughts of love. Does that apply to older men also? And I ask myself, do I really want a man who has confessed he is hopeless in the kitchen, is not even on nodding terms with the cooker, which he laughingly refers to as that strange object he dusts every now and then? He does keep the house looking immaculate - maybe he's a neat freak, come to think of it, I've never seen a thing out of place! And would I eventually come to hate the pipe he smokes and is so attached to, even though he never did light it in my presence? I know he was dying to, because I noticed he clutched it in his hand at times, like a security blanket, waiting for the moment when he could puff away on it.

On the plus side, he is a very nice looking man. He has a kind face, he still has a fair amount of silvery hair, he has his own teeth, appears to be in good shape, and is quite slim, his five foot nine frame still upright. Even at 76 he would be considered quite a catch by many women.t I'm not sure I am one of them, but on the other hand, I could easily change my mind!

Meantime, there's always the mysteries of the computer to keep us connected and the comfort of an old and trusted friendship, and time will tell. To use another old cliché, whatever will be, will be.

CHAPTER TWENTY-NINE

THE GRASS IS STILL GREEN

Although it is forty-odd years since I and my two young children sailed up the River Mersey that warm, sunny April day, returning home to England – for good I thought - I can still vividly remember the emotions of absolute joy surging through every pore of my being as we finally docked and saw the welcoming familiar landscape of my birthplace and the green grass of home. Much water has flowed under the bridge and many years have gone by since that eventful day in my life. I have returned many times to touch my roots, always with anticipation and pleasure, and soon I shall be doing it once more. I know this time though that there is going to be a new and different scenario, with a different script, and since I'm one of the players, I can only hope for a happy ending, but I can't predict it. I fear it is going to complicate my complex life, even further. I'm trying very hard to live in the moment, but my foolish heart wants to participate in the dance to come. At times I feel like a twenty-year-old again. Of course two seconds glance in the mirror soon dispels that myth, but it still keeps me awake at night thinking crazy thoughts and what–ifs, which fill my racing mind.

I wonder with amazement how Arthur and I arrived at this point in time. What suddenly changed a year ago after having fifty years of normal, ordinary friendship? There was never the smallest hint or random thought of anything other than that. I suspect it happened over dinner in the warm, intimate ambience of Cloisters Restaurant where we dined that evening. I felt the chemistry between us then and told myself it was my active imagination going into overdrive at the sight of a man sitting opposite me, his warm eyes lit up with an equally warm smile, as we chatted away like the old friends we are. That image has been hard to forget.

Whatever the magic ingredient was, time ran out. I was leaving the next night to make other visits before I flew back to Canada, promising to keep on writing as in the past. The letters though came more frequently, flying between us over the electronic airways. Much longer letters, warmer letters, compliments and always encouragement to keep on writing.

Which brings me to the present, and the adventure or misadventure which lies ahead. I wait impatiently for June 22nd to arrive. This time, Arthur will be waiting for me at the airport, not my brother Ray, who has always been the one to hug and welcome me home. My fatigue, after the long journey, will I'm sure, vanish the moment I see him.

I try not to think about the ending to this scenario. It is fraught with dangerous emotions and endless possibilities, which bombard my brain without me finding any solutions. My thoughts run from ecstasy to anxiety and apprehension at sharing space with a man for the first time ever, apart from my husband. It washes over me frequently in the melting pot of emotions, which include sheer panic and thoughts that I'm crazy to be doing this and should never have accepted his invitation to stay with him, when plans for the loan of Bridgette's little house did not materialise as promised. She was still waiting for the lawyer to complete her purchase and hand her the keys for her new home in nearby Birkdale Village. I had been delighted at the prospect of being able to entertain my sister and friends and even thought it might be nice to invite Arthur over for dinner, but it all fell through at the last moment before I was due to get on the plane for England.

I sit and stare at the photograph of Stan on my sideboard, seeking answers from the kind, blue eyes looking back at me. I'm sure he knows of the turmoil and excitement I'm feeling as the clock ticks swiftly by, and I wonder what he's thinking as my departure races to meet me. He just continues to smile at me, as always. It is too late now to change my mind, too late to run in a different direction, and I know in my heart I have to let myself experience this dance, whatever the outcome is when the music finally stops.

CHAPTER THIRTY

THE MIRACLE
OF MICHAEL

At times my life has been a roller coaster with tremendous highs and devastating lows to equal it all out. That's life I guess, for most of us. This chapter is the story of my latest 'high', which I'm happy to share with anyone who will listen.

Last September my companion Arthur was here from England and we spent a few days in Las Vegas. It was an enjoyable visit, but we were happy to be returning to Vancouver. We were very tired as we finally climbed into the taxi on the last leg of our journey home. It was 10.30 pm and we'd had a long day because of a delay with the return flight and spent four hours sitting in the plane ready for take-off. No explanation for the long wait, just the offer of a free drink, which did nothing to sooth the frayed nerves of the passengers. Terrorism and 9/11 were on the minds of more than a few of us!

As we rode through North Vancouver we were quiet, each lost in our own thoughts. I know I was thinking mainly of what we could have for a snack which wouldn't take a lot of time and effort in the kitchen, relishing the delicious thought of climbing into bed as soon as possible. No matter how wonderful it is to get away for a vacation, coming home is of immense pleasure to me. There is always that special moment as you turn the key in the lock and know you are back in familiar surroundings. That's the way I felt that night – so happy to be home.

Arthur took the cases into the bedrooms and I caught sight of the red flashing light on the answering machine and decided I would ignore it until morning. Then I groaned to myself 'I'd better just check the messages'. I pressed the 'on' button and heard the stilted electronic voice telling me I had eleven messages. I groaned again and almost decided not to listen to them and just wait until the morning, but somehow I didn't.

The first two messages were unimportant and I continued to listen, at the same time kicking off my shoes and removing my earrings and necklace to hasten the process in my quest for bed, impatient to get through the messages just to catch the names.

The third message was my son Christopher and it was hard to catch his low, quiet tone of voice. I thought he said 'Aileen's pregnant' but knew that couldn't possibly be right. I must have misheard him. I just carried on and listened to the next message, which was not important.

Message five was my son's voice again. Louder this time, more urgent and easy to hear him say 'Please phone me when you get home, no matter how late it is. Aileen's pregnant'.

My stomach lurched, along with my heart, which skipped several beats. It was a tremendous shock to hear those words. My son and his wife, both in their forties, had been trying to have a baby for twenty years. They had gone through all the usual expensive and unpleasant medical procedures, only to be disappointed and heartbroken each time it failed. It seemed Aileen would never be able to carry a child. Finally, they gave up trying and settled for two cats, which became their children and for me the closest thing I was ever likely to have as a grandchild. I used to receive Christmas and birthday cards addressed to Grandma from Harrison and Champagne, the cats. I would be amused or sometimes irritated when I received them, even though I was fond of the cats and understood why they were family to Chris and Aileen, and as cats go they were two perfect specimens and easy to love.

I stood by the answering machine absolutely stunned, then ran to tell Arthur the news. By now I was laughing and crying at the same time. All traces of the earlier exhaustion had completely vanished. It was so difficult to absorb this astonishing news and the torrent of emotions which rushed through my head like a riptide. Who expected to be a first-time Grandma at the age of seventy-six, and how did my son and his wife feel? Reality began to raise so many questions in my mind at the prospect of them starting a family at this time in their lives.

Of course I phoned them and realised they were still in shock themselves. There wasn't much sleep that night or the next few nights, but eventually in time we all calmed down and agreed this event was nothing short of a miracle, a wonderful gift, and that age didn't matter. We held our breath as the weeks turned into months and everything went well and continued to do so and on April 13th 2005 – the date chosen by Aileen and Christopher for the birth of their son – I would be in Calgary waiting to greet my grandson, Michael Stanley Becker Holt, who was to arrive by C-Section at 8 am, requiring us to get out of our beds at 5.15 am to keep the appointment at the hospital. I didn't think I would have a problem with that. After all, it isn't every day you get to witness a miracle.

That day arrived and we drove to the hospital. I chose not to be in the operating room at the birth, but Christopher was and I knew he would rush to give me the news when the actual delivery was over. I sat in a small room off the corridor not far from the OR and tried in vain to read a magazine. I couldn't have repeated a single word of it. My mind was focused on one thing only. I glanced at my watch every few minutes, listening for the sound of feet hurrying to tell me the news.

At 8.30 am I heard the clatter of cartwheels coming towards me in the corridor where I sat. It was Christopher with his brand new son, Michael, a small scrap of humanity. What a moment that was! We hugged each other, laughed and cried at the same time. Michael looked beautiful (of course!) not a bit like a newborn. His dark blue eyes were wide open, looking very alert and thank God, healthy and perfect. His cheeks were quite rosy and he had a smattering of dark hair on his head. It was a memorable day, one of those unforgettable events which will remain with us all forever.

From the time he was born he was a very active little boy, with beautiful blue eyes, light brown hair and a heart-stopping smile, interested in everything he discovered. Like most boys, he loved Thomas the Tank Engine and knew every single engine name. The same applied to the Sesame Street Gang. He also loved cars, trucks, puzzles and painting and was fond of 'cooking' and helping Mummy bake, covering himself from head to foot in flour!

He has now reached the age of eight and his interests have changed quite a lot. He became fascinated with dinosaurs after visiting the large museum at Drumheller, which is not too far away from where they live. It houses a very large collection of artifacts and a trip there is always enjoyed. Michael also loves a day at Calgary Zoo and they go there frequently in the warmer weather. They have spent a few days with me in Sechelt on the Sunshine Coast of British Columbia, and he spends hours looking for eagles and owls. While it is quite rare to spot an owl, we do have an abundance of eagles. They fly above the houses, circling in ever-decreasing circles, then zoom down on their prey in the surrounding bush. They must have wonderful eyesight.

Michael is very articulate and intelligent and has abundant energy. It is hard not to feel worn out at the end of the day, but he still hates to give in and sleep, though I think it is getting easier for the exhausted parents now that he has a very busy day at school and a fairly long one.

Aileen was forty-three and Christopher was forty-seven when Michael arrived and life for them has changed drastically, but I know they wouldn't have it any other way. They adore this little boy. The Miracle of Michael is still just that – an unexpected wonderful gift from Heaven.

I wrote a poem for that first Christmas, had it printed and framed and I've included it here.

THE FIRST CHRISTMAS

Our hearts will be lighter this Christmas Day, a time full of promise and love
With visitors coming from far away, sent by the one above

Now who can it be visiting me, not three wise men from the east
It's a tiny wee boy with bright blue eyes and restless little feet.

He's a gift of love from heaven above, priceless from the start
And a smile from his is surely enough to melt the coldest heart.

This year I don't need presents or baubles of any kind
Already I have the most treasured of gifts that anyone ever could find.

He's Michael Stanley Becker Holt, a very important name,
and I know from now on that Christmas will never be quite the same.

CHAPTER THIRTY-ONE

A HAPPY ENDING

Frank Sinatra was a favorite singer and performer to many of my generation through countless years of great music. I remember one particular song he sang called 'Love is Wonderful the Second Time Around', but I never dreamed it would ever apply to me.

I made another trip to England in 2003, after spending the previous year exchanging countless long emails with Arthur. Since that visit we have rarely been apart.

We married on June 4th 2007 in a civil ceremony in my small apartment, with just family present. Arthur's eldest daughter Jane and husband Phil flew from England, which was wonderful for both of us. This year as I write this, we will celebrate seven years of marriage and it is almost ten years since we got together after that amazing dinner when Cupid shot his arrow straight into our hearts!

Arthur and I spend six months in Canada and six months in England. It is mandatory that we keep the doors open in each country since we just don't know when it is all going to end. We feel blessed with the years we have had together. To me it is wonderful compensation for the time I had to spend away from my birthplace. Now, I have the best of both worlds. My husband has an apartment just outside of Southport, where my father spent so many happy years.

It is a strange feeling to walk through Hesketh Park and sit on the same seat where he and I sat many times, forty-odd years ago – history repeating itself. It is a very appealing seaside town with easy access to beautiful parks and woods, which we walk frequently when we are there. It is also just two hours' drive to my beloved Lake District and we have enjoyed several visits there.

Two years ago, Arthur very bravely hiked over our favourite Wythop Fell, not easy for him with his arthritic knees. I was so happy though to share that special place with this man in my life, just once, so he could understand my love of that area. It will always have a special place in my heart.

This is the last chapter of my journey through a life I could never have imagined happening and certainly one I couldn't have written a script for, some of it sad and some gloriously happy and rewarding. I have acquired three lovely stepdaughters and a host of extended family members, Jane, Kate and Helen, along with their husbands. I am grateful for them all - 'my pennies in the grass'.

There is of course a sadness in my heart that my only grandchild, Michael, lives in Alberta, a long way from Vancouver. I try to see him whenever possible, sometimes travelling to Calgary, driving through the beautiful Rocky Mountains to spend time with him and Christopher and Aileen. We talk on the phone frequently to stay in touch. He is a very bright child and absolutely crazy about hockey. He is on a team and is apparently a valuable asset. He does well at school and we hope that will continue. As a mother and grandma I just want him to be happy in whatever he chooses to do, and I pray he will grow up to be a good person and to use the valuable gifts bestowed on him.

I have always loved my family and stay in close touch with my own children and my two brothers, one in Canada, the other in North Wales. My only sister died in 2006 after a long illness fighting cancer. Her youngest son Stephen, who spent several years teaching English in China, has just died of the same disease, on October 25th 2013. He was flown back to England at the beginning of August and was in hospital close to where Arthur and I live. I visited him many times and was thankful to be there for him as surrogate mother.

The close family we were are scattered around the globe, like leaves in the wind, but still close at heart, with the help of technology. Life has gone full circle. The reluctant Canadian immigrant has come to terms with the vast array of surprises it has offered. I can now truthfully say that I have a deep affection for Canada and I'm grateful for what it has given me.

Of course I still love my birthplace, and whenever I make that journey to England and the aircraft makes its approach to land, I pin my eyes on the beauty of the green patchwork quilt below. My heart sings with pleasure, and I know that will never change. The stunning countryside of England fills me with emotion and has the power to move me to tears, and I never tire of seeing it. Friends I made in Canada and those I left behind in England and other places are still my friends, and I see them whenever I make a trip to my birthplace. I treasure the many friendships which have enriched my life.

I feel very blessed and thankful for all those 'pennies in the grass' which soon might be gone into obscurity, but will never forgotten. They are part of my own fairy story – one with a happy ending.

ND - #0463 - 270225 - C0 - 203/127/24 - PB - 9781861512321 - Matt Lamination